The War We Could Not Stop

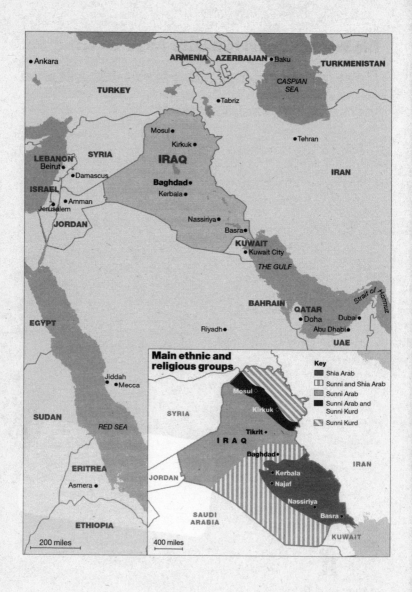

The War We Could Not Stop

The Real Story of the Battle for Iraq

EDITED BY RANDEEP RAMESH

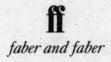

faber and faber

First published in 2003
on behalf of Guardian Newspapers Ltd
by Faber and Faber Ltd
3 Queen Square London WC1N 3AU

Typeset by Country Setting, Kingsdown, Kent CT14 8ES
Printed in England by Mackays of Chatham plc, Chatham, Kent

The right of Randeep Ramesh to be identified as editor
of this work has been asserted in accordance with
Section 77 of the Copyright, Designs and Patents Act 1988

The Guardian is a registered trademark of
the Guardian Media Group plc

Guardian Books is an imprint of Guardian Newspapers Ltd

A CIP record for this book
is available from the British Library

ISBN 0-571-22110-6

10 9 8 7 6 5 4 3 2 1

Contents

Preface

by Alan Rusbridger

Of all the predictions one can make at the end of Gulf War II this is the safest: that entire library shelves will one day be filled with books about the conflict. There will be long books, short books, picture books and map books. There will be gritty treatises about soldiering and diplomacy; trainspotter tracts on military hardware and numerous learned dissertations on the hermeneutics of war reporting. They will still be writing them in 50 years' time.

But here, for starters, is the *Guardian*'s book of the war. It is an 'instant' book, with all that that implies. It has been written against the clock and without the benefit of either official papers or hindsight. Even the very first sentence on this page – with its confident reference to the 'end' of Gulf War II – risks the derision of time future. Whatever else this is, it's not a tablet of stone.

It is, on the other hand, more than a simple slug of eyewitness history – vital though that in itself would be. Suzanne Goldenberg pitched up in Baghdad in the third week of January. She left 89 days later having seen at first hand the most devastating attack on any city in modern times, with all that that spelled in horror, pity, death and despair. Other reporters travelled – both 'embedded' and as free agents – with the coalition troops on ship and on land. At one point the *Guardian* and *Observer* between them had a dozen reporters and photographers inside Iraq. No future history of the war will be possible without reference to the daily dispatches of these, and many other, journalists. Each report they filed became a fragment of a temporal mosaic – tiny splinters of an overall picture that accumulated hour by hour, day by day.

Elsewhere around the world other hands were also at work on the mosaic. Half a dozen reporters in America and three Arabic speakers around the region brought different perspectives. Defence, diplomatic, environmental and political correspondents

d their essential parts. Towards the end of the fighting
eeled off from day-to-day writing to re-interview some
central players in a story which, by any standards, had
en the world.

The journalist and broadcaster Alastair Cooke explained in
these terms why he so loved working for the *Guardian*: 'No staff
members of a daily paper that I have heard of, on either side of
the Atlantic, are so free from instruction or the subtler menace
of editorial "guidance".' That spirit – as true today as when Cooke
was writing in 1959 – may help explain the breadth and diversity
of the paper's war coverage. Certainly, millions of Americans
flooded to the Guardian Unlimited website over the past months
in search of a texture and range of both reporting and comment
they felt lacking in the United States. So this book glues in place,
for the first time, that mosaic of fragments. Some parts of the
diplomatic and political narrative are as well sourced as any
future historian could reasonably aspire to. Some parts of the
action on the ground are vivid pieces of first-hand witness that
no historian will be able to match. The result may be 'instant',
but it should confidently earn its place on the library shelves –
whatever the subsequent company.

Alan Rusbridger is the Editor of the Guardian

Acknowledgements

The book's main contributors, who between them generated at least half of the words it contains, were Martin Kettle, Luke Harding, Brian Whitaker, Jamie Wilson, Patrick Wintour, John Vidal, John Hooper, Martin Woollacott, Matthew Engel, Kevin Maguire, Stuart Millar, Charlotte Denny and Richard Norton-Taylor. Randeep Ramesh pulled together the rest of the words and edited the book.

Without the efforts of the *Guardian*'s and the *Observer*'s brilliant team of reporters, none of this would have been possible. Most important, for this effort, were those on the ground in Iraq: Suzanne Goldenberg, James Meek, Audrey Gillan, Patrick Graham, Jason Burke, Paul Harris, Michael Howard, Jonathan Steele, Peter Beaumont and Burhan Wazir. Rory McCarthy in Qatar read between the lines of generals at US Central Command. Julian Borger did the same indispensable job in Washington with America's politicians and policymakers. Without their observations this book would not have made it into print.

There are also a number of experts, writers and reporters whose views and copy were used extensively for background material. Those whose words were helpful include: David Aaronovitch, Kamal Ahmed, Jackie Ashley, Amatzia Baram, Stephen Bates, Ian Black, Owen Bowcott, Martin Bright, Oliver Burkeman, Emma Brockes, Madeleine Bunting, Duncan Campbell, Jonathan Freedland, Timothy Garton Ash, Jon Henley, Amelia Hill, David Hirst, Simon Hoggart, Mark Lawson, Dan De Luce, Ewen MacAskill, Chris McGreal, Seumas Milne, Dan Plesch, Peter Preston, Hani Shukrallah, Polly Toynbee, Alan Travis, Simon Tisdall, Professor Julian Thompson, Jeevan Vasagar, Ed Vulliamy, Nicholas Watt, Michael White, Faisal al Yafai, Hugo Young and Gary Younge.

Newspapers don't just happen. Behind every talented writer is an equally impressive team of people who decide what is and what is not important every day. Their work is largely unheralded outside of any paper's office. But it is they who design and produce a newspaper daily by commissioning, organising, editing and finally pulling the coverage together. At the *Guardian*, thanks must be directed to the paper's deputy editor (news), Paul Johnson, and assistant editor, Brian McDermott, and to the foreign desk, run by Ed Pilkington and his colleagues Amelia Gentleman, David Munk and David Hearst. At the *Observer*, the war effort was similiarly directed by deputy editor Paul Webster, executive editor (news) Andrew Malone, and foreign editor Tracy McVeigh.

The *Guardian*'s excellent research team of Richard Nelsson, Ruth Merry, Luc Torres, Isabelle Chevallot, Allan Price, Sam Luton, Dominique Smith, Alan Power and Gavin McGuffie spent many hours finding cuttings and trawling the paper's archives. Finbarr Sheehy produced the *Guardian*'s graphics and those found in this book. On the *Guardian*'s news desk, Julian Glover and Simon Rogers also helped fill in the gaps with parliamentary intrigue, timelines, dates, pictures and graphics. Michael Hann pointed out useful material from around the globe. And the paper's home editor, Harriet Sherwood, vacated her very quiet office for a month – an act of kindness that proved invaluable in a newspaper office echoing with the din of war.

The editor of the *Guardian*, Alan Rusbridger, had the foresight to get the book started as the first bombs dropped and then ensured the smooth running of operations in fraught times. Finally, without four people this book would not have happened. They are owed the greatest debt. One is the *Guardian*'s book publisher, Lisa Darnell. This was her idea. Two are Anne Sacks and David Marsh. Without their copy-editing and proofreading skills, this book would never have escaped from the *Guardian*'s computer network. The last is Raekha Prasad, for being there.

Newspapers are produced by so many people that you could fill a book with their names and job titles. Apologies if anyone was inadvertently left out.

Introduction

It is often said that journalism is the first draft of history. This book attempts to be the second for the three weeks in Iraq that shook the world. Doubtless you will have read about the war in newspapers, seen it depicted on television, heard it fill the airwaves and pointed your browser at the innumerable excellent websites. All were a vital source for anyone who wanted to understand this agonising conflict. But despite the embedded reporters, cogent analyses and rolling news reports, Operation Iraqi Freedom was clouded for the most part by the fog of battle. This coiling miasma enveloped much of the battlefield for much of the time. Those behind the lines had one version of the truth while those on the edge of battle told another. In this respect, the best in war reportage has not changed. Sifting the truth from lies, the assertions from facts and the information from the disinformation is still what reporting does best.

Using the *Guardian* as the primary source of material, this book tries to explain where the war came from, why it happened when it did and how it finished. The book was designed to tell the story from as many perspectives and places as possible. There was as much to be found out from Baghdad to Jerusalem, or on the road to Damascus, as there was from crossing the Atlantic. It also becomes clear that for all the talk of a form of clean, technological war, the conflict resembled that fought decades ago by troops taking orders from those far from the battlefield. This and the eerie but bloody silence of the dead were stories worth telling.

In recognising the book's expanse, it is also worth noting its borders. Things change, events that now loom large later fade into insignificance. There will be arguments about what has been emphasised and deemed of merit, and whether today's morality will not be dissipated like the Iraqi sand before the

wind. Of course, in editing, rewriting and writing this book I will
have made mistakes in pointing out similarities where none
existed.

Central to this book is the idea that the war of Iraqi liberation
was a vehicle for advancing American interests. Some of these
are undeniably noble: democracy and liberty were scarce com-
modities in Saddam's Iraq. Britain signed up to the cause early
on and has to bear the cost of innocent blood spilt. This nation,
along with George Bush, also risked smashing the international
order and first bending and then breaking global laws carefully
constructed since the end of the Second World War. Whether
the disorder wrought was worth it, and whether the United
States understands the price of imposing freedom, will only be
worked out once Iraq is put back together. Those things are
about salvation and are for another book. This one, for better or
worse, is about destruction.

Randeep Ramesh, April 2003

Cast of characters

KOFI ANNAN Secretary-General of the United Nations

TARIQ AZIZ Iraqi Deputy Prime Minister

HANS BLIX Chief Inspector of Unscom

TONY BLAIR Prime Minister of the United Kingdom

ADMIRAL SIR MICHAEL BOYCE Chief of the UK Defence Staff

BRIGADIER GENERAL VINCENT BROOKS US Central Command spokesman

GEORGE BUSH US President, 1989–1993

GEORGE WALKER BUSH US President, 2001–

AIR MARSHAL BRIAN BURRIDGE Commander of British Forces

AHMAD CHALABI exiled leader of Iraqi National Congress

DICK CHENEY US Vice-President

JACQUES CHIRAC President of France

LT-COL TIM COLLINS Commander of the 1st Battalion, Royal Irish Regiment

GENERAL TOMMY FRANKS Commander of US and coalition forces

JAY GARNER Head of the Office of Reconstruction and Humanitarian Assistance

SIR JEREMY GREENSTOCK Britain's Ambassador to the UN

AYATOLLAH MOHAMAD BAKR AL-HAKIM Iran-based leader of the Supreme Council for the Islamic Revolution in Iraq

GEOFF HOON Britain's Defence Secretary

SADDAM HUSSEIN President of Iraq, 1979–2003

QUSAY SADDAM HUSSEIN younger son of Saddam, head of National Security Bureau

UDAY SADDAM HUSSEIN elder son of Saddam, head of the
  Iraqi Olympic Committee

IZZAT IBRAHIM Vice-Chairman, Iraq's Revolutionary
  Command Council

GROUP CAPTAIN AL LOCKWOOD spokesman for British forces
  in the Gulf

GENERAL ALI HASSAN AL-MAJID cousin of Saddam, known
  as Chemical Ali, Commander of southern Iraqi forces.
  Reportedly killed in US bomb attack

RICHARD PERLE Pentagon adviser

COLIN POWELL US Secretary of State

VLADIMIR PUTIN President of Russia

TAHA YASSIN RAMADAN Iraqi Vice-President

CONDOLEEZZA RICE US National Security Adviser

DONALD RUMSFELD US Secretary of Defence

GENERAL AMER HAMMOUDI AL-SAAD Saddam Hussein's
  scientific adviser

MOHAMMED SAEED AL-SAHAF Iraqi Minister for Information

GERHARD SCHRÖDER Chancellor of Germany

GRAND AYATOLLAH ALI SISTANI spiritual leader of Iraqi Shia

SHEIKH MUZAHIM MUSTAFA KANAN TAMIMI former
  Brigadier-General in Iraqi army and British-appointed
  governor of southern Iraq

BARAZAN IBRAHIM AL-TIKRITI Saddam Hussein's half-
  brother. Regime presidential adviser and former head of
  the secret police

COLONEL CHRIS VERNON British military spokesman

PAUL WOLFOWITZ Deputy US Secretary of Defence

The War We Could Not Stop

Special relationship: Tony Blair and George Bush, friends in war and peace
(AP/Pablo Martinez Monsivais)

1 Crossroads in the desert

The policies of all powers are inherent in their geography.
Napoleon, Emperor of France, 1769–1821

The path that led to the overthrow of Saddam Hussein was a long one. It led through many countries and it took many turns. But it might be said to have started on an unmarked stretch of the Basra to Baghdad highway in the southern Iraqi desert, somewhere south of the Euphrates river. It was here that the decisive implementation of a key decision taken thousands of miles away at the end of February 1991 set the scene for all that was to follow over the next 12 years. The decision was the cease-fire order ending the Gulf War. The man primarily responsible for it was General Colin Powell, then chairman of the United States Joint Chiefs of Staff. And the effect, unintended and un-expected by those who took it far away in Washington, was the withdrawal of American forces from Iraq and the reconsolidation in power of Iraq's brutal dictator.

Saddam Hussein had invaded neighbouring Kuwait in August 1990. He caught the Kuwaitis and the world napping, but the international response was instant. On the day Iraqi troops rolled into Kuwait, a hastily convened meeting of the United Nations Security Council in New York called unanimously on Saddam to withdraw immediately and unconditionally. The following day the Arab League met in Cairo and echoed the UN's call.

By January 1991, more than half a million troops from more than 30 countries, mostly North American, European and Arab, led by the United States, had assembled in Saudi Arabia and other Gulf states to enforce the UN's demands. On 16 January, Operation Desert Storm began with the first bombing raids on Baghdad. Thirty-nine days and 91,000 air missions later, the decisive ground offensive was launched on 23 February.

The ground war lasted less than five days. Iraqi troops defending Kuwait's border with Saudi Arabia were overwhelmed within hours. A massive flanking movement – the so-called 'left hook' that the theatre commander General Norman Schwarzkopf later attributed to his study of Hannibal – quickly cut the main Basra to Baghdad road, isolating Iraqi forces in Kuwait. Surrounded, the Iraqis fell apart, abandoning their positions, vehicles and equipment and heading for home. Saddam's men surrendered in their thousands or just disappeared.

On the evening of 27 February, President George Bush met his security advisers in the Oval Office to discuss the ending of the war. The chief advocate of a quick finish was Powell. He told the President that the four victory conditions that had been set by the US in August 1990 had now been fulfilled. Iraqi forces were leaving Kuwait, the Kuwaiti government was able to return, the security of the Gulf region had been restored, and American lives were no longer at risk. Bush went along with Powell's recommendation. If he moved quickly, someone pointed out, he could say that the war had been won in 100 hours. The military men and the politicians were agreed. That evening Bush issued the ceasefire order and went on television to broadcast to the nation.

'Kuwait is liberated,' he announced. 'Iraq's army is defeated. Our military objectives are met.' Then he continued: 'Seven months ago, America and the world drew a line in the sand. We declared that the aggression against Kuwait would not stand. And tonight America and the world have kept their word.' It was, Bush stressed, a victory for the United Nations and a victory for the rule of law.

The Gulf War had been an overwhelming military success for the United States and its allies. To a nation still haunted by the national humiliation and international debacle of the defeat in Vietnam a generation before, it was a cathartic moment. It seemed to reconsecrate the armed forces of the United States in the eyes of the nation, and to relegitimise America's place in the world, still reeling from the fall of communism in Eastern Europe. It also did wonders for the President's poll ratings, seeming to tee him up perfectly for the re-election campaign that would begin in earnest in a few months.

But the victory was not everything that it seemed. The ceasefire immediately caused controversy. Critics argued that it came too soon, forgetting or ignoring the fact that the UN mandate authorised all necessary means to eject the Iraqis from Kuwait, but no more than that. At every level in the Bush administration, officials assumed that Saddam would be overthrown in the immediate aftermath of defeat. But the Iraqi leader was more resilient than they knew. When Saddam seized the opportunity afforded by the ceasefire to crush a rising among Iraq's southern Shia and to drive the country's northern Kurds north towards and over the Turkish and Iranian borders – creating massive humanitarian disasters in both cases – the self-congratulation and celebration began to look first premature and then shameful.

The men who took the decision, from Bush downwards, nevertheless defended it resolutely. In the months and years to come, Bush would patiently explain that the UN resolutions under which the war was launched did not authorise a free-ranging war against Iraq. 'We did not have a mandate to invade Iraq or take the country over,' wrote Britain's Gulf War commander General Sir Peter de la Billiere in his memoirs. 'And if we had tried to do that, our Arab allies would certainly not have taken a favourable view. Even our limited incursion into Iraqi territory had made some of them uneasy.'

The other criticism, which was to echo down the coming years through countless discussions on the Iraq issue, was that this was a golden missed chance. Why was Saddam not overthrown when the opportunity presented itself? Why, when Schwarzkopf's 101st Airborne Division cut the Baghdad-Basra road (accompanied, ironically in the light of what happened in 2003, by French forces), did they turn right, turning the screw on Basra? Why did they not turn left, and head for Baghdad, and unseat Saddam himself?

'In purely practical terms, there is no doubt that British, American and French forces could have reached Baghdad,' de la

Billiere thought. 'We would have been there in another day and a half.' What held them back at that crossroads in the desert, he explained, were international law and international politics. To have moved on Baghdad would have been to move outside the remit of UN authority and would have split the coalition between its Islamic and its non-Islamic elements. In 1991 such considerations mattered far more than they seemed to do in 2003.

The military commanders were convinced that the decision they took at the crossroads in the desert in February 1991 was the right one. But as the years went on, criticism of the decision mounted. In particular, it came to be seen in the United States, and among conservative Republicans in particular, first as an error, then as a source of embarrassment, and finally as a deed of shame that could only be expunged in one way: by invading Iraq again and doing what they thought should have been done in 1991.

All that, though, remained far in the future when Iraq agreed to the ceasefire on 28 February 1991. Two days later, back at the United Nations, the Security Council adopted a permanent ceasefire resolution of its own and, a month after that, passed Resolution 687, demanding that Iraq should now 'unconditionally accept the destruction, removal, or rendering harmless, under international supervision' of any chemical or biological weapons and agents and of any ballistic missiles with a range of more than 150 km.

It was the start of a policy that came to be known as containment. At its heart were three processes. The first was a disarmament process consisting of an arms embargo and international inspections to rid Iraq of what would later be known as 'weapons of mass destruction'. The second was the so-called 'Oil-for-Food' programme, also administered by the UN, under which Iraq was permitted to sell limited amounts of oil internationally, in return for which it could import specified food and medical supplies. The third was a military enforcement regime, initially under UN sanctions over parts of northern Iraq – the so-called 'safe havens' for Kurdish refugees – but extended in

1992 by the US, Britain and France to include what were called 'no-fly zones' in both the north and the south of Iraq.

Periodically, Iraq tried to break the bounds of containment. When it did so, the US and its allies struck back. One such moment came in June 1993, when President Bill Clinton, the Democratic challenger who had succeeded Bush earlier that year, ordered a missile attack on an Iraqi intelligence centre in retaliation for an unsuccessful Iraqi assassination attempt on Bush during a visit to Kuwait in April.

A further flashpoint occurred in September 1996, when Saddam moved troops into the Kurdish safe havens; on that occasion the US fired missiles at targets in southern Iraq. For the next three years, the trigger for further tensions was invariably the deepening game of cat and mouse between Saddam and the weapons inspectors. This reached climaxes in October 1997, again in February 1998 and finally – after the withdrawal of the inspectors – in December 1998, when Clinton, who was about to be impeached by the Republican Congress in Washington, launched four days of missile attacks on Baghdad in an assault dubbed Operation Desert Fox. Periodic military actions by the US and Britain continued in 1999 and beyond, but by this time the original Gulf War coalition of 1990–91 had dissolved significantly. Containment continued, in the shape of the Oil-for-Food programme and the enforcement of the no-fly zones, but the weapons inspectors had been withdrawn.

The story of how Iraq 1991 led to Iraq 2003 is the story of a very American crusade. It is, at bottom, a story about how a small group of politicians, policymakers and intellectuals, who came to be known as the neo-conservatives or 'neo-cons', came to get their way. It is the story of how they evolved a theory of America's place in the world that had as its first great objective the ousting of Saddam by American military might. And it is the story of how, as opportunities presented themselves and challenges arose, this small group of rich, powerful and influential ideologues seized them to make a reality of their long-nurtured dream.

Of all the neo-cons, none mattered more than Donald Rumsfeld and Dick Cheney. The two men went back a long way. Bright, witty and ruthless, Rumsfeld was the senior of the two. Cheney, nine years his junior, was a colder person, less socially assured, but just as determined and every bit as conservative.

In the 1970s, Rumsfeld was Gerald Ford's White House Chief of Staff, then his Defence Secretary (he was the youngest civilian Chief in Pentagon history – later he would also become the oldest). When Rumsfeld moved to the Pentagon, Ford promoted his deputy, Cheney, to be Chief of Staff. But under Ronald Reagan and, in particular, George Bush Sr, Cheney overtook his old boss in the seniority stakes. In 1989, Cheney became Defence Secretary while Rumsfeld remained in the business world.

As Bush Sr's National Security Adviser Brent Scowcroft makes clear in his memoirs, the fundamental divide in the administration was between Cheney on the one hand and everyone else (Bush and Powell included) on the other. In particular, Cheney took a much more aggressive stance on international politics and military options. He was opposed to negotiation with Mikhail Gorbachev, while Bush and Scowcroft were in favour. He opposed Powell's idea that the US should withdraw its tactical nuclear weapons from Europe and South Korea. And as part of the preparations for the Gulf War he asked Powell for a study of how small nuclear weapons might be used against Iraq units in the desert.

Even at this early stage, Cheney's relations with Powell were complex. It was Cheney who reached down to select the recently promoted General Powell as Chairman of the Joint Chiefs, bypassing 14 more senior candidates. But Cheney's Pentagon was not Powell's preferred milieu. It was, Powell wrote in his memoirs, 'a refuge for Reagan-era hardliners'.

Bush Sr's defeat in the 1992 presidential election was a defining moment on the neo-con journey back to Iraq. The 1980s had been golden and validating years for American right-wing politics. To the new Republicans of the Reagan era, there was always something a bit unsatisfactory about the patrician Bush as the populist Reagan's successor. Next time, they decided, things would have to be different.

If Bush Sr's presidency helped to push the neo-cons into a more aggressively conservative direction, his influence was as nothing to that of the man who ousted him from the White House in 1992. Bill Clinton's victory traumatised the American right. To have a Democrat in the White House was bad enough, an unscripted interruption in the triumphalist progress of the American right. But Clinton himself was even worse. He offended every instinct of born-to-rule Republicans. He was poor. He was smart. He was naughty. And, worst of all, he had opposed the Vietnam War. One of Cheney's Pentagon advisers in those years, Eliot Cohen, later wrote of the 'humiliating defeat by the governor of a small, poor southern state, Bill Clinton, who had avoided the draft during Vietnam'. It was a verdict that managed to combine all the neo-cons' grievances against the 42nd President in one spluttering sentence.

Thrown out of office in 1993, the neo-cons did what American political exiles always do while the other party is in power. They joined corporations and made money, as Cheney did in the Halliburton energy engineering group. They took academic jobs, as one of Cheney's former deputies, Paul Wolfowitz, did at the Johns Hopkins University School of Advanced International Studies, or as former White House aide Condoleezza Rice did at Stanford. They got involved in campaigns, as Douglas Feith did in trying to stop the chemical weapons convention that the Bush administration had negotiated. And they eyed their futures.

One central theme in the emerging neo-con worldview was to rethink the position of the United States in the aftermath of the collapse of the Soviet Union. The end of the Cold War had left the United States as the sole superpower in what Bush Sr had dubbed the 'New World Order'. Yet Bush and most of his advisers – people such as Scowcroft and the former secretaries of state James Baker and Laurence Eagleburger – believed that this created dangers as well as opportunities. The United States was 'the necessary power' in providing security and stability around the world, but also had to reassure the world of its good faith. Clinton's new National Security team, headed by Warren Christopher and Tony Lake, seemed to see things much the same way.

The neo-cons were crafting a very different approach even before they were ousted in 1993. In February 1992, Paul Wolfowitz, then Pentagon Under-Secretary for Policy, and Zalmay Khalilzad of the White House National Security Committee staff wrote a paper that Cheney had commissioned. Cheney's brief to the two men had been to articulate America's role in the post-Cold War world. In their paper, titled *Defence Planning Guidance*, Wolfowitz and Khalilzad set out a number of themes that would in time set the agenda of George Bush Jr's foreign policy a decade later.

America's mission, they wrote, was to ensure that no rival superpower emerged in any part of the world. America could do this by making absolutely clear that the US stood for democratic and free market values and by an equally emphatic assertion of military might. America must 'maintain the mechanisms for deterring potential competitors from even aspiring to a larger regional or global role'. The Pentagon, they argued, should take all measures, including the use of force if necessary, to prevent the proliferation of nuclear and other mass destructive weapons systems.

This could best be done by 'ad hoc' coalitions of nations. The US, the authors said, should be 'postured to act independently when collective action cannot be orchestrated'. There was no mention of any role for the United Nations. The guidance envisaged a policy of pre-emptive strikes against states bent on acquiring nuclear, biological or chemical weapons. Among the countries that Wolfowitz and Khalilzad identified as potential targets of such a policy, which they illustrated by means of a series of hypothetical war scenarios, were some former Soviet republics, North Korea – and Iraq.

Wolfowitz was already well on the way to becoming the intellectual driving force behind the policies of 'regime change' and the democratic transformation of the Middle East. In his younger days he had been a Democrat, a follower of the influential Senator Henry 'Scoop' Jackson of Washington state, liberal on social issues but hawkishly interventionist on foreign policy. He is still both. Along with his brash contemporary Richard Perle, Wolfowitz moved to the Republicans in the 1970s, fired by determination to break the influence of Henry Kissinger's doctrine of détente with the Soviet Union.

By the time Saddam invaded Kuwait, Wolfowitz was at the Pentagon. Even then, he was always the administration's strongest advocate of intervention. When Bush Sr pulled US troops out of southern Iraq after the ceasefire, Wolfowitz was dismayed. His dismay grew during the Clinton years. As the post-Gulf War policy of Iraqi containment, begun by Bush Sr, took root under Clinton, Wolfowitz gave vent to his disdain in articles for the rightwing *Wall Street Journal*. In one such article in 1996 he derided 'our passive containment policy and our inept covert operations'. The following year, he explicitly proposed 'the military option', unilateral if necessary, of ousting Saddam.

But Wolfowitz was no lone voice in the Republican wilderness in the Clinton years. On the contrary, he was just one of a number of formidable and angry conservatives who were growing ever more frustrated by the turn of events in US politics and at what they saw as America's diminished authority abroad. Perhaps the most flamboyant of them all was Perle, famously dubbed the 'prince of darkness' when he was Assistant Secretary of Defence during the Reagan years for his unremittingly confrontational views on arms control. Then there was Josh Bolton, who had said on one occasion: 'There is no such thing as the United Nations. There is an international community that can be led by the only real power in the world, and there is the United States, when it suits our interests and when we can get others to go along.'

And there were others. There was J. D. Crouch, formerly a Pentagon policymaker under Bush Sr, who led efforts to prevent the United States from signing up to the chemical weapons convention and who, in 1995, advocated a US military strike against North Korea. There was Douglas Feith, a Perle protégé and longtime opponent of the 1972 anti-ballistic missile treaty that Nixon had signed with the Soviet Union.

Clinton's victory in 1992 had been followed by a sensational Republican win in the 1994 mid-term congressional elections, led by the confrontational conservative Newt Gingrich. But Gingrich's political tactics backfired. In a trial of strength with Clinton he tried to shut down the federal government. The confrontation discredited Gingrich and relaunched Clinton's presidency. In November 1996, to the renewed consternation of conservatives, Clinton was re-elected for a second term, defeating Senator Bob Dole.

Clinton's personality, Clinton's policies and, above all, Clinton's presence in a White House that the Republicans believed was truly theirs had become a standing affront to conservatives. During Clinton's second term, many conservatives would devote themselves to trying to oust him from office. The neo-con intellectuals, on the other hand, devoted themselves to trying to destroy his Iraq policy. Clinton's policy of containment towards Iraq may have begun with Bush Sr but, to the neo-cons, it had come to embody everything that the neo-cons despised and detested about the successor president. To the true believers in the think tanks such as the Project for the New American Century, the Centre for Security Policy and the American Enterprise Institute, where the neo-cons worked out their years of exile, the overthrow of Saddam gradually became a test of foreign policy virtue that the sinful Clinton would inevitably fail. By the 2000 presidential election, regime change in Iraq had become the partisan incarnation of a 'not Clinton' foreign policy.

In late 1997, the neo-cons' house magazine, the *Weekly Standard*, headlined its cover 'Saddam Must Go: A How-To Guide'. Inside, the lead article was written by the familiar team of Wolfowitz and Khalilzad. 'We will have to confront him sooner or later – and sooner would be better,' the pair wrote. They called for 'sustained attacks on the elite military units and security forces that are the main pillar of Saddam's terror-based regime'. A few weeks later, John Bolton joined the chorus. His article, also in the *Weekly Standard*, called on the Republican Congress to lay bare 'the decline and fall of America's Iraq policy since Clinton took office' and to spell out for the administration, in both political and military terms, what 'a real president' (in Bob Dole's phrase) would do with Saddam Hussein.

'History will record,' Bolton continued, 'the progressive collapse of the Gulf War coalition in Clinton's first term, caused largely by his administration's inattention to Iraq. And the record will show, in the last year, the accelerating decline of US influence in the Gulf and the increasing likelihood that Saddam Hussein will break out of the ring so laboriously built around his regime. In default of executive leadership, Congress must detail the steps necessary to bring Saddam's regime back under control or to make it pay the full price of its transgressions.'

Shortly after Bolton's article was published, an event occurred that in retrospect seems to some like a formal declaration of intent by many of those would be at the heart of the Iraq invasion policy of George Bush in 2003. It took the form of an open letter to Clinton on Iraq policy and was signed by 18 conservatives. The letter was organised by the two founders of a new think-tank, the Project for the New American Century. William Kristol is a journalist who also edits the *Weekly Standard*, in which Bolton's article had appeared, while Robert Kagan is a Reagan-era State Department policymaker who was to achieve international fame in 2003 as the author of a book, *Paradise and Power*, which argued that Europeans had become afraid of power while Americans were happy with it.

The Project for the New American Century, they wrote, was 'dedicated to a few fundamental propositions: that American leadership is good both for America and for the world; that such leadership requires military strength, diplomatic energy and commitment to moral principle; and that too few political leaders today are making the case for global leadership'.

The open letter to Clinton is dated 26 January 1998. It said that the policy of containment had been eroding, that the Gulf War coalition had fallen apart and that the weapons inspection regime was becoming increasingly ineffectual. American policy, they said, should no longer be 'crippled by a misguided insistence on unanimity' in the UN Security Council. 'The only acceptable strategy,' the writers concluded, 'is one that eliminates the possibility that Iraq will be able to use or threaten to use weapons of mass destruction. In the near term, this means a willingness to undertake military action as diplomacy is clearly failing. In the long term it means removing Saddam Hussein and his regime from power. That now needs to become the aim of American foreign policy.'

The signatories were a who's who of American neo-conservatism. In addition to Kristol and Kagan, they included Rumsfeld, Bolton, Perle, Khalilzad and Wolfowitz, all of whom were to play central roles in the George W. Bush administration from 2001.

If it was a conspiracy, it was an exceedingly public one. But it was also an immensely powerful one. It helped to generate a drive on Capitol Hill that year, led in particular by Jesse Helms, which led to many of these propositions becoming adopted as the law of the land, signed – reluctantly – into law by Clinton himself. The Iraq Liberation Act contained a series of instructions to Clinton to channel money and military aid into Iraqi opposition groups. It baldly stated that US policy was 'to support efforts to remove the regime headed by Saddam Hussein from power'. Clinton, fighting for political survival over the Monica Lewinsky affair and facing crucial mid-term elections, agreed to sign it into law in October 1998.

Clinton did not take the new law seriously, and nor did his officials. 'A regime change cannot be done by imposing a new regime by military force from outside, even assuming that would be possible,' said Clinton's Under-Secretary for Defence Policy, Walter Slocombe, in 1999. 'You can produce a lot of trouble. You can produce a lot of dead people, but you can't produce success unless it's properly prepared.' The administration's military chiefs were even more scathing. The Iraq Liberation Act was 'harebrained', in the view of General Anthony Zinni, then head of US Central Command and the man in charge of any military moves in Iraq (his job was held by General Tommy Franks when the invasion finally took place in 2003). 'I don't think this has been thought out,' Zinni added. 'A Saddam in place and tamed is better than promoting something that causes Iraq to explode, implode, fragment into pieces, cause turmoil.'

The Iraq Liberation Act is not a blueprint for everything that happened in 2003. It posited a much more important military role for Iraqi opposition groups, which the US would train and arm. It foresaw a deposed and arrested Saddam being tried for crimes against humanity by an international criminal tribunal. And its chief proponents seemed to believe, at this time, that the liberation of Iraq would be best achieved by creating large liberated areas within central and southern Iraq, protected by US air power, from which attacks would be launched – by Iraqi opposition forces – into the parts remaining under Saddam's control. But there is no doubt that the act was a spearhead of conservative Republican thinking about foreign policy as the end of the Clinton era approached.

The outgoing President's disdain towards the Iraq Liberation Act acted as just one more provocation to the Clinton-haters. White House aides were quoted as saying that Clinton had no intention of 'passing one rifle' to the Iraqi opposition. The anger this approach caused to the true believers was intense. 'In 31 years in Washington,' Perle told a Senate committee in the final summer of the Clinton presidency, 'I have not seen a sustained hypocrisy that parallels the current administration's public embrace of the Iraq Liberation Act and its dilatory tactics aimed at preventing any progress taking place under the act.' Everything would be different after the election, Perle added. 'Governor Bush has said he would fully implement the Iraq Liberation Act. We all understand what that means. It means a serious and sustained effort to assist the opposition with a view to bringing down Saddam's regime.'

George W. Bush did not come to Washington with a plan to oust Saddam Hussein in his back pocket. He never pretended to know much about foreign policy. On the campaign trail, Governor Bush made few references to foreign affairs or to security policy. When pressed, he said he would take advice from people who knew more than he did. These advisers, it later transpired, were known as the Vulcans, a group that was chaired by Rice and Wolfowitz.

It has become apologist orthodoxy to say that Bush and his running mate Dick Cheney never mentioned Iraq on the campaign trail in 1999 and 2000. In fact they did. In a December 1999 debate among the Republican hopefuls, Bush was asked what he would do if he discovered that Saddam had weapons of mass destruction. Bush replied that he would 'take 'em out'. The moderator, Jim Lehrer, followed up. Had Bush said he would take Saddam out, he asked? 'Take out the weapons of mass destruction,' Bush replied.

Nor was Cheney entirely silent on the subject. In an interview on NBC in September 2000, he was asked about the crossroads in the desert. In retrospect, did he believe that the Bush Sr administration was right not to have turned left and attacked Baghdad? Cheney replied that he did. The United States should not act 'as though we were an imperialist power, willy-nilly moving into capitals in that part of the world, taking down governments'. In the current situation, a Bush-Cheney administration wants 'to maintain our current posture vis-à-vis Iraq', he assured his interviewer.

On another occasion during the campaign, Bush put his wider uncertainties into words: 'When I was coming up, with what was a dangerous world,' he said, 'we knew exactly who the "they" were. It was us versus them, and it was clear who the "them" were. Today we're not so sure who the they are, but we know they're there.' On another, speaking in Charleston, Bush said that we lived in a time of America's 'unrivalled military power' but gave few hints of how he proposed to use it. 'What is most curious about these speeches,' wrote the historian Frances Fitzgerald, 'is the combination of triumphalism and almost unmitigated pessimism about the rest of the world.'

In November 2000, George Walker Bush won the most controversial presidential election in United States history. Though he lost the popular vote by more than half a million votes, he won in the electoral college thanks to a five-votes-to-four judgement in his favour in the US Supreme Court. Bush took over the White House in a bitterly divided country, and for the first few months of his presidency he made few moves on foreign policy of any kind.

What he did do, however, was to stock the defence and foreign policy parts of his administration with many of the most prominent figures in neo-conservative circles. Cheney had been elected Vice-President on Bush's ticket. Rumsfeld went to the Pentagon for the second time, accompanied by Wolfowitz, Feith, Crouch and, in an advisory role, Perle. Bolton was put in the number three post at the State Department, under Powell. Khalilzad joined the National Security Committee (and would later become special White House envoy to Afghanistan and then to the Iraqi opposition), which was headed by Rice. The new foreign policy team were well to the right not just of their Clinton administration predecessors, but also of the Baker-Scowcroft-Cheney line-up under the new President's father a decade earlier.

George Bush has said privately that in those first months of his presidency he rarely considered any other policy towards Iraq than the continuation of containment. On 16 February 2001, less than a month after he had been sworn in, the new President ordered the bombing of Iraqi command and control centres near Baghdad, and signalled that the new administration would take a tough line against the Saddam regime. Yet an early drive against Saddam was not on his agenda, he later told Tony Blair. Others offer a different view. US policy towards Iraq 'continues to be driven by the Iraq Liberation Act', Rumsfeld told a congressional committee that spring. Within a few weeks of taking over at the Pentagon, Rumsfeld and Wolfowitz were making good on something that Clinton's team had persistently avoided. Iraqi oppositionists began to receive weapons training from US special forces based at College Station in Texas.

But conspiracy theorists should be careful. Though Bush undoubtedly arrived in the White House with a deep grievance against Saddam – 'He tried to kill my dad' was his answer on one occasion when questioned about his view of the Iraqi leader – there is little evidence to support the claim that the new President was obsessed with overthrowing Saddam to settle a family score. His attention in those early months seemed to be more focused on China and North Korea, and the Rumsfeld-led National Missile Defence project, than on the Middle East and Saddam. For Bush to turn his attention to Iraq, something else was required.

The al-Qaida terrorist attacks on New York and Washington that came out of a clear blue autumn sky on 11 September 2001 redefined every aspect of American foreign policy and defence thinking. Bush's own view, as told to Blair at Camp David a year later, is that before 9/11 he was in favour of aggressive containment, but that after 9/11 he was open to regime change. Rumsfeld's views, in contrast, were barely changed by 9/11, merely hardened. Just five hours after the hijacked American Airlines Flight 77 had ploughed into the very building in which he himself worked, and with the rescue crews still scouring the smoking debris, Rumsfeld sat in his office, poring through intelligence reports and jotting down notes. If most Americans were still shellshocked by the unprecedented horror of the al-Qaida attacks which, even then, most observers assumed were the work of Osama bin Laden, Rumsfeld was astonishingly focused in another direction. According to CBS News, the Defence Secretary wrote that he wanted 'best info fast'. And then he wrote this: 'Judge whether good enough hit SH at the same time. Not only UBL. Go massive. Sweep it all up. Things related and not.'

Seven hours later, Bush convened a meeting of his top defence and security advisers in a White House bunker. 'We have made the decision to punish whoever harbours terrorists, not just the perpetrators,' Bush told them. What he meant, he then went on, was that this was 'showtime'. The discussion then focused on Bin Laden and the two countries where his al-Qaida forces were known to be most heavily entrenched. Those countries were Afghanistan and Pakistan. Only towards the end of that first strategy discussion did Rumsfeld raise another subject. What about other countries that supported terrorism, he asked. Bush's reply, according to the investigative reporter Bob Woodward's later account, was succinct. 'We have to force countries to choose,' he said.

On the first weekend following the attacks, Saturday 15 September, Bush called his main advisers to a much longer discussion at his Camp David retreat. The agenda was what was now defined as 'the war on terrorism' and focused principally on Afghanistan. Again, though, both Rumsfeld and Wolfowitz (whose presence there surprised Powell, who had assumed deputies were not invited) turned the discussion to Iraq. Afghanistan was a notoriously difficult military theatre, Wolfowitz argued. 'In contrast,' writes Woodward, 'Iraq was a brittle, oppressive regime that might break easily. It was doable. He estimated there was 10 to 50 per cent chance Saddam was involved in the September 11 terrorist attacks. The US would have to go after Saddam at some time if the war on terrorism was to be taken seriously.'

Powell was sceptical. The chances of building a coalition would disappear if the US went after Iraq, he told the meeting. 'If you get something pinning September 11 on Iraq, great – let's put it out and kick them at the right time. But let's get Afghanistan now. If we do that we will have increased our ability to go after Iraq – if we can prove Iraq had a role.' Bush agreed with his Secretary of State. Iraq could wait, he decided.

But Bush does not appear to have waited very long. The war plan against Afghanistan finally reached the President's desk two days later, on 17 September. He put his signature to a two-and-a-half-page document. But at the end of the document was a direction to the Pentagon to draw up military options for an invasion of Iraq. According to the *Washington Post*, in an article published 15 months later, 'longtime advocates of ousting Hussein pushed Iraq to the top of the agenda by connecting their cause to the war on terrorism'. Over the next 9 months, the *Post* argued, 'the administration would make Iraq the central focus of its war on terrorism without producing a rich paper trail or record of key meetings and events leading to a formal decision to act against President Saddam Hussein'.

The decision to attack Iraq, the *Post* claimed, was 'in many ways a victory for a small group of conservatives who, at the start of the administration, found themselves outnumbered by more moderate voices in the military and foreign policy bureaucracy'. The conservatives' view, the *Post* continued, was quickly embraced by Bush and Cheney soon after 9/11.

According to the *Post*'s account, as corroborated by other witnesses, 'the important thing is that the President's position changed after 9/11'. In March 2003, an anonymous senior administration official confirmed this at length in a *New Yorker* article: 'Before September 11, there wasn't a consensus administration view about Iraq. This issue hadn't come to the fore, and you had administration views. There were those who preferred regime change, and they were largely residing in the Pentagon, and probably in the Vice-President's office. At the State Department, the focus was on tightening up the containment regime – the so-called "smart sanctions". The National Security Council didn't seem to have much of an opinion at that point.'

The Defence Policy Board at the Pentagon, chaired by Perle, began meeting to carry out the President's order on 19 and 20 September. Little more than a week after the 9/11 attacks, therefore, the US government was actively preparing for an attack on Iraq which – officially – was not government policy until well into 2002 at the earliest.

Over the following weeks in the autumn of 2001, while Bush and most of Washington concentrated on Afghanistan and the domestic impact of 9/11, the Pentagon increased its momentum on Iraq. 'The issue got away from the President,' an official commented later. He was conceding the initiative to people who were obsessed with the issue. 'I do believe certain people have grown theological about this,' another official said. 'It's almost a religion – that it will be the end of our society if we don't take action now.' When Colin Powell attended such meetings at the White House, he came back to the State Department in disbelief, telling his officials: 'Jeez, what a fixation about Iraq.'

Publicly, Iraq was not on the agenda through most of this time, even though speculation was rife that plans were afoot. Bush himself said little in public until the State of the Union speech on 28 January 2002 when he spoke about Iran, Iraq and North Korea constituting an 'axis of evil, arming to threaten the peace of the world'. He would not wait on events, while dangers gathered, Bush told his audience on Capitol Hill – an audience that included Tony Blair. Even then, White House officials tried to steer journalists away from the full significance of the reference. One briefer told reporters 'not to read anything into any name in terms of the next phase'.

Yet this was deceitful. Not only had Bush signed off the 17 September war plan, which included the section about planning for an attack on Iraq, but around the turn of the year 2002, he also signed a secret intelligence order directing the CIA to undertake what the *Washington Post* called 'a comprehensive covert programme to topple Hussein, including authority to use lethal force to capture the Iraqi President'. There is also evidence to suggest that, by February 2002, Blair knew that key decisions had been taken in Washington. According to a *Sunday Telegraph* front-page article in April 2003, based on Russian intelligence documents allegedly found after the fall of Baghdad, Blair complained to Italy's Prime Minister Silvio Berlusconi in Rome on 15 February 2002 about 'negative things decided by the United States over Baghdad'.

Somewhere in the first half of 2002, everything went up a gear. 'The President internalised the idea of making regime change in Iraq,' the previously quoted official told the *New Yorker*. It was time to figure out 'what we are doing about Iraq', Bush said to Rice during a meeting in April. 'I made up my mind that Saddam needs to go,' he told the somewhat surprised British media at the Bush-Blair summit in Crawford, Texas, early the same month. 'That's about all I'm willing to share with you.'

Speculation about whether Iraq would be attacked was intense all through the spring and early summer. Even when Bush unveiled what would come to be called the 'Bush doctrine' of preemptive military action, in a speech at West Point on 1 June 2002, there was still a sense that the issue had not been settled. The fiction that no decision has been taken continued to be well concealed, not just from the public, but from senior members of the administration itself. 'Time is getting short for decisions that have to be made if the goal is to take action early next year, before the presidential election cycle intrudes,' the *New York Times* mused in early July 2002. That same month, the State Department's Director of Policy Planning, Richard Haass, thought he should raise the question during one of his regular meetings with Rice at the White House. Should we talk about the pros and cons of attacking Iraq, Haass asked the National Security Adviser. Rice's reply, as reported later, was terse and true. 'Don't bother. The President has made a decision.'

By August 2002, the neo-cons had won. The issue was now not whether to attack Iraq, but how. Whether, without 9/11, the neo-cons, above all in the Pentagon, above all Rumsfeld and Wolfowitz, would have won so soon, so clearly and so totally is doubtful. The decision to attack Iraq had little or no direct connection with 9/11, yet 9/11 made it possible. The decision came because powerful and influential people had prepared, in some cases obsessively, for this moment. When the moment came, they had an answer which pre-empted the question. They were the right people in the right place at the right time. It was time to return to the crossroads in the desert and take a new direction.

2 Disunited nations

Nescis, mi fili, quantilla sapientia regitur mundus .
(Know, my son, with how little wisdom the world is governed.)
Count Axel Oxenstierna, Swedish statesman, 1583–1654

It was turning into the darkest weekend of Tony Blair's career – and the news from Iraq was making it worse. At home, the media were in a frenzy over the flat-buying allegations that would soon be dubbed Cheriegate. The tale of the Prime Minister's wife, the lifestyle guru and the conman lover had put Downing Street under siege, sending relations between the Prime Minister and his top strategist Alastair Campbell plunging to an all-time low. Inside and outside Downing Street, temperatures were plummeting even faster than the PM's approval ratings. As the first snows of winter fell over southern England on 6 December 2002, the Blairs had retreated to Chequers to lick their wounds and defy the world.

That weekend came the news from Baghdad. On Saddam Hussein's behalf, one of the Iraqi President's top scientific advisers had handed over a dossier to United Nations weapons inspectors. It contained Saddam's answer to UN calls for a complete account of Iraq's weapons of mass destruction programme. All told, the dossier ran to 12,000 pages and weighed 60 kg. But it all boiled down to a single assertion: Iraq's denial that it had possessed chemical, biological or nuclear-related weapons and missiles for more than 10 years. When Blair heard the WMD declaration that weekend, he thought to himself that war with Iraq was now virtually inevitable.

The reason was that the Prime Minister had until now pursued a strategy that relied upon convincing people that Iraq was a threat, in George Bush's words, that 'Saddam Hussein's regime is a grave and gathering danger'. The trouble was that no one had been convinced. Not Iraq's neighbours. Not Britain's near-est friends in Europe. Not all the members of the United Nations Security Council. Not the UN's weapons inspectors. Certainly not opinion at home. Baghdad, sensing disarray, added to the con-fusion by saying it had nothing to hide. Blair was failing to make his case because no credible, independent evidence had emerged so far of Iraq's intent and its ability to terrorise the world. He was not helped by the fact that bombing Iraq was a pet project of the American right, whose ideas are influential in the US and Israel but reviled by the rest of the world.

But Blair was convinced, and after 11 September so was the White House. On Saturday 7 September 2002, Bush and Blair met at the US President's mountaintop retreat at Camp David in Maryland. As they took a walk, they reflected on how the world had changed. Bush said that, exactly a year before, he and his foreign policy advisers had been discussing plans to tighten sanctions against Iraq. War against Saddam had not been on his agenda then, as it was now, he said. A year ago, Blair told the President, he had seen himself as the one who was putting on the pressure over Iraq. In Blair's view, intervening against Saddam was all of a piece with intervening against Slobodan Milosevic in Kosovo. But 11 September had changed everything. After 11 September 2001, Blair and Bush agreed, America's world view had been transformed.

In the immediate wake of 9/11, according to Sir Christopher Meyer, then British Ambassador to Washington, Blair pushed to divert the Bush administration away from an attack on Iraq. He argued that there was little credible intelligence to suggest a link between the Islamic fundamentalists of al-Qaida and the Arab totalitarianism of Saddam. But Meyer repeatedly told Blair that the Bush administration was coming under pressure from the Pentagon to turn its guns on Saddam after Afghanistan.

Before Blair was due to meet Bush at his Texas ranch in April 2002, Meyer briefed him on the profound impact of 9/11 on the American psyche. 'Everything had changed in America,' he recalled. There was much talk of regime change in Iraq, he reported, and overwhelming pressure on Bush to adopt a new pre-emptive military doctrine. Blair saw this as an opportunity rather than a threat. Conscious of the discomfort among his Labour backbenchers at Washington's growing hawkishness, he publicly put forward his own brand of liberal interventionism in a speech at the end of his Texas visit, given at the George Bush Sr Presidential Library at College Station.

'The moment for decision on how to act is not yet with us,' he said. 'But to allow WMD to be developed by a state like Iraq without let or hindrance would be grossly to ignore the lessons of 11 September and we will not do it. The message to Saddam is clear: he has to let the inspectors back in, anyone, any time, any place that the international community demands.' Importantly, he went on to refer to three conflicts he had been involved in that had involved regime change: 'If necessary, the action should be military – and again, if necessary and justified, it should involve regime change.'

In the upper reaches of the British government, private anxieties were starting to spread about the way the US debate was developing. At a televised press conference in a draughty school hall in his Sedgefield constituency, the Prime Minister admitted that the debate on Iraq had moved faster than he had expected. In a phrase that had been agreed over the August summer holidays, Blair also said he wanted the issue of Iraq to go to the UN, but only so long as it was 'a way of dealing with the matter rather than a means of avoiding it'. It was a phrase he was to repeat many times in the months ahead.

With the debate growing in Washington over whether to go down the Security Council route, Blair travelled to see Bush at Camp David on the weekend of 7 September. By the time he arrived in the US, however, the argument seemed to have been settled. Colin Powell, the Secretary of State, had seen off the hawks in a series of stormy meetings. After a four-day stay at his parents' summer house in Maine, where the President had 'in-depth conversations' with his father about Iraq, Bush seemed committed to taking the dispute with Iraq down the UN route.

He would call for UN weapons inspectors, who had been withdrawn four years previously, to be sent back in on a tight timetable.

Blair and his team saw Camp David as a great success. In the short term, the British believed the chief achievement had been to convince Dick Cheney, the Vice-President, who had derided the UN process in August, to come onside. Cheney's language made it clear where he and the aviary of hawks in the White House stood. 'A return of inspectors would provide no assurance whatsoever of [Hussein's] compliance with UN resolutions,' the Vice-President had warned. 'On the contrary, there is a great danger that it would provide false comfort that Saddam was somehow "back in his box".'

In the long term, Blair believed that the Americans had agreed to follow a process which, if Saddam co-operated, would avert war. The outcome of the conflict was now in Saddam's hands, he thought.

A script was agreed at Camp David that Bush would deliver at the UN. On 12 September, the US President gave his speech. For London it was a triumph, but it was nearly a disaster. As Bush delivered his speech, the vital reference to adopting the UN route dropped off his teleprompter, apparently because of a technical problem. Bush's response was both brilliant and flawed. Unfazed, he spotted the omission and ad libbed the key commitment. But, as he did so, he made an inadvertent error. He referred not just to the need for a new UN resolution on enforcement of weapons inspection. He referred to new 'resolutions'. That use of the plural was to have big consequences as the diplomatic campaign now went into overdrive.

One immediate result was that Bush's comment prompted Dominique de Villepin, the flamboyant French Foreign Minister, to suggest, at a lunch at the Hotel Pierre in New York with his counterparts in New York the following day, that there should be two resolutions: one to send the inspectors back in, and a second to authorise military action. The French, he said, would be prepared to vote for the second only if Iraq had been given a chance to comply, and had failed to do so. France's immediate concern was to ensure that the first resolution should not give the US a free hand to resort to force whenever it judged Saddam to be in breach of his obligations. 'Be sure about one thing,' Powell told Villepin. 'Don't vote for the first unless you are prepared to vote for the second.'

The diplomatic task of constructing a resolution on the inspections process and punishment for non-compliance began in earnest on 16 September. The overall aim was to satisfy the US hawks and at the same time be reasonable enough to win the support of the French, the Russians and the Chinese. The wrangling over the wording and the ordering of paragraphs took nearly six weeks. From the start, divisions in Washington made themselves felt. Both Britain and the US diplomatic mission in New York wanted to start the draft with relatively mildly phrased language in the resolution, and then resist all calls for concessions from the French. But hawks in Washington suggested an approach in which concessions could gradually be offered. For instance, Donald Rumsfeld was demanding that UN inspectors should be guarded by US troops. Blair would have none of that idea, and said so to Bush.

As the transatlantic diplomacy continued, Blair made his case against Iraq and its threat to the world in Parliament on 24 September. He had promised to publish a dossier drawing on British intelligence that would prove to the public and the Labour Party that Saddam possessed weapons of mass destruction. What he did not reveal was that the dossier already existed – it had been prepared in March 2002. When it arrived the 50-page document was, at first glance, devastating.

'I am in no doubt that the threat is serious and current, that he [Saddam] has made progress on WMD, and that he has to be stopped,' wrote Blair in a foreword to the government's dossier. Iraq's arms were a 'threat to the UK national interest', affording Saddam 'the ability to inflict real damage upon the region and the stability of the world,' he warned. In case the urgent nature of the menace was still unclear, Blair added for good measure that chemical and biological arms were held at a maximum state of readiness. 'Some of these weapons are deployable within 45 minutes of an order to use them.'

The report claimed that Iraq could strike as far as Israel and Turkey. It also included a declaration that Baghdad was developing nuclear weapons and that uranium had been 'sought from Africa that has no civil nuclear application in Iraq'. The trouble was, in the coming months, much of the dossier's claims were demolished. British journalists in Baghdad visited several 'facilities of concern' highlighted in the report and found nothing sinister. Most spectacular was the collapse of the nuclear allegations in the face of rebuttals from the Director General of the International Atomic Energy Agency and the UN weapons inspector Mohamed El Baradei.

The search for a UN resolution was made no easier when, in the middle of the Labour Party conference, the first draft, with the harshest possible language, was leaked to the *New York Times*. Blair and Jack Straw, the Foreign Secretary, found themselves in a tiny overheated room at the Imperial Hotel in Blackpool, discussing the wording with the British team at the UN, the Foreign Office and Washington.

The text was agreed at the end of September. It referred to 'all necessary measures' (UN code for military action), but deferred action until the inspections process was clearly over. Immediately after the Labour conference, Straw went to Paris to try to persuade Villepin it was in the French interest to go along with this. He travelled to the Middle East, including Iran, where President Khatami confided that he would tolerate a war. He would prefer it to come through the UN route and to involve a quick strike, the Iranian leader said, even if for domestic reasons he dare not say so in public. His country needed no reminding of the dangers of weapons of mass destruction in Iraqi hands. 'Iranians still die here every week from the chemical attacks by Saddam,' he told Straw, referring to the Iran-Iraq war of the 1980s.

This was a coup of sorts for the coalition, which had no support for military action in the Middle East. Jordan's King

Abdullah II believed a war with Iraq would bring a virtual Armageddon to the region. Saudi Arabia's Crown Prince Abdullah warned that the United States could not count on using Saudi air bases in any conflict – an extraordinary position for a country that US troops still defend against Iraq.

The delay in reaching agreement on the resolution was caused as much by internal discussion in Washington as international disagreement, but Sir Jeremy Greenstock, Britain's ambassador to the UN in New York, explained: 'What happens is, a product emerges from two or three days of intensive telephone diplomacy between the permanent five members [the US, Britain, Russia, France and China] and diplomats here, and then you wait several more days for Washington to decide on their position for the next round . . . If you tick off the days that went by between 16 September and 8 November when the resolution was agreed, the days waiting for the next US position were many more than the actual negotiation over language between members of the Security Council.'

On 8 November the UN finally agreed Resolution 1441. 'To the bitter end the French tried to get a commitment that the Security Council would have to make a further decision after an assessment by the inspectors,' Greenstock said. 'That proved a red line for the Americans, who would not be tied to a second resolution, or anything that relied on the recommendation of the inspectors.' The final wording merely allowed for the Council to meet if Iraq did not fully comply with the resolution. In retrospect, some British officials – although not Straw – now admit that it was a mistake to try to secure unanimity. It led to a confused resolution from which either side could extract the meaning they liked. With hindsight, Greenstock concedes that too many ambiguities were left.

It is important to put into context how the UN works – or does not. Despite the 250 or so wars since its inception, the world's government has punished aggressors on just three occasions: in 1950 with North Korea, 1991 with Iraq and 2001 over Afghanistan. Part of the UN's ineffectiveness was its role as a shouting shop during the Cold War. Since the Berlin Wall came down, the UN has been slightly more energetic. In the 1990s, it retrospectively endorsed armed interventions in Liberia, Sierra Leone and Kosovo, while failing to stop genocide in Rwanda. But the 191 countries of the UN hold two principles dear: one is a dedication to nonviolence by nations, the other a commitment to collective action against those who threaten international peace. If Iraq broke either, Baghdad would breach these central tenets of the UN charter and trigger war. But Resolution 1441 was not enough, a point conceded by John Negroponte, America's UN ambassador, in the Security Council at the time it was passed.

The inspectors went back into Iraq on 27 November. France, Germany, Russia and China were all resisting precipitate military action, but the points at which they were prepared to countenance hostilities varied. A key moment in this process was Iraq's dossier, produced on 8 December. Saddam failed to give a credible account of Iraqi weapons programmes, exasperating both wings of the Washington debate as well as the main British players. But he also gave France and Russia enough material to argue that the process triggered by 1441 was working.

In Downing Street, Blair and his government were sinking into the swamp of Cheriegate. The Prime Minister understood that if the inspection process was a lengthy affair, it would be a return to the cat-and-mouse game of the 90s, when Saddam blocked and parried an increasingly intrusive UN inspections regime. The most obvious fault in the resolution was the lack of a timetable by which the inspectors were to conclude their work. Hans Blix and his team suggested establishing 'tasks' for Iraq to carry out which were due to be listed on 27 March.

The British government, sensing public opinion settling in favour of peace and inspections rather than war without them, decided to go on the offensive. It released a 23-page document, *Saddam Hussein: Crimes and Human Rights Abuses*, which provided a horrifying account of abuses. Again this was widely criticised by human rights groups, MPs and others for recycling old information. At the launch, the Foreign Office had on the platform an Iraqi exile who had been jailed by Saddam for 11 years. Later, he disclosed that the handcuffs he had worn had been made in Britain. What was significant was that after three months of diplomacy, Blair was preparing the ground for another argument against Iraq: regime change of a tyrant and a dictator.

Blair was also coming under fire from Labour backbenchers. So, despite his misgivings, he persevered with the UN route – hoping that the tide would turn in his favour. He met Blix privately at Chequers in January to see whether the timetable in Iraq could be shortened. When this failed, the US and Britain demanded an interim report on 27 January. Both countries still hoped that Blix would be critical of Saddam's lack of co-oper-ation. In this context, Greenstock now advised that a second resolution could be framed and won, giving Saddam a tight deadline or the prospect of war.

Doubts had started to emerge in the UK government. A former close colleague of Blix rang the Foreign Office out of the blue to warn that he might not be the right man for the task. 'If you are looking for a man to come to decisive judgments, you have picked the wrong man,' was the message. Blix had been app-ointed chief weapons inspector after pressure from the French. The pivotal position of the French forced the Foreign Office into a long assessment of how President Chirac would behave when the moment came to judge whether Saddam was abusing the inspections process.

The UN Security Council's five permanent members, who wield the diplomatic equivalent of a nuclear device, the veto, have long been split over the issue of Iraq. They are America, Britain, Russia, France and China – the great powers at the end of the Second World War. Although French troops had taken part in the first Gulf conflict and had also patrolled the no-fly zones over Iraqi skies, in the 90s Paris had grown closer to the Russian and Chinese position that Iraq's disarmament was practically complete and that sanctions were increasingly hurt-ing the people of the country, not its tyrannical ruler. Of course all three had financial interests in Iraq.

But it was French intransigence, coupled with Chirac's belief that America needed to be curbed, that worried London. British sources now believe that Chirac made what they describe as the strategic decision not to support the Washington-London axis as long ago as the end of October 2002. 'He was off the leash ever since the end of cohabitation with the socialists,' said one cabinet minister, referring to Chirac's crushing re-election victory in May 2002.

When Germany arrived on the Security Council as a non-permanent member, the diplomatic dynamic changed. In part to secure his own narrow re-election in the German elections of September 2002, Gerhard Schröder adopted a robust position against military action in Iraq. Politically, it saved him. Now, as a powerful rotating member of the Security Council, Germany provided both an ally and a rival for France's emerging defiance of the US.

The crunch at the UN came as France and Germany were celebrating the 40th anniversary of the Franco-German treaty. 'This was not just going to be a symbolic event,' the Foreign Office recognised. At the anniversary celebrations in Versailles, Chirac and Schröder agreed to forge a united front to press for a peaceful solution to the Iraqi crisis. The litmus test of their reformed alliance became the willingness to confront American unilateralism. 'If Germany and France do not vote together on the Iraq question,' said Rudolf von Thadden, Berlin's co-ordinator for Franco-German relations, 'it will be difficult to pursue a common policy in the coming years.' A true anti-war alliance was born.

Straw tried to restrain Villepin. He complimented him for playing his cards well in the run-up to 1441, and insisted that Britain was not bent on war. He argued that middle-sized countries such as Britain and France had far more invested in the UN than a superpower like the US. He told Villepin: 'You realise that if Saddam complies, we are going to take "yes" for an answer. That's the end of the matter and the US knows that. I have told Powell that and he understands.'

Blair agreed with that judgement. He believed he had a clear understanding with Bush that if the UN route worked, there would be no war. Though Blair wanted Saddam to be ousted, he was prepared to override that wish if the Iraqi regime co-operated with the UN. At the same time, though, military preparations were now advanced, and were helping to secure some levels of Iraqi co-operation. US forces had been growing in the Gulf region since the summer. UK forces joined them through the autumn and winter.

As the military build-up continued, and with the Pentagon hawks continually raising the stakes, there was no lack of circumstantial justification for the emerging French view that the US was now bent on war. By mid-January, Paris decided to respond in dramatic fashion. Speaking at the UN on 21 January after a meeting on counter-terrorism, Villepin made his démarche on Iraq. 'Today, nothing justifies considering military action,' he said. Asked if France would use its veto, he added: 'Believe me that, in a matter of principles, we will go all the way to the end.'

Powell was furious. He had met Villepin privately the night before at the Waldorf Astoria Hotel in New York and had not foreseen this public rebuff. According to Meyer, who saw Powell soon afterwards, he was still spitting at the French. Worse, Rumsfeld had responded to Villepin's speech by provocatively labelling the French and Germans as 'old Europe'.

Rumsfeld's remarks only inflamed British and European anti-war opinion. Preparations were already under way for a big anti-war demonstration in London on 15 February to coincide with protests around the world. In Parliament, the anti-war mood among Labour MPs was hardening. Rumours swirled of potential ministerial resignations.

Blair desperately needed the political cover of a second UN resolution explicitly authorising war. The issue was discussed repeatedly in cabinet and Blair repeatedly expressed confidence that a second resolution could be achieved. On the BBC *Breakfast with Frost* programme in January, he had gone beyond the agreed line by saying he would only go to war if a veto was wielded unreasonably. The official position had been only to say that a second resolution was preferable, not essential.

On 23 January, Straw went to Washington to put the case for a second resolution and review the Franco-German position with Powell. The pair also discussed the need to rally European opinion, something partially achieved when 10 central and eastern European states rallied to a pro-US declaration signed by Blair and the Spanish Prime Minister, Jose Maria Aznar, a declaration that greatly offended Chirac.

Blair travelled to a brief summit at Camp David on 31 January to discuss the timing of the war and the gathering diplomatic impasse. It was not an easy meeting. Accounts differ wildly, a sign that in reality it was a bruising occasion. Officially, Blair persuaded Bush to make a further push on the Middle East peace process as part of the effort to win round international opinion to the attack on Iraq. Unofficially, according to one senior minister, 'Tony got very badly roughed up indeed. The Americans gave him a very hard time about the UN.' Matters were not helped when Blix popped up to say that the war clock stood 'at five minutes to midnight', a clear reference to how close to battle America was.

The consensus was that the coalition remained at least six weeks from war, and needed more time to persuade public opinion. It was agreed that Powell should make a high-profile presentation to the Security Council, drawing on intelligence reports to demonstrate that Saddam was not co-operating. Managing media expectations for such a global media event was never going to be easy, but the build-up suggested that Powell would produce the 'smoking gun' that Blix and his team had failed to find over the preceding weeks. The presentation was long on assertion and muffled taped phone calls, but short on killer facts. It fell flat.

To make matters worse, Powell's prolix presentation was followed by a succinct assault from Villepin, rapidly becoming the star of this new televised global parliament. When Villepin finished his response, the audience in New York broke into applause. It was a sign that Britain and the US were becoming isolated.

Russia took the opposite course to its former satellite states. On 9 February, it joined Germany and France in what later came to be known as the 'non-nyet-nein' alliance. Again Britain had misread the degree of opposition in a major European capital, and was surprised by the setback. With not just one but two veto-wielding members of the Security Council now signed up to the cause of delay, there was even speculation that the US could be diverted from its path.

A day earlier, Downing Street's plan to win over the British public ran into more trouble. The government thought it had scored a blow when it released a report entitled *Iraq: Its Infrastructure of Concealment, Deception and Intimidation*. A Downing Street production, the first sentence of the report said it was based on a number of sources, including intelligence material, but it turned out that much of it was lifted from academic sources. Even MI6 started privately complaining at the way No 10 had been over-egging intelligence material on Iraq.

Blair reacted aggressively. He decided to raise the emotional temperature of the argument, shifting the ground for his stance from the weapons of mass destruction into a broader assault on Saddam. It became what his communications director Alastair Campbell dubbed the 'masochism strategy', confronting hostile TV audiences and making more regular reports to parliament.

Despite this ploy, the polls were showing that the public still thought the US was straining every sinew to find an excuse for war. Blix was due to make another report to the Security Council on 14 February. There had been little sign in British eyes of fuller co-operation from Saddam. Downing Street was being reassured the report would be negative, but Straw started to smell a rat. He heard the report was not only going to attack the US, it was also going to praise the Iraqis for greater co-operation. 'Bloody hell, we are going to be in the dock,' Straw thought. He rewrote chunks of his speech to the UN while travelling to New York on Concorde.

Although some of the details in Blix's report were not un-help-ful to the Anglo-US cause, the crux was clearly that he was advocating more time for inspections. Moreover, no weapons of mass destruction had been found. Blix insisted he was produc-ing careful reports based on the evidence found by his inspec-tors, and that the inspections were 'effectively helping to bridge the gap in knowledge'. The Americans were sceptical, and held back from giving Blix up-to-the-minute intelligence. Britain was more helpful with intelligence, but the politicians were concerned that Blix was going beyond his mandate. 'He was always very worried that the responsibility was on him for war or not-war,' a minister recalled. 'He should have got on with the job and not thought he was in any position to arbitrate politic-ally. That was our job.'

The next day, millions of anti-war protesters from around the world took to the streets in what was perhaps the world's first global political demonstration. The anti-war bandwagon was rolling with extraordinary force. Three out of four Italians were opposed to military action, as was 80 per cent of the Spanish population. Blair's own personal standing was taking a battering and there was speculation on his chances of political survival. Private polling for Downing Street showed that George Bush himself was the big negative for British voters and Labour MPs.

On 27 February, 121 Labour MPs rebelled against their own government, backing a motion arguing that the case for war was unproven. London now repeatedly stressed to Powell the absolute imperative of winning a second UN resolution. Straw even gave the Secretary of State regular updates of the British parliamentary arithmetic. If the government did not get a second resolution it looked as if 190 to 200 MPs would be opposed. Figures like this could spell Blair's demise. To the Prime Minister's irritation, he learned that senior civil servants had begun to check the procedures that might be necessary if he was forced to quit.

Against this background Washington and London had to decide to push for a second resolution explicitly authorising war. Although US public opinion marginally favoured a second resolution, the Bush team felt the first resolution provided enough political and legal authority for war. For Washington, a second resolution was optional not imperative, and perhaps might only be a complication. The same could not be said of Blair, who desperately needed the protection of the second vote.

To secure a further resolution authorising military action, the US needed 9 of the 15 Security Council votes available. For weeks it had been clear that the US could count on only 3 other nations – the UK, Spain and Bulgaria. A further 5 states from among the undecided, or at least undeclared, non-permanent members – Pakistan, Mexico, Chile, Angola, Cameroon and Guinea – were needed. Given the resources with which the mighty United States can cajole and bully poor nations, this had not seemed to present an insuperable obstacle, but for the hardening opposition of France, Germany and Russia. On 7 March, the date of another Blix report, and after much internal discussion, Straw tabled a simple resolution giving Iraq a further 10 days to come into line. This was described as the reverse veto. If Saddam had not come into line by 17 March, and no objection was raised on the Security Council, the trigger for war would have been pulled. The aim was to put the onus on the French to veto military action.

The US and UK announced they would now put the pressure on the 'middle six'. 'No matter what the whip count is, we're calling for the vote,' Bush said. But, according to one British official, the US 'did not try that hard to win support for the second resolution. Although everyone talked about all sorts of arm-twisting and bribery, what was staggering was that there was very little of that. In fact there was none. They did not make much effort. They ran a come-to-us strategy. They did hardly any travelling.' By contrast, both Villepin and Lady Amos, the Foreign Office minister, made the rounds to Angola, Cameroon and Guinea in what became fruitless attempts to nail down firm support.

In reality, America's bruising behaviour and the battle talk of neo-conservatives had alienated friends and allies. President

Musharraf of Pakistan risked everything in backing the war on terror, and, deeply unpopular at home, there was a distinct possibility he could fall if forced to back a war on Iraq. President Vicente Fox of Mexico had been let down by the US when it failed to ease curbs on Mexican immigrants into America after promising to do so. One African official was quoted as saying: 'What can the Americans do to us? Are they going to bomb us? Invade us?'

In Blair's view, the best bet lay with the Chilean President Ricardo Lagos, the country's first left-wing leader since the CIA-backed overthrow of Salvador Allende in 1973. But Lagos was facing internal political difficulties too, and there was deep hostility in his party to an American-led war. The 'middle six' decided to stick together for mutual protection. None wanted to be the one that gave UN endorsement to war. The British diplomats in New York admitted frustration, with one saying: 'They found it a deeply uncomfortable experience with ministers marching around their capitals demanding their loyalty.'

Things seemed to be reaching a head when Lamine Sidime, the Guinean Prime Minister and leader of the six, was ushered into Greenstock's New York office on the afternoon of Sunday 9 March and invited to sit down on the plush yellow sofa. It was the vital meeting to see if they could break the impasse. The Guinean suggested a 45-day deadline by which the Iraqis had to comply. Greenstock, knowing the American position, had to reject the proposal flat. 'This is for the birds,' he said. 'It is a transparent way of arguing for six months because that takes us to the hot period and the US will not wait that long.' Sidime said the timing was negotiable, but 'we want to see some benchmarks set'.

Greenstock saw this as a possible breakthrough. Benchmarks – specific goals on specific subjects – might do the trick. On the other side of the Atlantic the same evening, Blair was on the phone to Chile's Lagos, pressing him on the idea of benchmarks and timing. It is a mark of how important this moment was to Blair that he even suggested he and Straw could fly to Santiago to clinch the deal. But the traction was not there among the other members of the 'middle six' to justify the trip.

It was now a crisis. In the next week, Blair regularly rang Greenstock to ask how many votes he had. Greenstock replied: 'I can only give you a clear four.' He later recalled: 'The Prime Minister was thinking I might be quite close to the nine. So he asked, where are the rest? I replied they are not there yet, they are still being fought for. He said, crumbs.'

After playing the UN game for six months, the US State Department was coming to the view that it did not want to wait for Blair any longer. On 12 March, a week after Bush vowed to force countries to take sides on the issue, Powell for the first time publicly admitted that the fight for a second resolution was going to be abandoned. Although Bush had made a serious attempt to pursue American aims through the Security Council, he had failed because of he had been captured by the hawks. Having invented Iraq as the main target of a co-ordinated terrorist front, and having in every policy advice and public pronouncement repeated the assertion that toppling Saddam was vital to global security, America – and Tony Blair – were caught in the trap of right-wing propaganda. The rhetoric of the neo-conservatives in Washington had become doctrine. This had not bewitched allies and friends. It had repelled them.

Instead of reaching for another solution, Britain and America reached for a scapegoat: France. For London and Washington the final nail in the coffin of the second resolution was hammered down by Chirac on Monday 10 March, when he announced on French television: 'My position is that, whatever the circumstances, France will vote no because she considers this evening there are no grounds for waging war in order to achieve the goal we have set ourselves – i.e. to disarm Iraq.' Chirac's use of the phrase 'whatever the circumstances' was seized on. None of the 'middle six' was going to pay the political price of supporting a war knowing France would veto the military action anyway.

The unmistakable implication was that if the UN refused to back military action at this time and Britain went to war

regardless, France would somehow be to blame. Straw nevertheless seized on the statement. There was a tense phone call
between London and Paris. But as a *Guardian* editorial pointed
out:

> The key words here are 'this evening'. What Chirac clearly meant
> was that, in circumstances pertaining at that moment in
> time, France would use its veto. He did not say that would be
> the case at all times; and indeed, since he spoke, several official
> statements have made it plain that France is anxious to pre-
> serve UN unity and will explore 'all opportunities' for compro-
> mise. That was the import, too, of his telephone conversation
> yesterday with Tony Blair. To the extent that Mr Chirac's
> meaning could have been misinterpreted, he made a tactical
> mistake. But the overall French position, that war may be sup-
> portable but only as a last resort, is not objectively in doubt.

Geoff Hoon, Britain's Secretary of State for Defence, felt he had
to phone Rumsfeld to warn him that without a second resolution the Commons vote might be lost. Britain's withdrawal, Hoon
now admits, would have represented a massive hole in US military planning. 'It would have been extremely difficult since our
forces were so intertwined.' Following the Hoon call, Rumsfeld
went straight into a press conference and told the world Britain
might not be showing up. He was trying to be helpful, but it took
an apologetic call from Bush to Blair to unscramble the mess. A
desperate Hoon, fearing that the comment would not help
efforts to breathe new life into the dying embers of diplomacy,
rang him to ask him to withdraw the statement.

Straw published the benchmarks on Wednesday, two days after
Chirac's declaration, despite Greenstock's overnight reports of
little progress. Blair and Straw met to consider whether to pull
the plug on the diplomatic process, but Blair decided to keep
going over the weekend. He had been preparing to hold a last-
ditch summit with Bush, originally scheduled for Barbados but
switched at the last minute to the Azores. Blair, with an eye to
the coming parliamentary debate in the Commons, wanted to

extract some kind of commitment to a UN role in the post-war reconstruction of Iraq.

On Monday 17 March at the UN headquarters in New York, Greenstock served the last rites on UN diplomacy. In the face of certain defeat, the US and Britain withdrew their resolution. Greenstock summed up the failure of the strategy: 'Maybe we were naive, but we always thought the combination of tough inspections, the military build-up and catching Saddam red-handed with weapons of mass destruction would persuade the people round Saddam that this is not worth the regime's suicide. As you can see we were wrong.'

Whether or not an attack was legal was still a muddy issue. America and Britain said it was and claimed they were 'author-ised to use force' by earlier Security Council resolutions. In fact, the UN confers legality on war in only two circumstances, described in a pair of articles under Chapter VII of its charter. Article 42 says that the Security Council may 'take such action by air sea or land forces as may be necessary to maintain or restore international peace and security'. Article 51 allows the use of armed force in self-defence. Neither of these appeared to apply at this point in time to Iraq. So Blair and Bush fell back on an earlier resolution, 687. This, both nations claimed, suspended but did not terminate that use of force.

The same reasoning was used twice in the 90s to justify US and British bombing of Iraq after disputes about weapons in-spections. France, China and Russia all disagreed – arguing that in that case Washington could bomb Iraq in perpetuity to restore peace in the Middle East. Iraq was clearly not an imminent threat to world peace. Neither was there a humanitarian crisis, as there had been in Kosovo. The UN Secretary General questioned the war's legitimacy. Taking part in an illegal act could have been the conclusion of the Attorney General, Lord Goldsmith, when he published his legal opinion. But it was not. Elizabeth Wilm-hurst, Deputy Legal Officer at the Foreign Office and a former legal adviser to the UK mission at the UN, resigned – but never gave her reasons.

3 Blair's moment of truth

Man is by nature a political animal.

Aristotle, Greek philosopher, 384–322 BC

At 10.11 p.m. on 18 March Labour's chief whip, Hilary Armstrong, leaned across the front bench and gave Tony Blair a number. The Prime Minister leaned back on the green leather seats of the House of Commons, folded his arms in relief and could be seen to mouth: 'So that's all right, then.' Blair, his fine features worn away with worry, had wrestled his own party to the ground and won. Britain was on its way to war.

For Blair, and Britain, it was a historic mandate. But not only was the future uncertain: the past few weeks had unravelled alliances that the Prime Minister had carefully been knitting together since he had stepped over the threshold of 10 Downing Street almost six years ago.

His unwavering support for the United States and the use of force in Iraq had produced the biggest anti-war, and by extension anti-Blair, demonstrations ever held in Britain. He had been slow-handclapped on live television by mothers and lovers of those killed by al-Qaida in New York and Bali. One cabinet minister, another two ministers and four ministerial aides quit before the Prime Minister rose to address MPs. Broken too were carefully cultivated friendships with European neighbours.

The elective dictatorship of the British parliamentary system had been shaken by two parliamentary revolts on Iraq. One was tonight's vote. The other was on 26 February. Together they comprised the greatest trauma of the Blair years. They continue to cast a long, strong shadow and will do so for years to come. Iraq was Tony Blair's political near-death experience. It has been to him what the exchange rate crisis had been to John Major and Westland to Margaret Thatcher.

When Thatcher left for the Commons to defend herself in the climactic Westland debate in early 1986, she told her officials in Downing Street that by the evening she might no longer be Prime Minister. Before Blair departed for the 18 March Iraq debate, Downing Street had drawn up contingency plans for the withdrawal of British troops from the build-up in the Gulf and also for the Prime Minister's resignation, should the votes have gone against him. Blair himself talked through the possibility of resignation with his family. It was recognised that the whole cabinet would have to tender their resignations. In the hours before the vote Labour whips, who are the Prime Minister's eyes and ears, had told undecided backbenchers that he was not prepared to stay in office, even if he won, without the backing of a majority of Labour MPs. That is how serious it was.

What the Prime Minister called the 'final stages' and President Bush the 'moment of truth' had begun two days earlier on an island in the mid-Atlantic. On the Sunday morning of 16 March, Blair boarded the chartered British Airways 777 he had made his own to fly to the Azores to join Bush and his Iberian allies on the issue of Iraq: the Spanish Prime Minister Jose Maria Aznar and the Portuguese leader Durao Barroso. Lasting just 90 minutes, the talks were briefer than the journey to reach them, but they were a symbol of the Prime Minister's unwavering belief that action against Iraq was essential, even without the second UN resolution that he had worked so hard to achieve.

The message was not missed in London. As Blair's plane flew back towards Heathrow late the same night, one of his most senior ministers was preparing to end his career in front-line politics. Robin Cook, Leader of the House of Commons, had not spoken out in public against the Prime Minister's position on Iraq but in the privacy of the cabinet his views were no secret. His opinions could not be dismissed lightly. For nearly 30 years, ever since as a backbencher he began to raise questions about the role of Special Branch under the Callaghan government, and to challenge Labour's Cold War thinking on defence, Cook has been one of the few Labour MPs who understood that even

Labour governments could be threats to liberty at home and to security abroad.

As Foreign Secretary and Leader of the Commons under Blair he had been at the forefront of radical thinking. It was an irony that his finest parliamentary performance – and he was considered a great exponent of the art – was in opposition under Blair, when he demolished the Tories over the Scott Report into the arms-to-Iraq scandal. Soon after Cook's performance, Blair sent him a note. 'Dear Robin, I really thought your performance was one of the highlights of my time in parliament,' it read. 'You were not merely brilliant, you lifted the whole morale of our troops.'

But Blair could continue without this mercurial, brilliant talent. On the Thursday before the Azores summit Cook had told him that he would resign if war began without a second resolution. The next day the Leader of the House met the No 10 communications director, Alastair Campbell, to discuss how news of his departure would break. He did not attend another cabinet meeting.

In rather less measured tones – and, more significantly, in public – another cabinet minister had broken ranks over the issue of Iraq. The International Development Secretary, Clare Short, often described as the conscience of her party, had taken to the airwaves on 9 March. In an interview with the BBC she was characteristically forthright. 'If there is not UN authority for military action, or if there is not UN authority for the reconstruction of the country, I will not uphold a breach of international law or this undermining of the UN and I will resign from the government,' she said. She went on to describe the Prime Minister's behaviour as 'reckless'. But, unlike Cook, her threat was to be an empty one. Short, after being convinced by Blair, stayed – but kept the decision private.

The next time the government met was on the crisp morning of 17 March. At the end of Downing Street the sunshine and the daffodils lay over St James's Park like warm butter, but for ministers weighing the perils of war nothing could lift the gloom. At the Prime Minister's first emergency cabinet, Cook's place around the long oval table was filled by Lord Goldsmith, the Attorney General who had offered Blair the controversial advice that war without a second resolution was legally acceptable. Cook was seen leaving his official residence on the other side of St James's Park, but entered No 10 by the backdoor, unnoticed, to tell the Prime Minister in person that he had decided to go.

Two connected events mattered now. The first was Cook's resignation speech, expected that night, and its impact on MPs. The second was the parliamentary debate and vote the next day. At 9.45 p.m. Cook, flanked by two former cabinet ministers who had served the Prime Minister in his first term, Frank Dobson and Chris Smith, addressed a hushed chamber from the back benches. His resignation speech was a withering critique of the government's policy which found no answer from the front bench.

'History will be astonished at the diplomatic miscalculations' that looked set to bring war, he told the chamber. He urged MPs to block a conflict 'that has neither international authority nor domestic support' and warned that 'we delude ourselves about the degree of international hostility to military action' if Britain simply blamed the threatened French veto for the collapse of the diplomatic process.

Earlier that afternoon Downing Street had released the traditional exchange of letters between the Prime Minister and a departing colleague. The documents were friendly – Blair holding out the prospect of a future role in Europe for his former ally – but Cook took issue with the Prime Minister's jibe in his letter of thanks for years of hard work that as Foreign Secretary he had backed war in Kosovo without a UN vote. That war had been supported by Nato, the European Union and Serbia's neighbours, he pointed out.

The speech saw Cook turn on the Prime Minister's policy the same caustic skills he had used in opposition to taunt John Major's Tory government over the Scott Report on the arms-to-

Iraq affair. Iraq had launched Cook's cabinet career and Iraq ended it.

Robin Cook's careful positioning as a friendly critic was a coded message to other Labour MPs. In it were a set of arguments that could be deployed against the government but in such a way that they could only be read as constructive advice at best and criticism at worst. Labour MPs did not miss the subtext of Cook's potent speech. He had taken care to distance himself from hard-left figures in the party who hoped to use Iraq as a lever to bring down the Prime Minister. He stressed, as he had in his resignation letter, that he remained a supporter of Blair. His disagreement was about strategy, not personality. Cook was not reaching to pat the Prime Minister's back with a hand that concealed a stiletto.

The stakes were high. On the Monday evening of Cook's resignation, the word coming back to Downing Street was not good. That night MPs from all three main parties came forward to sign the rebel motion for the next day, which argued that the case for war was 'not yet proven'. More than 120 had signed it by the time the table office closed at 10.30 p.m. Such calculations were important in Parliament's increasingly febrile atmosphere. In February the Prime Minister had been shocked by the scale of the parliamentary opposition against him on Iraq. Then, 122 Labour MPs had voted for a rebel motion that argued that the case for war had 'not yet been established', by some measures the biggest parliamentary rebellion in history. This time, with all chance of a new UN resolution gone, at least 170 Labour MPs were thought to be considering opposing the government; some rebels claimed the figure could be even higher.

It is difficult to underplay the importance of the vote on Iraq on 18 March 2003. That date will be recorded as a milestone in the history of parliamentary democracy. It had taken a figure as large as Blair and an issue as substantial as war to force radical, unalterable change on parliament. The Commons was being offered a unique mandate, a constitutional shift as significant as anything since the Glorious Revolution of the 17th century that saw power shift decisively from the monarch to Parliament. Never before had elected representatives been offered an explicit vote on military action. Never again would Britain go to war without one. Labour, which in a sense had been captured and run by Tony Blair and his supporters, had ceded power to the Commons at a crucial moment. It was history. It was exciting.

The Foreign Secretary, Jack Straw, felt a special responsibility for the crisis since he had been insisting on a Commons vote, even though constitutionally none was required. He recalled in an interview later: 'It would have been ludicrous to make a speech saying, "We are facing the biggest crisis in 20 years and I now do beg the house to adjourn."' The whips also pointed out to Downing Street that it would never get closure on the issue unless there was a vote. Blair would have been hounded all through the war for denying his MPs a vote.

All stops were pulled out in an effort to persuade Labour MPs to stay loyal. In scenes reminiscent of the Tories' bloody battles over the Maastricht Treaty, party whips started work. Potential rebels were summoned to be told of the risks they were running; cabinet ministers, including John Prescott, Jack Straw and Margaret Beckett, phoned allies to ask for their loyalty. Over that Monday and Tuesday, the government in effect ground to a halt in the battle for survival. Ministers left their departmental offices and were assigned MPs with whom to speak. The whips had a list of around 40 waverers. Ten minutes before the vote Gordon Brown, the Chancellor, was still trying to persuade MPs. Normally Labour's massive majority made parliamentary votes a formality. This time things were different.

Such were the divisions in the Labour Party that even Blair's wife was drafted into the war effort. Cherie Blair, once an aspiring Labour politician herself, phoned friends in the parliamentary party on the morning of the vote to persuade them to back the government. It was a breach with tradition and set an uncomfortable precedent for her less political successors. As one of the *Guardian*'s reporters in the Commons pointed out, the Euphrates was now running through the Blair family flat in

Downing Street, just as Lady Eden had once complained that the Suez Canal ran through the drawing room at Chequers during her husband Sir Anthony's months of agonising over an intervention in the Middle East.

Apart from his wife, Blair's closest political soul-mate is Bill Clinton. The former President had seduced the Labour Party months earlier at its annual conference with the opening line to his speech: 'Conference, Clinton, Bill. Arkansas CLP.' He was now providing a political crutch for his friend in London at a crucial moment. Like Cherie Blair, he had been conscripted into action in an hour of need. Clinton pleaded in the *Guardian* with the doubting Labour Party. He could say the things that Blair never could. About the Republicans in the White House, about France and Russia, about how brilliant the PM had been. Like an Arkansas morning that makes the refreshing dew out of hot air, Clinton condensed the government's dry command of statistics into a persuasive argument of intent in his *Guardian* article, entitled 'Trust Tony's Judgement'.

> In the post-Cold War world, America and Britain have been in tough positions before: in 1998, when others wanted to lift sanctions on Iraq and we said no; in 1999 when we went into Kosovo to stop ethnic cleansing. In each case, there were voices of dissent. But the British-American partnership and the progress of the world were preserved. Now in another difficult spot, Prime Minister Blair will have to do what he believes to be right. I trust him to do that and hope the British people will too.

The issue of Iraq stirred as much passion in those fervently opposed to the war as those who fervently believed in it. In Parliament, MPs would have to satisfy themselves whether the war on Iraq was one of disarmament or whether it was about a superpower prosecuting its interests ahead of the world's. Whether events had provided an excuse to get rid of Saddam Hussein, a bogeyman for the Republican right. Whether the action would rent asunder the UN, the EU and Nato. Whether international bodies, where nations work together for the good of all, would ever function again.

What, many wondered, had happened to the arguments that Bill Clinton had aired the last time the former President had supported the current Prime Minister over Iraq? Then he had been addressing the Labour Party conference. "I tell you this,' he said casually, as if he was departing from the prepared text for a private chat with friends. 'Inspection had been effective, eliminating more arms than were ever destroyed in the Gulf War.' And he ran off with ease the list of hardware the inspectors had taken from Baghdad: 40,000 chemical weapons; 100,000 gallons of chemicals used to make weapons; 48 missiles; 30 armed warheads; and a massive biological weapons facility equipped to produce anthrax and other bio-weapons. Inspections worked, Clinton averred, even when Saddam got up to his old tricks, playing cat and mouse – while in war, no matter how precise or smart your bombs, innocent people would die. Nothing was more likely to prompt Saddam to use his weapons of mass destruction than 'the certain defeat by a US-led attack'. Pre-emptive strikes, he warned, might bring unwelcome consequences in the future. What had happened to those arguments; where had they gone?

On Tuesday morning MPs arrived at Westminster early. With the Commons now sitting earlier in the day – a legacy of Cook's time as Leader of the House – debate began at 12.30 p.m., and the session was extended to run to 10 p.m. It was to turn into a day of drama, plots and glorious debate, one that started with the unmistakable sound of the political knife being twisted and ended with Labour whips reacting in stony-faced delight to a result that was better than they had feared.

Those fears had grown during the morning as they listened to BBC Radio 4's *Today* programme. First the respected Health Minister, Lord Hunt, announced on air that he was resigning over Iraq; then John Prescott, the Deputy Prime Minister, retorted: 'I don't know who Lord Hunt is; he is obviously a minister of government . . . I'm sorry for my ignorance.'

It was a low blow and possibly a political misjudgement but it reflected the determination in government ranks to quash a rebellion that could have destroyed the Prime Minister. Meanwhile another minister was summoning up the courage to quit the government. John Denham, a respected Home Office Minister seen by everybody from the Prime Minister down as likely cabinet material, made it clear that he was joining Cook and 4 junior ministerial aides on the back benches. The news stiffened the backbone of potential rebels – and set the scene for another difficult ministerial resignation statement.

By 10 a.m. the parliamentary Labour party was gathering in a Westminster committee room to hear the Prime Minister put his case in private. Such was the crush that some ministers, including Kim Howells and John Hutton, could not get through the door and found themselves trapped in the corridor outside with a small knot of journalists. Inside, Blair was in high-octane mode, warning that the French strategy was to create rival poles of power: the US and its allies in one corner; France, Germany and Russia in the other. 'That's not diplomacy, that's lunacy,' he told assembled MPs. Blaming the French had become official government policy and it was popular to the extent that it swung, according to one Paris diplomat, 20 votes for Blair.

Several MPs stood up to defend the Prime Minister. Kevin Hughes said he had a son in uniform in Kuwait and there were people willing to defend democracy and freedom of speech with their lives. Without such soldiers, he added pointedly, MPs would have no division lobby to go through.

Lorna Fitzsimons, one of two former parliamentary aides to Cook, disagreed with her former boss. Hugh Bayley, a former minister who had been planning to rebel, said he had come back because of the French veto. Two London MPs under pressure from their constituencies said they would defy this and back the government. Outside, word seeped out that after reflection Clare Short had decided not to resign. The news was welcomed by Blairite loyalists, who quickly surmised that her career was all but over.

The PLP meeting ended just after 11.30 a.m.. The whips were first out, running, hyped up, clapping the Prime Minister as the doors opened. As MPs headed to the chamber for the debate, Cherie Blair walked across the lobby, embraced the portly figure of Charles Clarke, the Education Secretary, and headed for the visitors' gallery. Such is British politics that the Prime Minister had to give a repeat performance – this time to the Commons.

In a speech widely regarded by opponents and colleagues as the most powerful the Prime Minister had delivered, Blair sought to address both critics and supporters, recognising the ever-growing gap between two apparently irreconcilable positions, To a hushed House of Commons he talked as if his future depended on it – which of course it did.

This is the time for this house, not just this government or indeed this Prime Minister, but for this house to give a lead, to show that we will stand up for what we know to be right, to show that we will confront the tyrannies and dictatorships and terrorists who put our way of life at risk, to show at the moment of decision that we have the courage to do the right thing.

The question most often posed is not why does it matter, but why does it matter so much? Here we are: the government with its most serious test, its majority at risk, the first cabinet resignation over an issue of policy. The main parties divided. People who agree on everything else disagree on this and likewise, those who never agree on anything finding common cause.

Saddam Hussein was not the issue, Blair told MPs: the coming order of the world was. By the end he was shouting.

The country and parliament reflect each other: a debate that, as time has gone on, has become less bitter but not less grave. So why does it matter so much? Because the outcome of this issue will now determine more than the fate of the Iraqi regime and more than the future of the Iraqi people, for so long brutalised by Saddam. It will determine the way Britain and the world confront the central security threat of the 21st century; the development of the UN; the relationship between Europe and the US; the relations within the EU and the way the US engages with the rest of the world. It will determine the pattern of international politics for the next generation.

The speech, said to have been drafted by the Prime Minister in longhand the day before and toughened up later to include an implicit resignation threat, stunned many MPs. It was best captured in words by the *Guardian*'s parliamentary sketch writer Simon Hoggart:

One thunderous performance, passionate yet coherent, furious while icily controlled. Listening to it, you sensed that if things go horribly wrong this week he won't take the chance to flee. Instead it will be hand-to-hand fighting in Downing Street with the risk of terrible casualties. He blazed with conviction. His opponents may be equally sincere, but yesterday most of their attacks pinged off him like airgun pellets on a suit of armour.

At the end of the speech he heard behind him a noise which must have seemed as pungent, as nostalgic and as welcome as the voice of his late mother – the sound of Labour MPs cheering him. After a swipe at the Liberal Democrats, he said Saddam's claim that he had destroyed his weapons was 'patently absurd'. At this point he heard loud Tory applause but even louder Labour silence.

Then his attack on France, conveying a deeper bitterness, for we always find it easier to forgive our enemies than excuse our friends. There were mea culpas: he said wistfully how Europe should have figured earlier how to cope with America and its ambitions. And: 'For 12 years we have been a victim of our own desire to placate the implacable.'

There were dark warnings, the more chilling for being delivered in a quieter voice: 'A dirty radiological bomb is a real and present danger to this country.' He spelt out the dangers of inaction. 'To retreat now, I believe, would put at hazard all that we hold dearest, turn the United Nations back into a talking shop, stifle the first steps of progress in the Middle East, leave the Iraqi people to the mercy of events on which we would have relinquished all power to influence for the better.

Raising the stakes and kicking into what Hoggart called his Henry V at Harfleur mode, Blair put his leadership on the line. '[Are we to] tell our allies that at the very moment of action, at the very moment when they need our determination, Britain faltered? I will not be party to such a course.' The message to his own party from Blair was that if the vote went against war, he would resign.

To those who did not share his almost messianic belief in the cause, this was an imprudent and high-risk strategy. Peter Kilfoyle, a former Defence Minister, was the first dissenting voice to speak in the parliamentary debate.

We are having a 19th-century gunboat war in the Gulf, when the real dangers of terrorism should be isolated and dealt with as the first priority. [I] believe that this act would be illegal, it would be immoral and it would be illogical. [The Prime Minister] made much about the terrorist dangers and quite rightly so. But does that not point out the idiocy of fighting the wrong war, in the wrong place, at the wrong time, against the wrong enemy?

Blair faced a coalition of the unwilling. Dissent over the issue slipped over the floor of the house like mercury over metal. Charles Kennedy, the Liberal Democrat leader, opposed him as did Douglas Hogg, a Tory Foreign Office minister during the 1991 Gulf War. He framed his opposition to the war in moral terms.

If we were dealing with a situation in which Iraq had attacked another country I would vote for war. If Iraq had mustered troops on the frontier of another country I would vote for war. If there were compelling evidence that Iraq was delivering weapons of mass destruction to terrorists with which to attack another country I would vote for war. But none of those situations exist here.

Even friends of Downing Street sensed that this war could put into peril everything the Labour Party had built up since 1997. The *Guardian* columnist Polly Toynbee, reflecting on the debate, wrote:

> One MP murmured a fear that this could be Tony Blair's LBJ moment, recalling how all Lyndon Johnson's achievements in civil rights, Head Start for poor children, Medicare for the old and his whole Great Society programme were crushed under the wheels of his one mighty misjudgement on Vietnam. Many MPs and ministers who are deeply alarmed at the war nevertheless did not rebel, unwilling to risk the stability of the most successful Labour government for two generations.

It was this that in the end ensured that Blair's promise to resign if he lost was never tested. His arguments had won over some of his most vociferous critics – including Clare Short. After describing the Prime Minister as 'reckless', after saying she would quit if Britain went to war without UN backing, she failed to resign when it did so. In her mind, 'It would have been cowardly to quit.' To her colleagues it was a 'monstrous lack of principle'. Labour was more split than ever. But the Commons voted nearly 2–1 behind a war.

Even so, it was the biggest ever revolt by MPs. Among the ruling Labour Party 139 members rebelled, and 16 Conservatives, 53 Liberal Democrats and 11 others joined them. But because of Blair's massive built-in majority, it was still well short of the total that might have forced regime change in Britain.

As the *Guardian*'s leader of the next day made clear, the vote marked 'a really important moment in constitutional history'.

> Over the centuries, the decision to go to war has rested, first, with kings alone, then with monarchs in the Privy Council, more recently with the Council acting on the advice of the Prime Minister, sometimes (as in the Falklands war) largely

with the Cabinet. Yesterday, all this took a fresh twist. Though the formal prerogative power to declare war remains with the crown, the de facto authority passed yesterday to MPs. By allowing yesterday's debate and vote . . . it gave parliament the power to stop the war before it begins. Parliament did not take its chance, alas.

History's verdict will only be written in years to come, but no one doubted that it was a day of Westminster drama rarely seen since the death throes of the Thatcher and Major governments.

Shock and awe: Baghdad blasted (*Guardian*/Sean Smith)

4 The first casualty

George W. Bush announced the start of war on Iraq on Thursday 20 March 2003 at 3 a.m. GMT:

> My fellow citizens. At this hour, American and coalition forces are in the early stages of military operations to disarm Iraq, to free its people and to defend the world from grave danger. On my orders, coalition forces have begun striking selected targets of military importance to undermine Saddam Hussein's ability to wage war . . . We have no ambition in Iraq except to remove a threat and restore control of that country to its own people. I know that the families of our military are praying that all those who serve will return safely and soon . . . We will defend our freedom. We will bring freedom to others and we will prevail. May God bless our country and all who defend her.

The first confirmed casualty of Operation Iraqi Freedom was neither Iraqi nor American nor even British. Ahmed al-Baz was a Jordanian taxi driver on the busy road from Baghdad to Amman. Nobody knows if he had time to be scared or to cower under the first American attack, an undisguised attempt to assassinate Saddam Hussein in Baghdad. The cab driver, who was in his mid-30s, lost his life when a missile, whose provenance is unknown, struck a shop where he had gone to telephone his wife.

A few dozen cruise missiles had been launched from ships in the Gulf and the Red Sea in a lethal volley on the Ba'ath regime's stability 45 minutes before Bush stopped speaking. But al-Baz was innocent of any crime, imagined or otherwise, against which America had decided to administer justice. He had drawn up at Kilometre 160, a small, dusty settlement of shops and a petrol station where travellers on the 10-hour desert journey between the two Arab capitals frequently stop. There was no military site in the area, only a police station about a kilometre away. What offensive force the missile had locked on to will never be known, but its effect was devastating: the taxi driver was crushed when the ceiling of the shop crashed down on him. The two Iraqi passengers who had stayed in his cab were unhurt.

This would be a truly unequal battle. America's military might is both unprecedented and unmatched. The US accounts for more than 40 per cent of the combined defence spending of the world's 189 states with a budget of about $400 bn a year. Iraq, by comparison, was a bomb-blasted, sanction-crippled nation that could barely feed its people, let alone arm itself against a foe that historians regard as the greatest fighting force the world has ever seen. It spends about $1 bn a year on arming itself in a dangerous neighbourhood. Even at this level all Baghdad could muster were ageing tanks and barely airworthy jets. In gunning for a showdown with Saddam, the coalition had made the mistake of evoking the Second World War. We were the allies, they were part of the 'axis of evil'. Blair or Bush as Churchill meant Saddam was Hitler. But, terrible as he was, Saddam did not march across a continent and he had not created an industrial power with the military capability of a modern-day Wehrmacht.

At the heart of the coalition operation, which counted among its 40 or so supporters Albania, Eritrea, El Salvador, the Philippines and Estonia, were two anonymous, but identical, aircraft hangars painted grey and brown, set in a sprawling military camp in the Qatari desert, about half an hour's drive from the oil kingdom's capital, Doha. Inside each were two strategic control hubs, the military nerve centres from which US and British commanders would run the war in Iraq. This was Central Command. Running the operation was US General Tommy Franks, who until just over 18 months ago was was looking forward to a gentle ride towards retirement and an increasing concentration on his motorbike and golf clubs. Now he was about to become the most famous serving soldier in the world.

In war, even one such as this, it is the soldiers who along with the innocents suffer the strains and stresses of the conflict. And

Franks was a squaddies' general. They like his lived-in look, the fact that he earned his spurs the hard way (wounded three times in Vietnam) and his hints of humanity, such as getting up to warble country songs during concerts for the troops. He smokes cigars, he drinks margaritas, he eats Mexican food and he swears. But Franks had also achieved the second part of the trick: he had acquired the confidence of his political masters, no easy task in an administration whose civilians are convinced they know more than the generals. This may be because he, like his president, is a Texan down to his cowboy boots.

The US Joint Operations Centre in the centre of the 262-acre compound at Camp as-Sayliya was a mini-Pentagon. It was also Franks's ranch. Built over several months at vast expense, it was littered with technology and bravado, half Hollywood set, half computer game. The cramped, low-ceilinged room boasted six large plasma display screens, where commanders would watch their forces in battle depicted as small blue and green icons. Baghdad, in comparison, had to make do with a series of bunkers underground and a military communications system that relied on British radio sets brought in the 1980s. Trade sanctions made it difficult to get tractor parts, let alone access to the Macintoshes and Microsoft software that lubricated the American fighting machine.

It was around 4 a.m. in the Gulf when the word came that the attack on Iraq would begin. That word was 'asylum' and it was sent crackling over the coalition's secure radio system. Endlessly repeated over the airwaves, it was the signal coalition commanders had been waiting for. It was also a warning to all coalition helicopters and aircraft to get themselves below 250 ft – the height at which the Tomahawk missiles would be cruising. Ten minutes later the code changed to 'asylum is hot', signalling that missiles were now airborne. The Tomahawks being fired by US warships in the Gulf were put into a holding pattern above the fleet until each vessel had called 'barracuda' to show they had fired their full salvo. 'Greyhounds away' was the final call. The missiles were now en route to Baghdad.

In Baghdad, life was stirring on another fine spring morning on the Tigris. The city's pre-dawn chorus was accompanied by the sound of F-117A Stealth fighters blasting the urban landscape's western and southern perimeters. Only minutes before the sun broke across the horizon, US cruise missiles struck what the Pentagon said was a meeting of the Iraqi leadership command on the western perimeter of Baghdad. Not that much was captured by the world's television crews. For almost two hours, CNN's cameras – fixed on the roof of the Information Ministry in Baghdad – showed underwhelming scenes of traffic lights changing in the street below and occasional vehicles passing.

This was not the promised shock and awe of American might. It was more surgical strike than fatal body blow. The military operation that involved slicing the head of the Iraqi regime, Saddam, from the corpus, the Ba'ath Party, had failed. Just one and a half hours after the end of the American deadline for Saddam to give up and get out of Iraq, the bombing was, at about £25 m, expensive, brief and unsuccessful.

For ordinary Iraqis, the worst did not happen. The sky did not fall in nor did the heavens open and unleash a firestorm above their heads. According to Saddam's regime, 10 people died in the attack. Fittingly, the internet, spawned partly thanks to the efforts of the US military, allowed ordinary Iraqis to communicate their feelings to the outside world unmediated by a translator or the television lens. Here is one of the war's most eloquent chroniclers, Salam Pax, posting his terror and relief at the days' events on his weblog:

5.46 a.m. Air-raid sirens in Baghdad but the only sounds you can hear are the anti-aircraft machine guns.

6.40 a.m. There is still nothing happening in Baghdad. We can only hear distant explosions and there still is no all-clear siren. Someone in the BBC said that the state radio has been overtaken by US broadcast. That didn't happen, the three state broadcasters still operate.

4.28 p.m. Now that was really unexpected. When the sirens went on, we thought we will get bombs by the ton-load dropped on us but nothing happened, at least in the part of the city where I live. Anti-aircraft guns could be heard for a while but they stopped too after a while and then the all-clear siren came.

Today in the morning I went with my father for a ride around Baghdad and there was nothing different from yesterday. There is no curfew and cars can be seen speeding to places here and there. Shops are closed. Only some bakeries are open and of course the Ba'ath Party centres. There are more Ba'ath people in the streets and they have more weapons. No army in the streets. We obviously still have electricity, phones are still working and water is still running. We watched Saddam's speech this morning. He's got verse in it!

The Iraqi President was a skilled propagandist and his appearance on television was brandished like a trophy won in the war of words. To show that the message had not been recorded in advance, the Iraqi leader began with the date: 'At the time of dawn prayers on this day, 20 March 2003, the reckless criminal little Bush and his accomplices committed his crime, with which he had threatened Iraq and humanity . . .'

Addressing his fellow Iraqis, the President tried to stir the patriotism of his people by laying claim to the legacy of Arab nationalism and pledging the eternal defence of Palestine. They were rousing words, but there was little doubt Saddam looked more tired and puffy-faced than his usual TV appearances, his moustache a little greyer than usual. Dressed in military uniform with a black beret and large, dark-rimmed spectacles, the President spoke with a single Iraqi flag at his side and a blue curtain behind him. More curiously, his speech included 16 lines of verse, written in the style of a classical Arabic ode but with several jarring non-classical words.

Despite the Geneva Convention and a presidential ban on assassinating foreign leaders, the attempt to assassinate Saddam was declared legal by experts in international law. The Iraqi leader, it was argued, could be treated as a fair target because he was chief of his country's military at a time of war.

For those sifting the disinformation from the information, there were doubts over whether this was the real Saddam or one of the many doubles he used to trick his population and the world at large. Yes, he took to the airwaves, but read his speech from handwritten pages in a stenographer's notebook – suggesting that it had been scribbled in haste. The President could demonstrably get to a studio, but his surroundings were unusually modest. The spin, depending on who you listened to, was either that the house that Saddam built still stood or that its timbers were rotting.

The calculated psychological war saw rumours spread that Tariq Aziz, Iraq's Deputy Prime Minister, had either defected or been killed. To stop a rumour gathering such force that it became accepted truth and damaged the regime's morale, Aziz was forced to call a hasty press conference to prove he was still alive.

The spin from the White House was that America had picked up some red hot intelligence on the Iraqi leader's whereabouts. The CIA and MI6 had heard from informants in Baghdad that Saddam and some of his top Ba'ath Party officials had gone to a villa in the southern suburbs of Baghdad. This was enough for the dawn raid on 20 March. F-117A Stealth fighters dropped 2,000 lb bunker-buster bombs and 6 US navy ships fired 42 Tomahawk cruise missiles at Dora Farm, a heavily guarded compound belonging to Saddam's daughter, Hala, near Baghdad University in the south of the city.

The intelligence so excited the White House that senior US officials contacted the press pack to emphasise how good the information was. The CIA insisted a report that Saddam and his sons Uday and Qusay were at the farm was 'as iron-clad as you can get'. 'Even if we didn't get him, he now knows he must have been betrayed,' said an American official. 'He was paranoid before, but now he must be going crazy.'

The covert war had begun months before the first bombs landed on Baghdad and the first troops invaded the country.

It was not only a remarkably intrusive operation in a notoriously secretive state, but also heralded a new partnership between American and British secret services. Two hundred SAS soldiers, nearly half the total, were operating in secret in the deserts of western Iraq looking for Scud missile launchers and nuclear, biological and chemical weapons sites. They were also trying to seal the border with Syria. And they were communicating with Iraqi informants. For months MI6 and the CIA had been in regular secure radio contact with Iraqis in what, more than any other, military commanders wanted to be an 'intelligence-led' war. But relying on intelligence – and informants – is a notoriously uncertain business.

The Iraqi President, obsessed with his personal security, had numerous doubles and had avoided appearing in public for years. But, reasoned Washington, he had made a speech a day earlier and then disappeared into one of his bunkers – possibly the military compound where he was directing a council of war. This was the spot that Washington wanted to level, proving that the long arm of George Bush could rain blows on Saddam and his cronies with impunity.

It was a difficult call to make. The US war plan depended on striking multiple targets simultaneously in an attempt to reduce the chances of Saddam responding by blowing up oilfields or mounting missile attacks on US-led forces gathered over the border in Kuwait. The coalition also wanted to use the cover of darkness. By the time the deadline for Saddam to step down had passed, it would be 4 a.m. in Iraq, leaving only another couple of hours of night in which to mount an attack. But the temptation of killing Saddam and his leadership in the first action of the campaign, possibly triggering the collapse of the regime and avoiding a full-blown war altogether, proved too strong to resist.

For Bush, the moment of truth had arrived. It had come with the CIA director George Tenet, who bore the news that someone in Saddam's immediate circle had leaked his whereabouts. Ending a war before it could begin was a dream scenario – and Tenet

pushed hard to pre-empt the White House's plan for war with a
missile strike at Saddam.

It would mean beginning the hostilities early, but the chance
to kill Saddam might not come again. He made the case not just
to the President but to his National Security Adviser, Condoleezza Rice, his Chief of Staff, Andrew Card, and to the two senior
hawks of the administration: the Vice-President, Dick Cheney,
and Donald Rumsfeld, the Secretary for Defence. Whether it
was illegal – breaking the 1976 Ford administration directive
barring assassination attempts on foreign leaders – or whether
it would blunt the impact of the military campaign were discussed, but ultimately the decision lay with the President. In
keeping with his risk-taking style, Bush gave the operation the
green light. The clinching argument was that the proposed
'decapitation strike', if successful, would have brought the war
to a halt even before it had properly got under way.

The assassination plan was approved at the end of a four-
hour meeting that ended in the early evening – just in time for
the President to have what the White House described as a
'relaxing dinner' with his wife. After his meal, Bush made his
way back to the Oval Office to have one last session with his
speechwriter, Michael Gerson, and to practise the four-minute
address he would deliver from behind the simple square desk
known as the Resolute. It was from behind that desk that in
October 1962 John F. Kennedy had told the country of the Cuban
missile crisis and the current President's father had announced
the start of the 1991 Gulf War.

Before Bush finished speaking, the electronic codes had
flashed from the CIA headquarters in Langley, high above the
Potomac River in Washington's Virginia suburbs, to the fighter
squadrons in al-Udeid airbase in Qatar, home to the computer
systems of America's most deadly aerial force, its Nighthawk
fighter jets.

It was an intelligence-led attack that started the war – two
days earlier than planned. But the bombing raid angered MI6.
British intelligence sources say Saddam was not there. White-

hall was deeply unhappy about the decision to bomb the farm, which had disrupted the entire agreed strategic plan. The promised 'shock and awe' devastating bombing of Baghdad never materialised. Military sources claimed later that there was no point in a massive bombardment of the Iraqi capital, with the risk of heavy civilian casualties.

One person apparently crucial to Bush's battle plans had conspicuously not been consulted about when the war was to start: Tony Blair. The British Prime Minister was informed about the timing of the start of military action in a rerun of the events preceding the 1991 Gulf War, when the White House informed rather than consulted the then Prime Minister, John Major, even though he was a senior member of the coalition. Blair, Downing Street assured reporters, was involved in the discussions about launching the main military campaign. But it was clear that the timing and the manner of the attack was dictated by 'hot' CIA intelligence about the likely whereabouts of Saddam and the decision was made to strike fast.

Seeds of confusion were sown in the British public's mind over who was running the show and how. Bush had not helped in his speech to the American people, which dispensed with diplomatic niceties when he said the forces had been dispatched 'on my orders' rather than after discussion with Britain. Instead, it was Israel the Americans first called. This is understandable given that Tel Aviv was the target of most of the 39 Iraqi Scuds that hit Israel during the previous Gulf War. The Secretary of State phoned the Israeli Prime Minister, Ariel Sharon, to tell him that an attack was about to begin. This prior notice of conflict was also one of several means of keeping Israel out of the war.

The bombing of Baghdad did not start in the way the public had been led to believe. The first hours of the invasion were a repudiation of what had been said and written before the war began. The first attacks were meant to be massive – to shock and awe. But here was a limited attack aimed at killing Saddam Hussein. 'E' bombs were supposed to rain down on the city, cutting out all electric circuits. But the lights stayed on and water still flowed from taps. Saddam would not start burning the oilfields. Not so: a few had begun to burn. Whatever the rights and wrongs, America was conducting the war in a different way from the talk beforehand. Perhaps this was because Bush wanted to scare Saddam into submission.

Even the assumption that the war would be quick was undermined. The American President floated the notion that the war could take longer than previously thought. There was a possibility that America had miscalculated, reckoning that Iraqis would rise up against an undoubted tyrant. In not turning one of the Islamic world's great cities into a shooting range, it might also be easier for American and international opinion to accept the coming devastation, because the US had shown that even at the last minute it had genuinely tried an attack that would limit civilian casualties. Of course it could be the greatest act of presidential hubris: that toppling dictators could now be done after a fireside chat with some buddies and then throwing a switch in the Oval Office.

Memories of the first day's bombing were to be erased in the days to come, yet it was clear that the public's expectations had been raised to build support for pre-emptive military action and then lowered so people were ready for the inevitable return of soldiers' bodies and failed missions. So, as several missiles flew towards Kuwait from hidden Iraqi missile launchers, western opinion had to revise the hitherto accepted fact that hundreds of bombing missions in the southern no-fly zone had destroyed all of Saddam's air defences. It was clear that a real fight was on. And that victory in the court of public opinion meant voters – and Saddam – would be surprised by the tactics employed.

For the Iraqis the oppressive weight of expectation of an American attack had been growing day by day. In Baghdad, the mood of terror – both from an American assault and from Saddam's regime – was tangible. The reality of war finally came to Baghdad, a centre of Islamic civilisation since the seventh century. Sandbags sprouted on football fields and roundabouts.

Peace demonstrations had been rustled up by the authorities. The number of fatal car accidents surged as drivers panicked to get home, or to get out. Chemists sold out of Valium. Queues at petrol stations stretched for miles in a country where fuel is ridiculously cheap and plentiful. The price of mineral water doubled. Tinned foods and packaged soups disappeared from supermarket shelves. People had lived with the threat for so long that they had become used to burying their fears. One technique was to recount their survival stories of other US and British bombardments: in 1991, after Iraq's invasion of Kuwait, in 1993, and again in 1998.

The *Guardian*'s Suzanne Goldenberg was based in Baghdad and noted the rising panic in the days before the war broke out:

> Although Iraqis have talked of little else but war since last September – when it would break out, how long it would last, would their soldiers fight or flee, would Saddam Hussein let his grandchildren be slaughtered in a final stand – it never seemed entirely real. But now, after months of waiting and worry, the prospect of imminent attack was here, all too suddenly, and horribly real. In the kitchen of the Abdel Hamid family you could see it had arrived. A young boy, Amr, was making his own final preparations for the onslaught. He was performing the last rites of a four-year-old. In his hand he brandished a plastic gun. Whacking the ammunition clip into the toy, he held it to his stomach and put on a fierce expression. Then he raised it to the heads of the surrounding adults. 'Where are my bullets?'
>
> Amr's mother, Myasaa Abdel Hamid, is four months' pregnant and bone-tired. 'I've started talking to him about the war during these last few days,' she said. 'I told him, "If you hear loud noises outside the house, don't worry, they aren't coming in." But he doesn't really get it. He wants to know why there is going to be a war. He wants to know what Bush looks like. He wants to know if Bush is very angry with us. He wants to know if Bush has planes and guns. I tell him, "Bush has everything."

America was a hyperpower, the mightiest military force in the world. The war with Iraq, launched with high-tech missiles and bombs, marked a new mission for America's troops: to keep weapons of mass destruction out of dangerous hands and destroy nations that refused to respond to diplomacy. There was a hit-list drawn up after 11 September: Iraq was the priority. Iran and North Korea were next. Syria followed closely behind. America was not just a global policeman but the judge, jury and executioner in a dangerous world. A new era in world history began when the Twin Towers in Manhattan collapsed on 11 September 2001. Amr Abdel Hamid's mother was right: Bush had everything. His B-52 bombers and cruise missiles were what America meant by devastating 'force projection' – being able to hit an enemy from so far away that you cannot be hit yourself.

If it reminded the world of another age, there was good reason to suspect George Bush. This was the New American Century. Just as Britain, Holland and Spain had had their time. After all, it was a little more than 100 years ago that the English poet Hilaire Belloc, writing of the British army's machine-gun defeat of the Mahdi's forces in the Sudan, quipped: 'Whatever happens, we have got / The Maxim gun, and they have not.' The irony was that America, conceived as an anti-imperial project, was sounding a lot like the empires of old. No surprise, then, that in the soap opera of their daily lives, it was the US President, not the British Prime Minister, who had the biggest role.

Hours after the attempted assassination of Saddam, the plaintive wail of the air-raid siren sliced through the night sky of Baghdad. From the western banks of the Tigris – site of ancient Mesopotamian civilisation – that, though silted now, still define the heart of Baghdad, the anti-aircraft guns clattered into action. Iraqi soldiers took to their stations. But the attack was already upon them. Two projectiles hit the dome of one of Saddam's palaces in a thunderous explosion. The building collapsed in flames, and great billows of smoke drifted towards the river. The city was shaking in the night. The heralded but unknown Salam Pax again filed a vivid account on the internet.

10.33 p.m.   The all-clear siren just went on. The bombing would come and go in waves, nothing too heavy and not yet comparable to what was going on in '91. All radio and TV stations are still on and while the air raid began, the Iraqi TV was showing patriotic songs and didn't even bother to inform viewers that we are under attack. At the moment they are re-airing yesterday's interview with the Minister of Interior Affairs. The sounds of the anti-aircraft artillery is still louder than the booms and bangs which means that they are still far from where we live, but the images we saw on al-Arabia news channel showed a building burning near my aunt's house. Hotel Pax was a good idea. We have two safe rooms, one with 'international media' and the other with the Iraqi TV on. Everybody is waiting – waiting – waiting. Phones are still OK, we called around the city a moment ago to check on friends. Information is what they need. Iraqi TV says nothing, shows nothing. What good are patriotic songs when bombs are dropping?

Not in my name: on 15 February in London, Britain's biggest protest (*Guardian*/Dan Chung)

5 The home front

*Not even in the darkest days of Thatcherdom did my wife and
I feel so thoroughly ashamed to be British.*

Iain Banks, author, March 2003

Two days after the beginning of the bombing of Baghdad, the
country felt the weight of opposition to the Prime Minister.
Some 200,000 people marched in London – the largest wartime
demonstration ever in Britain. It was an angrier affair than the
previous month's march, which was the biggest protest in
British history. But with the bullets flying and the British army
in action, the large coalition of a million that had taken to the
streets before the war melted away.

For all its numbers, the anti-war support was broader than it
was deep. This made the event on a sunny Saturday during the
war in late March a more sombre event. Gone were the ranks of
the well-dressed middle-classes who swelled the event last time.
Instead, bizarre groupings such as the South London Home
Educators Sex Workers of the World Unite were almost lost in
the river of Muslim Association of Britain, Campaign for Nuclear
Disarmament and Socialist Workers Party posters that was wen-
ding its way through London, signalling determined resistance.

Gone, too, was the levity of previous anti-war marches in
peacetime, replaced by a sobriety brought on by the knowledge
that blood was being shed. 'Weep with the widows of Iraq'
summed up the feelings of many, as did the slogan: 'Just because
it's started doesn't make it right.'

With Tony Blair trudging somewhat wearily to war, his
opponents over Iraq were smaller in number but revitalised by
the military action, perhaps discovering a moral certainty in uncertain times. The battle for Iraq, unjustified and unendorsed
by the international community, was simply wrong. That it was

taking place at all merely emphasised their principled opposition, encapsulated by one of the peace movement's most effective slogans: 'Not in my name.'

The day before, a sombre mood hung over Friday prayers at the Jamiah Masjid in Wakefield, West Yorkshire. The mosque was packed with 200 faithful, listening to a sober sermon about Iraq by the mosque's imam, Maulana Islam Ali Shah, given first in Urdu, the Persian-influenced language of 200 million subcontinental Muslims, then in Arabic, the language of the Koran and the Middle East. 'Muslims want peace in this country because we are part of this country. When the bodies of troops come back there will be a backlash against Muslims, like there was after Afghanistan. We will see attacks on mosques again.'

There was a strong sense that Britain's Muslims were under attack. The iman urged the gathering to stay strong.

> This time for the Muslims is a test from Allah. If we bear this hardship lightly we will get two results, in this world and after death. War is not the solution to these problems. This is not how civilised people solve their problems. If we attack Iraq, we are no better than terrorists. Civilised people talk – and if they fail, they talk again and again.

After the prayers, people clustered together outside before returning to work. A group of Iraqi doctors spoke softly in Arabic. 'I have two brothers, a sister and my mother in Baghdad,' said Khalil al-Ani, a GP who came to Britain in 1981. 'They feel it is a war of aggression but are resigned to their fate. I am very worried about them. I'm worried about a siege in Baghdad, about a possible civil war. My wife has been crying because she has a lot of family there. I will never vote Labour again. This is a criminal war, in all senses of criminality. Blair talks about Saddam killing his own people, but he didn't kill a million of us – the sanctions did.'

A month earlier it had all seemed so different. On 15 February there was a global protest few arguments can inspire. It buried many myths. People were supposed to be disengaged from politics in the modern era; globalisation was reducing voting intentions to parochial concerns. But that Saturday the world was witnessing a very global, very public discontent. In America, hundreds of thousands made their voices heard above the silence of mainstream politicians, who refused to condemn the pending bombing of Iraq. The geographical spread of dissent – from Canberra to Cape Town, from Delhi to Damascus – showed the depth of passion against the war. In the age of the individual in Europe, millions took to the streets in a huge collective undertaking.

In London, the biggest protest march in British history took place on that cold Saturday in February. It was a turning point for British politics. The shout of 'Stop the War' rang through the capital's streets fom a million voices. Those opposing war included not only lifelong dissenters and critics of American foreign policy but also deeply conformist adults and children of all colours, faiths and ages. It was, in the words of one television reporter, the 'mother of all focus groups'.

As one column of marchers set off from Gower Street in the north of London, another left the Embankment – or tried to. Not a car or a bus moved in central London. The march from the north had to be diverted to accommodate the hundreds of thousands of people who had gathered at the meeting point. Stacks of placards waited to be picked up from the Stop the War Coalition, CND and the Muslim Association of Britain, the three groups that had organised the protest. But it was the home-made banners that bore the most striking, and humorous, messages. 'Peace and Justice in East London,' said one, carried by an elegant woman in a long black cloak. 'Make Tea Not War', 'Who Do You Think You Are Kidding, Mr Blair?', 'Stop Mad Cowboy Disease', 'Down With This Sort Of Thing', 'Peace Not Slogans'.

The great river of people that had begun to flow through London before noon was still in full flood long after nightfall. They ended up in Hyde Park, trampling the grass into a muddy field while they listened to the Rev. Jesse Jackson, whose gospel tones and preachy outbursts were so unBritish many could only connect with his passion, not his words. He was followed by the rap star Ms Dynamite.

The broad anti-war movement was a warning to Tony Blair that few were convinced that Britain should go to war. In an attempt to answer his critics, Blair gave a speech on 15 February to Labour's Spring Conference in Glasgow, just as the London marchers gathered. The mood among Scottish party members was far from sympathetic. The Prime Minister acknowledged the cost of conflict. Yes, he said, he understood the 'blood cost' of his conviction. Innocent lives would be lost if Saddam was removed by force, but others would lose their lives if he stayed. He was careful to say this was not the reason for action, but that it underpinned the 'moral case for removing Saddam'.

Protesters on the streets of London, and outside the conference centre in Glasgow where Blair was speaking, were not impressed. The *Guardian*'s Richard Williams best summed up the day of dissent: it was not a movement, it was a feeling. That feeling, he wrote, was not one of anger but of vast dismay directed at Britain's leadership.

> If you wanted to attempt the impossible task of identifying a typical marcher, you would probably settle for the middle-aged white man who walked past the barricaded end of Downing Street at about 1 p.m. carrying a hand-lettered sign. What it said, in neat black letters, came closest to summarising the message of the day: 'Labour Party Member No A128368 against the War.'

For although the river of people carried all kinds of flotsam and jetsam, the undercurrent was 'a mighty dissatisfaction with the performance of a leader who, 650 km away in Glasgow, was at that very moment attempting to justify a stance that few people appear to comprehend'.

That weekend proved to be the high point of opposition in Britain. The rift between the Prime Minister and the British public over war against Iraq was exposed by an opinion poll, taken over that weekend, which showed for the first time that a clear majority of British voters opposed a military attack. Blair had sustained significant political damage from the debate. His personal rating had dropped through the floor to minus 20 points, the lowest level since the petrol crisis two and a half years previously. Opposition to the war had risen five points in the past month to 52 per cent, with support for the war falling to 29 per cent.

The writer David Aaronovitch was not convinced by the marchers and set out to puncture the anti-war coalition's balloon: 'If I'd been a marcher, I would gloat, too,' he wrote soon after the march in February.

> Since the weekend it's been like one long sugary Coca-Cola ad: 'We are the world, we are the people . . .' All those years demonstrating about everything from abortion to Zimbabwe and now, when there is the biggest demo in British history, I can't clap along.
>
> In this moment of extraordinary success, I wanted to ask those who went on the demonstration some questions. I wanted to ask whether, among your hundreds of thousands, the absences bothered you? The Kurds, the Iraqis – why were they not there? Did some of the slogans bother you? Do you really believe that this parroted 'war about oil' stuff is true? What did you feel about the marchers wearing stickers bearing the Israeli flag and the words 'the fascist state'? Did you say to yourself, 'Actually, there's only one fascist state in this equation, and it's the one we're effectively marching to save'? Do you agree with Harold Pinter that the US is 'a country run by a bunch of criminals . . . with Tony Blair as a hired Christian thug'? What about rail union leader Bob Crow's suggestion that the government be brought down by civil action? Are you up for that?

The grassroots opposition to the conflict had emerged from the activist base of the anti-war movement. It combined the organisational abilities of the traditional left, the pulpits and minarets of religion and the energy of the anti-globalisers. This

trio would ultimately succeed in motivating the greatest number of people from the greatest number of households for any
cause in the history of British politics. The three groups had begun
working together when they organised resistance to the war on
Afghanistan that followed the attack on New York and Washington on 11 September 2001. They felt the road linking Afghanistan
and Iraq passed the same points: American aggression against
an enfeebled Muslim state, access to energy resources – a gas
pipeline in Afghanistan , oil in Iraq – and the right-wing Bush
White House assault on any nation that sought to stand up to its
unilateralism. But there was a crucial difference. Afghanistan
could be rationalised by most non-Americans as connected
with 9/11 – but Iraq could not. This lack of justification swelled
the opposition. By Christmas 2002, with US troops heading to
the Gulf, the peace movement was still growing rapidly.

There are not many politicians who value popularity as much
as Tony Blair but his stance on Iraq was making him very unpopular indeed. It was becoming clear that he would be prepared to take Britain into an American-led war without a second
UN resolution. The public was growing wary of the arguments,
suspecting that the rhetoric was being attenuated, circumscribed
and distorted by political calculations. The anti-war mood was
prone to sudden eruptions. When Blair visited Tyneside in late
February, he was met by an unexpectedly hostile audience at
the Baltic Arts Centre and outside as well by an impromptu
demonstration of children, lawyers and office workers keen to
register their disgust. 'I feel more strongly about this than any
other issue for many years,' said one floating voter, who admitted to being largely uninterested in politics.

With war appearing to be just weeks away, the peace movement turned increasingly to direct action and confrontation.
A peace camp was set up at RAF Fairford in Gloucestershire,
where 13 American B-52 bombers bound for Iraq had arrived.
On 5 March, students and schoolchildren walked out of colleges
and schools for the first time in response to an international day
of action called by American students. Other activists, steeped

in environmental or anti-globalisation protest, tried to stop bombs being moved from one base to another across Britain.

But the crescendo of anti-war fervour in the country came to an abrupt end in March. It was not drained of emotion but it lost its numbers. The French could be blamed for no second UN resolution. War was inevitable. More than 45,000 British troops were sitting under a hot sky willing to die in a fight against a tyrant. As this sank in, many protesters simply shrugged, packed away their placards and went home. For many, the anti-war movement was to become more a memory than a feeling. Opinion polls for the *Guardian* showed that from mid-February to the start of the war, a period of less than five weeks, the pro and anti-military action supporters switched from 52–29 per cent against war to 52–30 per cent in favour – an extraordinary swing of 22 per cent.

There was one group still prepared to take to the streets: the children of the suburban middle classes. With no real opposition to the government over university tuition fees and no Tory Party worth speaking of, the young became the active citizens politicians yearned for – and turned out for spontaneous demos against the war. A few thousand students and schoolchildren walked out of their classes on 5 March with barely anyone noticing. On Wednesday 19 March, hundreds of thousands walked out of class in at least 20 countries. The authorities everywhere were taken by surprise, both by their numbers and their passion. The opinion polls had consistently shown that 18- to 24-year-olds were some of the most opposed to the war, but student radicalism was thought to be moribund in Britain. Nobody in authority considered what impact a looming war would have on children.

In cities and towns across the country, thousands of schoolchildren and university students blocked traffic. The police were furious, accusing demonstrating children of wasting police time and playing truant. Schools were nonplussed. Some tried to bar children from demonstrating. Neela Dolezalova, an 18-year-old pupil in Hampstead, north London, asked: 'I wonder how this looks to the rest of the world? British schools imprison students during lunch breaks for fear that they will take initiative? Suddenly the politicisation of youth looks unattractive to those who have called us apathetic for too long. Ironically, it's fine for our government to encourage political interest through our citizenship lessons, but action against this war is suddenly condemned.'

The next morning, with the certainty that war was just hours away, a YouGov poll showed more than 54 per cent of people dissatisfied with Blair's conduct and 41 per cent thinking he should go as Prime Minister after the war. It was to be the last poll to give the peace movement any comfort. That afternoon of 20 March, news of the bombing of Iraq was flashed on television screens.

Blair appealed to a deeply divided Britain to unite behind the country's armed forces as they joined the attack to deliver the Iraqi people from their 'barbarous rulers'. The howl of despair at the Prime Minister's decision was put into words by the writer Iain Banks. In a letter to the *Guardian*, he spat out his frustration.

This immoral, illegal war is not being waged in our name, yet now we're told we must support 'our boys'. What sort of support is it to accept a course of action which places them in such mortal jeopardy? We wish these service people well. We wish that none of them had to risk being killed or maimed or disfigured or injured. We hope that not one of them ever suffers Gulf War syndrome II, or wakes up screaming, remembering the comrades they lost or the Iraqis they killed. So to merely wish the troops well is to be disloyal, to wish to put them put in harm's way is to be supportive. This is nonsense. This is the support a noose offers a condemned man and we reject it without reservation. Not even in the darkest days of Thatcherdom did my wife and I feel so thoroughly ashamed to be British. Because of this, and for whatever it may be worth, we have destroyed our passports and sent the remains to the Prime Minister's office.

Iain Banks, North Queensferry, Fife

   The protests had not failed because the war began. The anti-war movement was a spectacular success in two big ways. One, it forced the biggest change for more than three centuries on a parliamentary system that is democratic by reputation but dictatorial in practice. And second, the White House was dragged back to the UN by a British Prime Minister who faced unrelenting opposition from the streets.

   In America, land of the brave, the anti-war movement had always felt as if it was in the minority. But its finest moment came at the Oscars, after the bombing had started. The Academy Awards are permeated by a culture of self-congratulation that entrances the billions who watch it. But it was there that the film-maker Michael Moore won the best documentary prize for *Bowling for Columbine*, a movie that pinpointed Saddam Hussein's rule as the creature of the US and actually showed a clip of the planes crashing into the World Trade Center to the ironic accompaniment of Louis Armstrong's 'What a Wonderful World'.

   Moore unleashed the fiercest and boldest speech in the Academy's history. Shouting over the boos and cheers, he said: 'We like non-fiction and we live in fictitious times. We live in a time where we have fictitious election results that elect a fictitious President. We live in a time where we have a man sending us to war for fictitious reasons.'

Death in the desert: an Iraqi solder killed by British troops on the Al-Faw
Peninsula in Southern Iraq (Reuters/Stephen Hird)

6 Liberation

Liberation is not deliverance.
                Victor Hugo, French poet and novelist, 1802–85

Barely had the desert dust been shaken off the boots of the invading forces than the Stars and Stripes had been raised in the tiny Iraqi port of Umm Qasr. Just across the border from Kuwait, the country's only deep-water harbour had a name in the Arab world as a smugglers' haven. The town, where a few thousand people live in tough neighbourhoods, is made up of a series of docks and low buildings. It may have surprised the American and British forces how easily it seemed to fall and injected over-confidence into the veins of foreign soldiers. One British defence spokesman went as far as to claim that US and British forces would be in Baghdad in days. After all, Umm Qasr was secured in the first hours of the invasion, said Central Command in Qatar.

But nothing was to turn out as predicted. Instead, Umm Qasr was everything that the campaign was not supposed to be. True, much of the the Iraqi army, ragged and tired, gave up without much of a fight, but fierce resistance burst forth from guerrilla units. Secreted within the civilian population, Saddam's fighters popped up in supposedly secure areas, attacking the marine corps, who had expected not shots but smiles from liberated Iraqis. One marine was killed by a sniper, said to be from Saddam Hussein's Republican Guard. A few dozen Iraqis managed to hold out for days against tanks, heavy machine-gun fire and helicopters. The Stars and Stripes came down and the first Arab-American war had begun.

Not far away in Safwan there was no rose-petal welcome for the invading army, no cheering crowd and no Stars and Stripes. A crumbling, dead-end place, full of poor, restless young men, and reliant on the tomato trade for its income, Safwan was too afraid of the future and the past to notice the invaders – much. On the second day of the war, the US forces rolled into town – spreading chaos. The departure of Iraqi troops meant looting where there had once been law. Everywhere was the lingering fear that the revenge killings that swept the area in 1991 – a product of US encouragement and then abandonment of the revolt by the Shia population of southern Iraq – could happen again. 'Now we are afraid [Saddam's] government will come back,' a farmer called Haider told the *Guardian*'s James Meek, as the local agricultural co-operative was being looted behind him. 'We don't trust the Americans any more. People made a revolution, and they didn't help us.'

The marines, who took Safwan without loss, drew up in the border town after bombarding it. Their actions killed a dozen locals. Haider, who knew one of the men killed, said: 'Killing some is worth it, to end the injustice and suffering.' Afraid that the US and Britain would abandon them, the people of Safwan did not touch the portraits and murals of Saddam hanging everywhere. It was left to the marines to tear them down. It did not mean there was not heartfelt gladness at the marines' arrival.

Ajami Saadoun Khlis, whose son and brother were executed under the Saddam regime, sobbed like a child on the shoulder of the *Guardian*'s Egyptian translator. He mopped the tears but they kept coming. 'You just arrived,' he said. 'You're late. What took you so long? God help you become victorious. I want to say hello to Bush, to shake his hand. We came out of the grave.'

'For a long time we've been saying let them come,' his wife, Zahara, said. 'Last night we were afraid, but we said: "Never mind, as long as they get rid of him, as long as they overthrow him, no problem." ' Their 29-year-old son was executed in July 2001, accused of harbouring warm feelings for Iran. 'He was a farmer, he had a car, he sold tomatoes, and we had a life that we were satisfied with,' said Khlis. 'He was in prison for a whole year, and I raised 75 m dinars [£27,000] in bribes. It didn't work. The money was gone, and he was gone. They sent me a telegram. They gave me the body.'

Such sentiments were what the American-led coalition had hoped would bring down Saddam's regime without the need for much fighting. But Safwan proved to be the exception, and there were few cheers for the coalition elsewhere. Soldiers were often looking too hard for the enemy to realise that they were in another country with a distinctive history and culture, one that did not take too kindly to being shoved aside in the search for Saddam and his weapons of mass destruction. For the first few days of the Iraq invasion, British and American opinion had been in danger of slipping into a fool's paradise. Buoyed by perhaps its sense of technological, political and moral superiority towards Iraq, and precipitated by the preference for short, sharp, scheduled outcomes, the American-led coalition risked falling prey to a delusion that modern war is easy, cost-free and entertaining – when it is none of these things.

On the western front, from where it was feared the Iraqis could attack Israeli targets with Scud missiles, US troops secured the main airfields in the region and dropped cluster bombs – the weapon controversially used in Afghanistan and blamed for the deaths of civilians who confused the unexploded bomblets with food packages. The Iraqi airfields in the western desert, known as H–2 and H–3, were taken without much resistance from Iraqi troops, though coalition control appeared tentative. The H-3 airfield, 240 miles from Baghdad, had been one of Iraq's primary air-defence installations. Allied pilots had bombed it in September. The destruction of the airfield's radar would open up a clear route from the west to allow US and British warplanes to mount raids on Iraq.

In many cases, the campaign's progress was rapid simply because it did not meet much resistance. When it did, the perils of war became painfully clear. The south of the country, its Shia heartland which had been brutally repressed and was potentially Saddam's biggest internal threat, would not revolt against the country's tyrannical regime just because foreign armies had displaced Saddam's. From Safwan, just north of the Kuwaiti border, to the Persian Gulf port town of Umm Qasr, 15 miles to the south-east, to the highway leading north to Basra, Iraq's second city, the next few weeks saw bloody fighting rage between British troops and soldiers loyal to Saddam, whose regime largely rested upon Sunni recruits and members of his own Tikriti clan. The Shia population, who formed 60 per cent of Iraq's people, were content to sit and watch the two armies slug it out.

In the skirmishes, it was the coalition firepower that almost always triumphed. In the battle for the 5 bn barrels of thick black oil in the Rumaila fields, US forces attacked Iraqi soldiers. Seven of the Rumaila wells were set on fire, sending swirls of thick black smoke across the southern region, as the Iraqis put up a sturdy defence. The fight to take the blazing oil wells of Rumaila was not the walkover America had counted on.

For Kyle Brisebois, who at 33 had already fought one Gulf War, the hours of combat and chaos in the first two days of fighting were worse than anything he had experienced 12 years ago. His account was one of the first to reveal the intensity of that first night across the border, and the blunders and breakdowns which are the bleak, farcical reality of war. 'It was a nightmare,' he said, spitting regularly from a plug of chewing tobacco as he waited on a motorway bridge near Basra, preparing to move west. 'It was the worst fucking night of my life.'

Brisebois, a staff sergeant, commands an M1 tank in the marines' 5th regiment, which drove deep into Iraq in one of the first moves of the invasion. In an interview with the *Observer*, it was clear that the 5th and another marine regiment, the 7th, with helicopters and British artillery, had broken the will to fight of the Iraqi division which held the keys to Basra.

The sergeant's tank was one of a platoon of four attached to a unit of marine infantry charged with seizing the Rumaila oil-fields, one of the richest prizes in Iraq. They set off in the dark-ness on the first night of battle. No sooner had they charged through the breach in the sand wall marking the border bet-ween Kuwait and Iraq than one of the tanks broke down and had to be left behind. Not long after that, the hydraulics col-lapsed on two of the tanks, including Brisebois's. Corrosive fluid from a broken hydraulics pipe poured over Brisebois's gunner. To make things worse, the thermal imaging system on Brisebois's tank – the equipment that enables the crew to see in the dark – went on the blink. Amid the chaos, the platoon fell behind the infantry, and when they went on after them they got lost. In a minefield.

'I had night-vision goggles on and I looked down and I could see the round shape of landmines. They were all around the tank,' Brisebois said. 'It took us about 50 minutes to manoeuvre out.'

All this happened before Brisebois and his platoon were involved in any fighting. As they approached the oilfields, they were operating under constraints: they were free to kill any Iraqi soldiers in their way, but were only allowed to use their small calibre machine guns, and only certain kinds of ammunition in the tank's big gun, for fear of harming the most precious thing out there: the oil installations.

Even with the breakdowns and near-disasters that befell their platoon, the marines outgunned the Iraqis. One marine lieutenant died of his wounds following a firefight in the battle for the Rumaila oil installations, but many more Iraqis were killed, and hundreds surrendered. 'They were coming out with white flags and the infantry would come in between the tanks and the prisoners of war and round them up,' Brisebois said. The battalion to which his platoon belongs captured between 300 and 400 prisoners. The story was the same across the whole front between Kuwait and Basra, where an Iraqi mechanised division, the 51st, was thinly spread out.

There was a brief panic in Whitehall and Washington, which saw Geoff Hoon, the British Defence Secretary, admit that as many as 30 wells were alight. But US and British troops soon regained control, blasting the limited resistance away. In the words of Lieutenant-Colonel Mike Oehl, commander of one of the marine tank battalions that made the initial push into the south: 'Arguably, it isn't a fair fight, but I'm all for unfair fights.'

Unimpeded by enemy fire and avoiding head-on confrontations with besieged towns, a gigantic mechanised force sped along the motorway towards Baghdad, occupying all six lanes. One American tank battalion moved 53 miles in that first night, the furthest ever for a marine armoured unit. The only sign of their passing was a cocoa-coloured trail of discarded army-issue 'Meals Ready to Eat' packages on the verge and refuelling by the roadside with burning hot engines ticking as they cooled.

This flying column of marines was towered over by trucks delivering racks of shells and rockets to American troops outside the gates of towns and cities still held by Saddam's troops. Like a realisation of the most vivid fantasy of one of Hitler's master tank strategists, the few outsiders to witness this spectacle were seeing a blitzkrieg on an autobahn, an entire gas-guzzling army surging forward in a haze of growling diesel, carrying everything it needed to eat, drink and kill as it went. No static graphic could accurately represent the US-British invasion of Iraq. The mechanised columns were flowing like water along the narrow channels of Iraq's beautifully maintained roads, leaving the hard places of towns and cities high and dry.

In some cases, such as that of Zubayr, a mainly Sunni Muslim town in the largely Shia south that lies between Kuwait and Basra, they left behind islands of Saddamdom in which the tyrant's image was still sacred. Iraqi troops patrolled the streets of Zubayr, and portraits of Saddam Hussein adorned public places and offices. Yet Zubayr, after just four days of war, was surrounded by US-British troops. As a result, civilians spent days knotted in fear, moving from Iraqi-controlled areas where they must not criticise Saddam to US-British controlled areas where they were afraid not to criticise him, and back to Iraqi areas where they were afraid that anything they said to westerners might be used against them.

'We still love our President,' said Ali Latif at a lonely, looted petrol station west of Zubayr. 'We don't accept the Americans. It's our country. We love it.' Khaled Yassir, who came over to join the conversation Mr Latif was having with the *Guardian*, leaned down to scoop the thick dust in the middle of the road and lifted it to his mouth. 'This is Iraq, this is part of my blood, I love it.'

This country is dear to us. It's valuable to us and we are not
very happy that American forces have invaded us for something that's not worth it. It's all excuses. First they said Iraq
has weapons of mass destruction, but the inspectors have
been here since 1991 and they haven't found anything. Now
they say they want Saddam Hussein to give up power. On
what basis, if people accept him?

In the spring of the desert, the most powerful armed nation of
the modern world had begun an immense attack of computer-
guided fire and steel on the land of one of the great civilisations
of the ancient world. Iraq, particularly the green heart of Mesopotamia, the fertile crescent of land between the Tigris and
Euphrates rivers, is the cradle of civilisation, the land of Nineveh, Babylon, Nimrud and Uruk, the world's first city. This is
where the Sumerians invented writing 5,000 years ago, where the
Epic of Gilgamesh – the model for Noah and the flood – was committed to cuneiform a millennium and a half before Homer. It is
the land of the Old Testament, the Tower of Babel and Ur, where
Abraham, the father of the three great monotheistic religions,
was born. As the British and US forces moved relentlessly on,
they passed pieces of history, without noticing.

  Basra, Iraq's second city and the country's oil and commercial
centre, was of such strategic importance that it has been fought
over since its foundation 1,400 years ago. The British had been
there before – in the days of empire, British-led forces took it
from the Turks in 1914 and again, in the face of an Arab revolt, in
1941. Less than 100 hours of strife in 2003 and there were already
signs of a closer, much more recent British involvement in Iraq.
In the heliport just outside Basra, troops from the Black Watch
regiment found cruise missiles and warheads hidden inside fortified bunkers abandoned by the Iraqi army in the south. Cases
of rockets, giant anti-shipping mines and other ammunition
were piled from floor to ceiling in dozens of bunkers at what
was marked on maps as the Az Zubaya heliport. Some of the
boxes, containing missiles date-marked 2002, were stamped with

the names of British manufacturers. One pile of boxes in a store housing rocket-propelled grenades bore the name of Wallop Industries Ltd, based in Middle Wallop, in Hampshire.

It was also in Basra at this time that Arabic television crashed into the lives of western audiences. The tiny Qatar-based broadcaster Al-Jazeera could have been created in a neo-conservative laboratory: fearless reporting, promoting sharp opinion and free from the shackles of state control. It raised its voice against rigged elections, corrupt sheikhs and Zionism – all issues discussed in Arab kitchens across the Middle East. It was phenomenally successful, with 35 million Arabic-speaking viewers before the start of the war in Iraq. The station captured another 4 million subscribers in Europe after just a week of the war. But Al-Jazeera saw the war through Arab eyes. In the battle for Basra it was Iraqi tanks, artillery and rocket-propelled grenades that were repelling invaders – as Arabs had done for centuries. The Anglo-American force, armed with Cobra helicopters, and the tanks of Britain's 7th Armoured Brigade, the Desert Rats, were cast as foreign fighters, comparable to the Franj of the crusades, in the hearts and minds of many Arab peoples.

In Basra, Al-Jazeera beamed horrific images of Iraqi civilians apparently killed by the coalition bombing. The footage included an Iraqi child with the back of its head apparently blown off and wounded people covered in blood being treated on the floor of a hospital. It apologised for showing disturbing pictures but said: 'The world should know the truth and what is going on.' Sensing a propaganda coup, the Iraqi Information Minister, Mohammed Saeed al-Sahaf, claimed in Baghdad that 77 civilians had been killed and 366 wounded in Basra, mainly by cluster bombs. Al-Jazeera put the number of civilian dead at 50. Across the border in Kuwait, Major-General Daniel Leaf of the US Air Force said the coalition forces were doing all they could to avoid such deaths, but added that he could not confirm or deny the specific Iraqi claims.

To Arabs, Al-Jazeera was a beacon of truth and light in murky, troubled times. For the coalition the station was often little more than a conspiracy movie, cinematic agitprop against American Central Command's Hollywood news producers. Al-Jazeera's shocking images were a potent weapon in the war for people's hearts and minds. Its power and reach were demonstrated when two British servicemen were killed in the war, and their bloody, inert bodies shown on Al-Jazeera. The victim of the ensuing row was not the Iraqis or the Americans but Tony Blair – who became the focus of the wrath of the families of the dead.

Sapper Luke Allsopp, 24, from north London, and Staff Sergeant Simon Cullingworth, 36, from Essex, belonged to the 33 (EOD) Engineer regiment, a specialist bomb disposal unit of the Royal Engineers. They had gone missing when separated from their unit after an attack on military vehicles near the southern town of Zubayr on 23 March. Three days later their bodies were shown on Al-Jazeera. The footage showed the soldiers lying close to their vehicle. A wound was visible on one of the men's chests but there were no obvious signs of injury to the other.

Defence chiefs are said to have told Blair that the way the bodies were lying suggested they had been dragged out of their Land Rover and killed in cold blood. The Prime Minister did not wait for a second before using the deaths in the propaganda war. 'If anyone needed further evidence of the depravity of Saddam's regime the atrocity proved it,' he said during a joint press conference with George Bush at Camp David. 'It is yet one more flagrant breach of the proper conventions of war. To the families of the soldiers, it is an act of cruelty beyond comprehension. Indeed, it is beyond the comprehension of anyone with an ounce of humanity in their soul.'

But for the family of Luke Allsopp it was Blair who was displaying the cruelty. The regiment had assured them that he had been killed in action. His stepfather, Michael Pawsy, told the London *Evening Standard*: 'Both I and Luke's sister are disgusted by the claims that he was executed. There is no way that happened. The only way he would have been killed is in action. He loved his job and he would have died fighting. That's what he did. That's what his colonel and sergeant told us.'

His sister, Nina, said the regiment's colonel had called to set the record straight. 'He came around to our house to tell us he was not executed. Luke's Land Rover was ambushed and he died instantly.'

Blair apologised for any offence that may have been caused to the family, but the claim was never withdrawn. A week later two Iraqi men – one said to be a leading Ba'ath Party member and the other his son – were arrested and questioned over the deaths of the two soldiers. Unconfirmed reports said the two soldiers had been held captive and tortured for three days before they were publicly executed. You can't blame the families for wanting to believe the army's version.

While there were setbacks, Anglo-American forces found that geography was on their side. The hard rolling plains to the west of the valley of the Tigris and Euphrates were easy going for British and American forces. The valley itself was more difficult to cross. The ground is wet and the soil is soft, cut with countless irrigation ditches dating back to the dawn of civilisation. A couple of main roads running through ancient small towns run north to the capital.

What struck many correspondents was that the American troops were barely out of childhood themselves. They came as liberators to a land steeped in history about which they knew very little. The Euphrates, by the town of Nassiriya, is a narrow, slow-flowing blue current. Nassiriya is at the western end of the waterlands once occupied by 200,000 Marsh Arabs, the Ma'dan, whose culture, thousands of years old, was all but destroyed by Saddam, with terrible loss of life. The tranquillity of this ancient land was shattered by the Americans' unstoppable advance.

On most days it had been possible to sit by the riverbank in Nassiriya and watch the green spring reeds that defined the marshes bending in the wind. From there, the *Guardian*'s James Meek, five days into the battle, spotted one of the Ma'dan's high-prowed canoes drifting from side to side on its mooring rope. But it was not long before the sounds of wildfowl and lapping water was drowned out by a pair of ash-grey Huey helicopters, chugging low past the palm trees beside the bridge, and the whine of the next tank to cross. Staff Sergeant Larry Simmons, a Floridian from a marine reconnaissance unit in a foxhole over-looking the bridge, was not impressed by what he saw. 'You learn about the Euphrates in geography class, and you get here and you think: This is the Euphrates? Looks like a muddy creek to me.'

A few miles from the bridge to the south lie the ruins of the ancient city of Ur, founded 8,000 years ago, the birthplace of Abraham and a flourishing metropolis at a time when the inhabitants of north-west Europe were still walking round in animal skins. Sgt Sprague, from White Sulphur Springs in West Virginia, passed it on his way north, but he never knew it was there. 'I've been all the way through this desert from Basra to here and I ain't seen one shopping mall or fast food restaurant,' he said. 'These people got nothing. Even in a little town like ours of 2,500 people you got a McDonald's at one end and a Hardee's at the other.'

Just a couple of hundred yards downstream, a group of Iraqis, some of them hiding out in the country from the fighting in Nassiriya, invited journalists to strong, sweet tea in a farmhouse of whitewashed mud. They spread carpets and cushions on the floor and generously allowed the guests not to take their muddy boots off. Light shone through a triangular window. Mohsen Ali, a devout Shia fingering amber beads as he spoke, said the Iraqi people would fight for Iraq, if not for Saddam, although he supported the dictator. The country needed a strong leader, he said – even a brutal one. 'If in Iraq there's a leader who's fair, he'll be killed the next day,' he said. 'Iraqis have hot blood. If he's not tough, he dies the next day.'

Dreams of a grateful Iraq joyfully liberated by US and British armies evaporated fast in the Euphrates valley as a sense of bitterness, germinated from blood spilled and humiliations en-dured, grew slowly but surely in the hearts of invaded and invader alike. Near Nassiriya, at a key strategic point more than 200 miles south-east of Baghdad, US marines attempted to take bridges over the river Euphrates – and quickly became bogged down in casualties. The marines, in turn, responded harshly. Out in the plain west of the city, marines in charge of a gigantic series of convoys north towards Baghdad also reacted to ragged sniping with an aggressive series of house searches and arrests.

America as a liberator from tyranny is not easy for Iraqis to swallow. There are many who cannot easily forget that the Americans abandoned the uprising in the Kurdish north and Shia south that George Bush's father incited in 1991. There is the running sore of Palestine in the Middle East and America's patronage of Israel. The link was all too easy to make: missiles, made in the USA, killed innocents in Gaza and now the same thing was happening in Iraq. Sanctions, which have been most ruthlessly enforced by the Americans, had hollowed out a country sitting on the world's second biggest oil reserves so that all that remained was a husk of a nation. Malnutrition and undernourishment afflicted young and old alike. Public services such as education, health, water and electricity only receive 10 per cent of the cash required from an impoverished government, albeit one whose ruling class live in palaces with ornate gates separating the flourishing and the withered.

Three months before the bombing started, a writer for the *Guardian*, visiting Baghdad where nearly a fifth of the population of the country live, noted its shabby, moth-eaten exterior.

The buildings of this Paris of Mesopotamia sag into the ground like elderly men on life-support machines. Pavements end inexplicably in mid-flow, petering out into haphazard piles of rubble. Shops operate out of shells which wouldn't survive heavy rain. It doesn't even look like a place that was once beautiful: its porridgey concrete buildings would be an eyesore even if they were brand new. This isn't Aladdin's cave: it's Stevenage 50 years after a nuclear holocaust.

The Ba'ath Party thrived off this humiliation at the hands of America. It was a shame and anger that the President and his regime wanted to harvest. It was to such sentiments that

Saddam spoke after some US forces had suffered heavy casualties in the battle for Nassiriya at the hands of Iraqi irregulars.
'The people of Thi Qar [the province where Nassiriya lies], the
people of civilisation, you all know that the enemy will concentrate his raids and bombardment whenever you concentrate
your fighting on him on the ground,' Saddam said in a televised
address.

In the first week of war, it was clear that the dictator's spell
had not been broken. Not only was there spirited resistance
from Iraqi soldiers and units but also a full-blown fightback was
getting under way. The spine of the war was the US 3rd Infantry.
More than 20,000 troops were driving west from Kuwait and
then north to Baghdad. These troops skirted around major cities
and stayed out in the desert. It was left to the smaller units to
take out key towns. In Basra, the invaders and defenders were
engaged in a dirty war. Saddam had given responsibility for the
zone south of Baghdad to his cousin, the most notorious Iraqi
after the President himself and his son, Uday – Ali Hassan al-
Majid, known as Chemical Ali for his campaign to suppress the
Kurds in 1988, which left 200,000 dead. A US State Department
official, speaking on condition of anonymity, told the *Guardian*
that intelligence had been received that General Ali had been
given authority to use chemical weapons against the Shias.

There was no doubt that Baghdad's tactics were intended to
scare the local Shia population into supporting Saddam and to
stiffen the local resistance with teams of Fedayeen and Special
Republican Guard, who had a reputation for ruthless, bloody
fighting. Basra was left to the British. One unit reported coming
under fire near a bridge on the outskirts of Basra airport. Troops
said two men dressed as civilians opened up with rocket-propelled grenades. Major Charlie Lambert, second-in-command
of the Royal Scots Dragoon Guards battle group, said the difficulties British troops were facing were caused by Iraqi reneg-
ades out of uniform who were 'not playing by the rules'.

The reaction of British troops to the unexpectedly severe opposition was mixed, with some showing little sign of concern, others

expressing fear that the war could drag on for months. Sgt Mark Smith, 38, a provost sergeant with the Royal Scots Dragoon Guards, said he remained determined to remove Saddam but expected a prolonged struggle. 'It's not the Iraqi army we have to worry about, it's the person with the Kalashnikov in the back garden,' he said. 'The Iraqis are smiling assassins. They wave at you as you go past, then shoot you in the back. I thought from the moment we left camp in Germany that this would go on for ages.'

The fog of war descended over much of the battle. In the marshy, fertile valley of Iraq and the hardened desert that surrounded it nothing, least of all the truth, emerged unscathed from the conflict. On the sixth day of the ground war, the British forces outside Basra reported an uprising in the city. This was what the soldiers had been waiting for: signs that the Iraqi people themselves would throw off the chains of oppression in which Saddam and his cohorts had bound them for decades. Al Lockwood, a British military spokesman in Qatar, said there had been an uprising in Basra against the Ba'ath Party. According to reports: 'The Shia population attempted to attack the ruling party. The ruling party responded by firing mortars.' It was not known how many casualties were caused by the artillery fire, which British forces described as 'horrific'. Tank commanders from the Black Watch battle group who wanted to intervene, it was reported, had to be restrained by their officers, while the risks of causing further civilian casualties were assessed.

The message was that British officers were out to save those who could not save themselves from Saddam. So why did a correspondent for Al-Jazeera, reporting from inside the city, deny that any uprising had taken place? No surprise that many felt that the line dividing information from propaganda in this war had been erased long before the bombs dropped.

Basra was on its way to becoming a tomb for many of its inhabitants. The 1.2 million residents of Iraq's second city were having to survive without fresh water or electricity. Communications had been badly hit, making it difficult for the outside world to get first-hand accounts of conditions. The *Guardian* managed, via relatives in London, to speak to two Basra residents. Their accounts speak of the harrowing experience that war casts over people's lives – a shadow that inevitably stains. First, Hussein, aged 70:

> We are building a bunker under the stairs, the bombardment is getting close to our home. We live in the centre of Basra, very close to the governor's house, and this area now seems to be a target. The shops are closed in this area. Three of my sons and their families are with me in the house. We have electricity from 7 p.m. to 11 p.m. from a generator which has to be paid for. But there is no drinking water. There is only what we call 'garden water' for irrigation, which comes through pipes at certain times. We are using that for drinking water. It is not good to drink. It is not even good for washing, but we are drinking it now. We have some water stored in drums and we drink that too. We will survive on the rations we were given: rice, oil, flour, salt, sugar, beans and lentils. Vegetables, meat and fruit are not included. Because of the bombardment, we are scared to go out.

And Kasim, aged 42:

> There has been heavy shelling in the city centre and in another area near the Mukhabarat [secret police] headquarters. The headquarters has been razed to the ground. This is a residential area and there have been casualties among civilians. In another area where we have relatives a funfair was bombed, and some houses nearby. The houses are old so when they bomb, even if the bomb doesn't hit them, they collapse because of the vibrations, the shock of the explosion. We don't know what to do. If we stay inside, we're afraid the house will collapse. If we go out we may be hit. Since yesterday we have had no water so we are drinking from barrels or going to the river. This is a very heavy bombardment. It was not like this before, not during the Iran-Iraq war. Everyone is afraid.

Iraq and Britain have spent many decades in the the 20th century peering at each other through the mists of time. Britain created the state out of the ashes of the Ottoman empire after the First World War. Its mining companies struck oil there and troops from India, then part of the British empire, put down rebellions by the Arab population. Britain even stationed soldiers in the desert. Whitehall installed and supported friendly monarchs. Foreign policy was made in London, not Baghdad. Iraq was a nation – it was a founding member of the United Nations – but one not in charge of its own destiny. This fanned the fires in people's hearts. Arab nationalism was born in the wake of Israeli victory in the first Palestinian war, which ended in 1949, and became a powerful, unstoppable force in Basra, Kirkuk and Baghdad after the then Iraqi Prime Minister, a friend of Britain, refused to condemn the Anglo-French-Israeli attack against Egypt over the Suez Canal in 1956. Two years later, on 14 July 1958, a military coup overthrew the ruling dynasty and ended Whitehall's grip on the Middle East. Britain's influence and standing in Iraq disappeared under the waters of the Tigris.

The *Manchester Guardian* front-page headline of the next day shouted: 'Iraq army sets up republic, US urges Security Council to meet today.' Then, as now, nobody could deny Iraq's importance. Empire and oil were the concerns of British Prime Minister Harold Macmillan and his Foreign Secretary, Selwyn Lloyd. Britain, along with France and the US, via the Iraq Petroleum Company, controlled Iraq's oil output, which then amounted to a sixth of what spurted from the Middle East. A Liberal MP, in that day's paper, was quoted as saying: 'This is the blackest day for Europe since September 1939: Europe will have no oil.' An exaggeration, to be sure, but a more prophetic analysis came from Lord Lambton, an Arabist of some note. He had warned for some time that British policy could not be based on the assumption that ruling princes and sheikhs in the Arab world would forever remain in power unchallenged. 'As oil-bearing Arab states grew richer and more confident of themselves, there would inevitably be a shift of power away from feudal rulers.'

The mingling of pasts put into context what was happening in Iraq today. History never repeats itself, but it is worth revisiting. When in the first 100 hours of fighting, British troops captured a man speaking with Manchester accent but fighting with an Iraqi militia unit, they were first speechless and then furious. Believed to be in his mid-20s, the man told soldiers he was Iraqi-born but a British citizen. He then taunted his captors, reportedly saying they could not touch him because of the Geneva Convention, and that under it he would be able to go home and claim benefits. Where was this man's home? The north-west of England or the Middle East? Whose side was he on? Was he British because the British had been here before?

Corporal Jonathan Duffy, 21, with the First Battalion Irish Guards, which is part of the Royal Scots Dragoon Guards battle group of the Desert Rats, questioned the man at the camp and said that he had received a gloating response. 'He was being very arrogant and offensive, swearing at everyone,' Cpl Duffy said in a pooled despatch from Martin Bentham of the *Sunday Telegraph* sent from the front line.

'He said he had come out here to fight against coalition forces because he didn't believe in what we were doing. But when it came to it he did not fight properly at all, he just surrendered. He was a coward.' Cpl Duffy, himself from Manchester, said the man had been quickly identified because he was the only fluent English-speaker among Iraqi captives. He had a Manchester accent so he stood out immediately. 'We were asking him to help us to be a translator with the other captives, but he was just being abusive, and saying, "Why should I help you? I don't have to."

'He told us that he was originally from Iraq, but had emigrated to Britain with his family and had British citizenship. He said he wanted to go back to England, to go back home, he called it. It was a joke. He was calling us mugs. I think he should be shot and hung.' The upshot was that this soldier, a British citizen fighting for the Iraqis, was not committing a treasonable offence. He had travelled to Iraq intending to fight the coalition forces, but wanted to be reunited with his family in Manchester. He was now a prisoner of war. For British troops it was hard to take. Soldiers could have been forgiven for regarding him as the enemy within, but as the past shows it is hard to capture succinctly why so many Iraqis had a jaundiced view of American and British intentions, no matter how benign their aims appeared to be.

As war progressed, the outlines of its strategy could be made out in the swirling dust that accompanied American and British advances. The first advance, on the eastern bank of the Euphrates, had been subject to the robust resistance in Nassiriya. The second, headed by the First Marine Expeditionary Force, heading for Baghdad between the Tigris and Euphrates, was advancing towards Kut along two converging routes. Ominously, Kut, defended by the Baghdad Division of the Republican Guard, had been one of the British army's greatest defeats during the First World War. In 1916, an attempt to reach Baghdad failed, and some 13,000 British troops were captured after being besieged by the Turks Few survived captivity. The third advance, led by the US Fifth Corps, had been along the western bank of the Euphrates approaching the capital through the Shia holy city of Karbala, 50 miles south of the Iraqi capital, close to where units from the Medina Division were located.

Just when the unstoppable force of military might was headed inexorably towards Saddam's immovable objects, the elements intervened. The prickly heat of the desert melted away and was replaced by something far more unconstrained and dangerous than bullets or bombs. By the end of the first week of fighting the weather took a turn for the worse in the valley of the Euphrates.

The sandstorm began as a strong breeze, spinning the fine dust thrown up by tanks and trucks into vortices. At first, it seemed that the long US marine convoys, picking their way with painful slowness along an unmade-up road north of the river Euphrates, were generating the dust themselves. The vehicles would stop and the dust would settle, and the forms of small children materialised by the roadside, shouting for the yellow humanitarian ration packs the Americans threw from their trucks. Some children had sacks full. Their fathers stood alongside them, holding up Iraqi dinar notes with Saddam Hussein's portrait on them, hoping to change them for dollars.

Further north, when the convoys stopped, the dust did not settle. It was a vicious, raging sandstorm, and it blew for most of the day, bringing the US war machine to a halt as it advanced steadily towards Baghdad. Sand raced in twining rapids along the road surface and in dark ragged sheets overhead. Vehicles had to keep only a few yards distance from each other to avoid losing sight and blundering off into the desert. Even wrapped up in their NBC (nuclear, biological and chemical protection) kit, helmets and sand goggles, the marines' faces were blast-coated with a fine layer of brown dirt. When asked how long it was since he'd had a shower, one marine thought for a moment and said: 'Four weeks.'

The convoy in which the *Guardian*'s James Meek was travelling planned to move 100 miles in a day. Instead, by nightfall, it had gone 15. Lt-Col Bob Weinkle, commander of the forward supply unit that made up this convoy, confirmed that senior commanders had been obliged to order a halt to most operations by the ferocity of the storm.

Anyone out in the storm without goggles had their eyes stung red raw. Uncovered hair took on the texture of a Brillo Pad. Light vehicles rocked on their springs in the wind. Lt-Col Weinkle said a lot of his men came from the desert base of 29 Palms in California. 'We're used to riding out these conditions, although not necessarily a day like this, or this large a convoy,' he said. 'The orders are to sit tight until the worst passes. I think it's definitely affecting the operation. It hampers delivery of logistics but it doesn't stop it.'

Forward units had two days of supplies, he said, so a one-day break in the relay system the marines were operating for their supplies shouldn't be a problem. Yet there was no doubt supply lines were becoming stretched. The marines were a long way from the sea. Their main armoured troop carrier, an enormous amphibious beast called an AAV, had become a ship of the desert, hardly the role it was designed for. This Vietnam-era vehicle, made of relatively vulnerable aluminium, was built to carry marines short distances from beach landings. Some would have travelled 200 miles in six days. Many had broken down and were being towed forward in the hope that they could be repaired in the field or cannibalised for spare parts. When the dust storm blew itself out, the marines would not have water for washing. Their limited supply was for drinking only. 'A marine can typically go up to 30 or 40 days if they have to without any kind of bathing,' said Lt-Col Weinkle. 'Baby wipes are the key.'

Nearly a week after the invasion began, the battle for Umm Qasr was over. Minesweepers finally finished their work clearing the waterway of the deep-sea port, and Coalition High Command were determined that nothing should stop the arrival of the first shipload of aid from being anything but a triumph. The arrival of *Sir Galahad* was the first proper good news story of the war and the dockside was a sea of vehicles with satellite dishes sprouting from their roofs, while dozens of journalists had been bused in from Kuwait.

The *Guardian*'s Jamie Wilson, along with two representatives of the *Sydney Morning Herald*, had been helicoptered in from HMAS *Kanimbla*. 'We've been told that getting you guys to the port for the *Sir Galahad* is top priority and takes precedence over everything else,' one of the officers said.

So important was the news of the arrival of the ship, and its cargo of aid, that its docking at Umm Qasr was delayed – for the sake of a press conference. Three days overdue, the *Sir Galahad* arrived on the morning of 28 March, escorted by a British minesweeper and a couple of US Coastguard cutters. Umm Qasr itself had been turned into a fortress. Giant Iraqi fork-lift vehicles, hotwired by the troops, had been used to create a steel perimeter made out of commercial shipping containers.

As *Sir Galahad*, right on cue, edged her way into view around the bend in the river the press conference began. Col Steve Cox, deputy commander of 3 Commando Brigade, a no-nonsense looking character with a moustache worthy of *A Bridge Too Far*,

stood on a makeshift rostrum and addressed the waiting journalists. His mission, he said, was to bring law and order to Umm
Qasr and the surrounding area and allow the population to feel
safe enough to go about their business. 'They are downtrodden
and frightened,' he said, 'and they do not trust the West. They do
not know if we are going to beat Saddam Hussein and they are
waiting to see. But each day we take a little step and each day
things get a little closer to normality.'

But the men of 23rd Pioneer regiment were having difficulty
convincing local people of their good intentions. By the weekend,
convoys laden with water and emergency rations were leaving
Shabiah airbase, morning and afternoon, bound for Iraqi civilian heartlands. It was undoubtedly a curious way to deliver aid:
the large processions were always accompanied by British tanks.

For the British, their job was to act as 'band-aid' until the UN
agencies, the experts, were able to take over. 'We cannot expect to
fix everything,' admitted Col Peter Jones, commanding officer
of 23rd Pioneer regiment. Puffing on a cigar, Col Jones added:
'What we can do is get the Iraqis some structure to their lives.
We can make them self-sufficient for the time being. After that,
the UN agencies take over.'

If this was the theory, it did not work out in practice. The
young man wearing the brown shawl in Zubayr summed it up
succinctly: 'We want you to go back home. We do not want your
American and British aid,' he said, his eyes flashing with anger.
If the soldiers from the British humanitarian task force had any
doubts that he meant his words, a sudden burst of gunfire from
a nearby building underlined the atmosphere thick with threat.

For the British troops in charge of pacifying southern Iraq
while American forces swept on to Baghdad, delivering much-
needed supplies was a vital component in winning over the hearts
and minds of the Iraqi people. But if the soldiers were expecting
that their efforts would be rewarded by a grateful populace gar-
landing them with flowers, they were to be sadly disappointed.

The first attempt to deliver aid to the Iraqi people occurred a
couple a days before the *Sir Galahad* made it into port. It was, in

all respects, a practical and logistical disaster. A convoy of vehicles, including two water tankers and as many Warriors, had set off earlier in the day carrying British military aid supplies. As the convoy pulled up inside the town, however, a crowd of predominantly young men ran towards it. Fights and skirmishes broke out for bottles of water. The Iraqis asked for food and cigarettes. And while a cordon was quickly created, hundreds rushed towards the trucks, overpowering soldiers.

'We have no water and no food,' said Ali Abdullah, 50. He stood away from the crowd, stroking his beard, and surveyed the scene intently as crowds of young men fought over boxes of bottled water. 'For five days now, we have been without electricity. Have you brought some electricity?'

For the aid agencies, the chaotic scenes in Zubayr, Safwan and other southern towns confirmed their fears that the coalition forces were ill-suited to double up as aid workers. Cooped up in neighbouring Jordan, Kuwait and Turkey, with tonnes of medical supplies, food and water purification equipment, aid workers were unable to get into Iraq because it was too dangerous for western civilians. In addition, non-governmental organisations were not prepared to compromise their neutrality by delivering aid under the protection of the military.

The result was that aid was delivered chaotically and under fire from unquelled Iraqi forces and militia. After the first disastrous drop in Zubayr, back at Shabiah airbase, one American soldier remarked: 'Hell, I wanna help these Iraqis, but I don't wanna get my ass blown off in the process.'

7 Baghdad bombed

We are not the doctors. We are the disease.
  Alexander Herzen, Russian political philosopher, 1812–70

Nothing had prepared Baghdad for this. Dense spring sandstorms were blanketing Iraq – engulfing the country's capital city and making it resemble not so much a modern Middle Eastern metropolis on the banks of the Tigris as a smoggy postwar London sitting above a grimy Thames.

The freak sandstorm – the worst in more than 10 years – coated the city, and its 5 million inhabitants, with a thick, grimy dust. Many saw the orange sky as an omen, or a curse – certainly not against Iraq, which in their belief had never wanted this war, but on the American and British enemies who were intent on invading their land. The Iraqi Defence Minister called it 'a divine gift'. But the seventh day of the campaign was one where the earth opened up and swallowed the misconceptions that many ordinary Baghdadis had harboured.

The Americans, people in the city believed, were after the regime – had they not bombed Saddam Hussein's house, built over an underground bunker in southern Baghdad? The city's denizens had endured days of the piercing air-raid sirens across Baghdad and seen Iraqi forces lace the sky with anti-aircraft fire. What were the targets of the deadly precision of volleys of missiles that sent plumes of smoke into the night? The presidential compound in central Baghdad and the government buildings in the western part of the city – both of which appeared to have been reduced to rubble. That false sense of security in US technology, and its precision-guided bombs, was abetted by the weather, an orange apocalyptic haze that engulfed the city.

Like many, the people of the Shaab neighbourhood on the northern perimeters of Baghdad never considered they were in

No way out: families flee from the bombing (*Guardian*/Dan Chung)

the way of harm. They had no an inkling that after the palaces, military installations and the ministries they would be next. On this seventh day of bombing, Iraqis had learned to adapt to the rhythm of the bombs, venturing out by day if they had to, avoiding official areas known to be the target of America's wrath. Nobody paid much attention to the roar of the planes overhead; it was the third or fourth sortie since daybreak.

At 11.30 on that morning shrouded in desert dust, the people of Baghdad lost their innocence over the war. Two American bombs fell out of the sky, and on to a crowded marketplace. If this was the result of precision bombing, as US and British military commanders initially claimed, then it wasn't precise enough. Dozens lost their lives. The first victims were said to be two local men, Tahir, 26, and Sarmat, 21. Both were idling away the day in a small shop that sold water heaters. In an instant the shop gave way, swallowing up the pair. The sideways force of the blast spewed chunks of masonry and body parts across a six-lane highway. Sizzling chunks of shrapnel tore through plaster facades, leaving pockmarks on the interior wall. Brick shopfronts collapsed, amid cascades of glass that extended for 200 metres. Two cars hurtled in the air, landing on their sides.

The lethal impact of the blast was augmented by cruel circumstance. Several witnesses said an oil tanker had been parked in the area moments before the bombing. Five cars along a slip road were carbonised, and flames licked the first-floor windows of buildings. One of the burnt-out cars had contained a family with three children, said Hisham Madloul, as he picked his way through the bloodstains and debris in flip-flops. 'There were three families in the building upstairs and many children,' he said. 'We have committed no sin. We are not guilty. Why are they doing this? We are innocent people.' He paused for breath, and went on. 'What does Bush want?'

It was not a question Alaa Ahmed, 12, was equipped to answer from his bed at Baghdad's al-Kindi Hospital. He lay on his pink pillow, with his head and right hand swathed in bandages, gazing vacantly with huge brown eyes at the circle of white coats

around him. Above his bed, the doctors said several of the 21
people travelling in Alaa's minibus had been brought to the hospital, some horribly burnt, some with grievous internal injuries,
and others dead on arrival. Alaa could barely follow the conversation, which was probably a mercy. He had boarded the minibus
with his best friend to go shopping. The doctors said the other
boy was even more badly injured. 'This enemy wants to kill all of
us,' said Tomma Hussein, a doctor working in al-Kindi's casualty
ward when the dead and injured were brought in.

'These were far more serious injuries than any we have seen
before in this war. I saw two people die in the casualty unit –
they were young, perhaps 17 and 25 – and I saw a young girl
whose hand was amputated.' That sense of shock and bewilderment travelled to the centre of the city from far-flung Shaab as
the day wore on, and drivers pulled up in cars to gawk at the
aftermath of the slaughter. But as night fell, and the pande-
monium subsided in the casualty wards of Baghdad's hospitals,
it was also mixed with rage. 'I want to see one of them – those
American soldiers,' Dr Hussein said. 'I want to kill one of them.'

The bombing of innocents could not be part of a war of liberation. Instead it threatened to bring people, divided over issues
of religion, language and geography, together under the banner
of nationalism. The following days saw a tussle for global public
opinion as both sides spun the tragedy to retail their own ver-
sions of the truth. The Iraqi Health Minister, Umeed Madhat
Mubarak, said 36 civilians had been killed and 215 wounded.
The British and Americans were 'targeting people to decrease
their morale', he said. Certainly more than a dozen were killed,
but Brigadier-General Vincent Brooks, the US Central Command spokesman, said the finger of blame was pointing in
Iraq's direction: 'We think it is entirely possible that this may
have been an Iraqi missile.'

Around about this time, something seemed to snap – both in
the minds of the Iraqi people and in the imagination of Washington's war planners. Just a few weeks earlier, on American television, the US Vice-President Dick Cheney had predicted that

US troops would be 'greeted as liberators'. But what had been slowly seeping into the western public's mindset was that the American and British troops were not being treated as friends but enemies of the Iraqi people.

This was partly because coalition efforts to win the hearts and minds of Iraqis had been complicated by the inability of the British and Americans to bring in sizeable quantities of aid. What was envisaged as a flood of supplies instead simply trickled in. This spelt catastrophe for Basra, where food, drinking water and medical supplies were running low. Instead of salvation, the troops were bringing destruction to Iraq. US and British troops fought Iraqi forces around key cities such as Nassiriya, Najaf and Basra – a key plank of the military strategy to secure the southern parts of the country before moving on the capital. And the clashes were getting longer and bloodier.

War is a dangerous and deadly business, not meant for the faint-hearted or supple-spined. The victims of US airstrikes or of British gunfire had done nothing wrong – but the price of liberating Iraq saw their blood spilt. Suddenly and swiftly, the invasion became not so much about determined resistance and the doughty push forward but death and disruption. It was now clear there would be no welcome and no swift surrender. Moral sensibilities were, at first, squashed and then pushed out of sight. This was now about rent limbs, dismembered, charred corpses, frightened American marines and cruel, insensitive, squaddie bloodlust. The enormity of war, it was now apparent, would consume as it conquered. This was something to fear.

Memorably, this change in the mood on the ground had been caught by the Pentagon's Lieutenant General William Wallace, the commander of the US army's V Corps overseeing ground operations. 'The enemy we're fighting is different from the one we'd wargamed against,' was how he put it.

There was unease among army officials that the 300-mile supply lines between the leading US forces and logistics bases in Kuwait were too vulnerable to mount a decisive assault on Baghdad. There were reports that not enough food and fuel had been packed. Two more divisions of American troops – from Texas and Germany – were mobilised, but they would take weeks to arrive. Sandstorms, mud and near-constant guerrilla attack had made advancing up the Euphrates valley difficult.

Carefully prepared plans that would have meant that US and UK forces respected local customs had been shelved. The projected Muslim burial of killed Iraqi troops, on their right shoulders, with their heads pointing towards Mecca, did not take place. The shift in thinking meant a change in how the war would be won. For the UK and US, it was not a time to waver but a time to overcome and overwhelm the resistance.

The Shawala neighbourhood of Baghdad is a collection of mean single-storey houses, lying at the southern extremes of Iraq's capital, far removed from the security installations and grotesque palaces of Saddam Hussein that had been the primary targets of US bombs.Yet on the ninth day of fighting, 28 March, the market stalls of Shawala, which were thronged with shoppers in the early evening, were atomised by a huge detonation. More than 50 Iraqis were killed in an instant.

The blast was heard a mile away in the Noor Hospital, where the victims of Shawala were brought. Inside the hospital, dark streaks of blood marked the final journey of the dead, and an elderly man in traditional robes leaned against a wall and sobbed into his red and white keffiyeh. Even for the battle-hardened doctors of Noor, who had endured three wars in a generation, the aftermath of the attack marked a fresh descent into horror. 'There were limbs torn off, and burns, multiple shrapnel injuries, head and chest injuries,' said Tarif Jamil, a doctor on the casualty wards. 'I saw about six children – all dead – and at least three women.'

The new thinking, whose shape could be discerned through the fog of war, was as simple as it was brutal. Gone was the talk of technological wizardry and the MBA-inspired military strate-gies of US Defence Secretary Donald Rumsfeld. Our boys, wait-ing for supplies, would not be left as sitting targets in the desert for snipers – because the coalition air force was to flatten Iraqi firepower and, with terror, sap its will to fight. Baghdad was blasted with the biggest weapons used to date in the conflict, two 5,000 lb satellite-guided 'bunker-busting' bombs, both dropped on what were described as key communication centres. In fact the targets were telephone exchanges in the eastern al-Alwya residential district. It was also the first blitzing of the civilian infrastructure of the city.

It was clear the gloves had come off. The violent nature of war had been exposed for all to see. It was so partly because of the unprecedented levels of reporting: the main British news networks on TV had extended their budgets by a combined £22 m. There was also an acceptance that not since Vietnam had a conflict been conducted against such widespread public opposition around the world.

Access was the key to resolving the tension between defensive American and British politicians and the perceived aggression of modern-day journalism. So there were far more live pictures from the front than had been the case in any previous war: sometimes, the screen split to take in feeds from Baghdad, Kuwait, northern Iraq and an aircraft carrier simultaneously. Iraq was the backdrop to the mother of all propaganda wars. The war reporting had become part of the US and British military operation. Journalists were embedded in units: coming to share the fear, excitement and (war planners no doubt hoped) the triumph. But right now what they saw were heaps of charred bodies and inert, dismembered Iraqi limbs.

American troops were singled out for their use of indiscriminate, excessive force. After suffering heavy losses in Nassiriya, US marines were ordered to fire at any vehicle that drove at American positions. In one of the most memorable dispatches of the war, Mark Franchetti of the *Sunday Times* described how one night he heard a dozen times 'the machine guns opening fire, cutting through cars and trucks like paper'. The next morning he said he saw 15 vehicles, including a minivan and two lorries, riddled with bullet holes. In the report he filed there were 12 dead civilians lying in the road or in nearby ditches. One man's body was still on fire. A girl aged no more than 5 lay dead in a ditch beside the body of a man who may have been her father. A father, baby girl and boy had been buried in a shallow grave. Franchetti said the civilians had been trying to leave the town, probably for fear of being killed by US helicopter attacks or heavy artillery. He wrote: 'Their mistake had been to flee over a bridge that is crucial to the coalition's supply lines and to run into a group of shell-shocked young American marines with orders to shoot anything that moved.'

Reporters also saw more than a dozen burnt-out buses and trucks and the bodies of at least 60 Iraqi men on the road north of Nassiriya. A photograph carried in the *Guardian* showed a bus that had been attacked by US troops. Bloodstained corpses lay nearby. Reuters wire agency reported there were 4 bodies outside the bus and, according to the marines, 16 more inside. The American troops said the dead men wore a mix of civilian and military clothing and were in possession of papers 'that appeared to identify them as Republican Guards'. But Brigadier General John Kelly admitted: 'We have very little time to decide if a truck or bus is going to be hostile.'

There were also unnecessary displays of exuberance from American soldiers. A British officer was alarmed when the US marines who were escorting him through the port of Umm Qasr let loose a volley of rifle fire at a house on the outskirts of town. The officer told Reuters reporter David Fox: 'They said they had been sniped at from there a few days ago so they like to give them a warning every now and then. That is something we [the British] would never condone.'

The *Guardian*'s James Meek told the story of a 50-year-old businessman and farmer, Said Yagur, who said marines had searched his house and taken his son, Nathen, his Kalashnikov rifle and 3 m dinars (about £500). The marines argued that the money was probably destined for terrorist activities. After protests by the father, who rose up against Saddam Hussein after the last Gulf War and had his house shelled by the dictator's artillery, they let the son go and returned the gun and money.

Cluster bombs were used in and around the holy Shia towns of Najaf and Kerbala. There were reports of sometimes unlucky, often hapless Iraqi civilians fleeing one danger only to die in a hail of bullets unleashed by trigger-happy American soldiers. And the sorties, delivering one deadly payload after another, continued to to streak across the skies. The use of cluster bombs was a sign that the Americans, in particular, would resort to brutal levels of power and force.

A surgical assistant at the Saddam Hospital in Nassiriya, Mustafa Mohammed Ali, told the *Guardian* that US aircraft had dropped 3 or 4 cluster bombs on civilian areas in the city on the first weekend of bombing, killing 10 and wounding 200. He said he understood the US forces going straight to Baghdad to get rid of Saddam, but added: 'I don't want forces to come into [this] city. They have an objective, they go straight to the target. There's no room in the hospital because of the wounded.' When he saw the bodies of two dead marines, he revealed that he cheered silently.

When cluster bombs fall, civilians die. They die in the initial attack, if the bombs were used against military personnel who were intermingled with civilians. But worse still is what happens for years afterwards when civilians, often children, stumble upon unexploded 'bomblets'. Such remnants from US cluster bombs dropped in the Gulf War in 1991 are still being found – 2,400 of them in 2002 alone. Some 1,600 civilians have been killed and 2,500 injured in the intervening 12 years from unexploded bomblets.

Used against tanks or concentrations of forces, cluster bombs are currently a legal weapon. But, just as in earlier conflicts, civilians are already being hurt by them. On 31 March, the American military bombed Hilla, a town six miles south of Baghdad, with cluster bombs. According to the chief doctor at Hilla's teaching hospital, 33 civilians were killed and 100 injured.

Far away from the war zone, the picture of a corpse of an Iraqi baby, killed during the US attack, defined the conflict in the collective imagination of many in the West. The tiny cadaver of the baby had been carried out of the morgue on a pink pallet, swaddled like a doll in a funeral shroud. Its body was laid face to face on the pavement against the body of a boy, who looked about 10.

Horrifically injured bodies were heaped into pick-up trucks, and were swarmed round by relatives of the dead, who accompanied them for burial. Bed after bed of injured women and children were pictured along with large pools of blood on the floors of the hospital.

'All of these are due to the American bombing of the civilian homes. Hundreds of civilians have been injured, and many have been killed,' said Nazim al-Adali, an Edinburgh-trained doctor at the hospital, who appealed to his 'colleagues' in England to protest against the bombings. Among the injured in the women's ward was Aliya Mukhtaf, who said her husband and 6 children had been killed in the attack. Television pictures, not broadcast in the West but shown to reporters at the scene, showed a teenage boy with bandages over the stump where his right hand was sheared off by shrapnel. 'There are not any army cars or tanks in the area,' said Dr al-Adali, who claimed cluster bombs had been used.

Further south, British artillery had fired cluster munitions against military targets near Basra and its million inhabitants. So sensitive is the British military about the use of such bombs that their use was immediately denied by army headquarters in Kuwait. The denial was later reversed by Geoff Hoon, the Defence Secretary, in London. A retired general, one whose mind perhaps was steeped in another age, asked us to 'harden our hearts'. War was cruel and insensitive and undiscriminating, but, as the *Guardian* in its editorial column said: 'In this screwed-up, divided, warring world, that dead Iraqi baby in the photo is our baby, too. And we grieve – for the child, for our own country as well as theirs, and for all the men whose hearts grow hard.'

Cluster bombs, like the depleted uranium shells used by British tank divisions in Basra, signified that there would be no limit on the amount of military power that could be used to destroy the will of Iraqis to resist. If a regime, army or civilian population needed to be shocked and awed into submission, then the message was clear: the coalition forces would not hesitate to do so.

Attitudes calcify because war, no matter how hi-tech, is waged as a low, dishonest affair. When blood is shed, the results are rarely pretty. True, the defenders of Saddam's regime were using all means at their disposal, no matter how low-tech, to repel the US forces. America's pre-eminence – superior airpower, superior weaponry – may have encouraged the Iraqis to fight dirty. Whatever the reasons, battles now raged across the southern half of Iraq, a nation as big as France, in ungovernable and messy ways. The result of the tactics used by the Iraqi units in resisting US forces meant fresh faces under helmets and twitching fingers on gun triggers. When a soldier is frightened, he or she will end up shooting anything that moves. So troops sent to cure Iraq of Saddam end up resembling the disease. This was certainly not what the war planners in Washington and London had wanted.

Wounded US soldiers were soon describing Iraqi tactics in gory detail. Staff Sergeant Jamie Villafane, 31, from Long Island, New York, was among 24 American servicemen recovering from combat injuries at the US armed forces' medical centre at Landstuhl in south-west Germany. The scout from 1st battalion, 30th Infantry Regiment, told the *Guardian* at the end of March how he and his six-man section survived an ambush by Iraqi soldiers posing as civilians on a bridge south of Nassiriya a week before.

> On Saturday, about 13.00 hours, we had a call to go down and check out some civilians . . . There were about two dozen civilians on two separate bridges. We moved up to find out about the civilians and they moved off the bridge. [Some] moved to the left of us and the ones to the front of us went underneath the bridge. As we were looking at the ones to the left of us my gunner, Sgt Horgan, announced 'RPG' [rocket

propelled grenade]. A rocket hit our truck from the front. It blew me out of the truck.

The next I remember I started engaging the group to the left of us who were firing at us: the civilians who were firing at us. At that time, another rocket was fired from the front. It was a wire-guided missile 'cos it came pretty close and I got to see the wire as it went by. If I hadn't moved it might have hit me. I announced to my soldiers behind me that it was a rocket and [yelled] 'Get down.' They all got down and moved out of the way and it hit the truck next to us. At that time, I realised that I was injured. I don't remember anything between the first and the second rocket but I must have got my weapon off the truck.

I moved off to the side of the bridge to start to get a good spot to start getting some fire down on these guys. When I went down there, there was one guy hiding behind one of the pillars. I yelled at him and he turned and dropped his weapon. He was no longer a combatant. He was a prisoner of war.

[Another three guys] just came round the corner. They seen I already had one guy at gunpoint. I'd put him in front of me. You could see they were terrified. Really. I mean, if you've ever had a gun pointed at you . . . They had AK47s. They dropped their weapons. They had robes on to look like the regular bedouins around there. The uniforms . . . one of them had four stripes [and] one of them had three stars. I'm not sure what rank that is for Iraqis. They were living underneath the bridge. Lotta weapons.

We were briefed that they might put on civilian clothes – that some of the soldiers were putting on civilian clothes to flee. We had no idea they would use that to ambush us. I guess they have to do whatever they have to. If I went back out there, I have to second guess every single civilian. I'd not be able to look at any man, woman or child without asking: 'I wonder what they've got on them.' Me and Sgt Horgan talked about it [later] and we figured out that getting shot at really was not that bad. It was just the getting shot part that sucked.

What had not changed was that under the battle gear, American and British soldiers were just flesh and sinew, blood and guts. They bled too. The push-button campaign of the first few days – connecting laptops to the cruise missile silos in warships – had gone. There was also an understanding that despite all the missile guidance systems, satellite imaging and precision bombing the troops crouching down beside a firing howitzer in Iraq looked much as they did 60 years ago in Europe. Television showed that young men and women were, like those on battlefields before them, dying for decisions made far from the war zone.

When an Iraqi suicide bomber in a taxi killed four Americans at a checkpoint north of Najaf, it indicated that there was a wellspring of hate being tapped by the invasion. Ali Jaffar al-Noamani killed himself and four American soldiers by blowing up his own car at a checkpoint – and put the final nail in the coffin of the 'liberation' scenario of the Washington-London alliance. The suicide attack, which killed four soldiers of the 3rd Infantry Division, happened when a taxi stopped close to the US checkpoint and the driver waved for help. As 5 soldiers approached the car, it exploded. The suicide bombing was the first against either US or British forces since the campaign began.

The invading Anglo-American forces now had to treat all Iraqi civilians as potential suicide bombers. A spokesman for General Tommy Franks, the US commander of the war, was unapologetic. 'Our checkpoints are being a little more aggressive out there,' he said. 'We will try to interdict potential suicide bombers earlier. Our kids can take the action they need to protect themselves.'

Such statements raised eyebrows in Britain. British soldiers had decades of dealing with such experiences – first in colonial insurgencies in Malaysia, then in Northern Ireland and peace-keeping operations in the Balkans. The actions of US troops would not endear the forces to the Iraqi civilian population nor convince them of their good intentions. British officers, off the record, were happy to describe the very different approaches of UK and American soldiers by pointing to Umm Qasr. 'Unlike the

Americans, we took our helmets and sunglasses off and looked at the Iraqis eye to eye,' was how one British officer put it.

The Iraqi regime felt the fear coursing through the US army and promised more suicide missions, despite the doubts raised over whether Mr al-Noamani had been a volunteer for jihad or coerced into carrying a bomb. Baghdad did not stop to consider that in encouraging such attacks Saddam and assembled generals would be committing a war crime. In battle there is nothing wrong with tricking the enemy. But if a suicide bomber gets to his or her target by pretending to be a civilian, it is a violation of humanitarian law because it endangers all civilians. The message from international lawyers was that if deceit was a government strategy, it was a war crime.

The suicide bombing completed the transformation of the war from a struggle for survival by Saddam's regime to what was billed in Baghdad as a patriotic rising of the weak against a vastly more powerful force of foreign invaders. 'This is the beginning, and you will hear more good news in the coming days. We will use any means to kill our enemy in our land, and we will follow the enemy into its land,' the Iraqi Vice-President, Taha Yassin Ramadan, told a press conference. 'The US administration is going to turn the whole world into people willing to die for their nation.'

The failure of a quick, clean victory in Iraq meant the failures in military strategy were examined more closely. 'Everybody's frame of reference is changing. The enemy always gets a vote. You fight the enemy and not the plan. I personally underestimated the willingness of the Fedayeen to fight, or maybe overestimated the willingness of the Shia to rise up,' said Col Ben Hodges, commander of the 101st Airborne's 1st brigade.

This oversight cost the US dearly in unnecessary casualties, wrecked vehicles and a lowering of morale. Donald Rumsfeld, the US Defence Secretary, came under pressure when reports suggested it was his fault that this conflict was not a technological, quick or 21st-century war. Indeed it resembled the bareknuckled fights of the 20th century.

On the ground, the effects were to destabilise and debilitate the American and British forces. There was also a physical effect on the ability to move supplies, leaving, say a number of credible reports, some units with only enough rations for one meal a day. 'We have almost outrun our logistics lines,' said one officer at a US unit at the northernmost stretch of the advance in central Iraq, close to Baghdad. To make matters worse, after 3 weeks of unusually cool weather, a heatwave was building up in Iraq.

Military strategists pondered where the Iraqis had learned these new tactics. Was it Mogadishu – where warlords routed a small group of US commandos? Was it from Palestinian suicide squads in the occupied territories? For James Fox, who had covered the Vietnam war, history's lesson for the American administration began in the paddyfields of south-east Asia.

The key book for the Iraqis was written by General Vo Nguyen Giap, the brilliant Vietnamese architect of the war against the French and the Americans. It was published in English in 1961, under the title *People's War, People's Army*, long before the US war in Vietnam hotted up. Though full of partyspeak, it shows how easy it is to hold up and demoralise a hugely superior army that has a long supply convoy. Giap exploited what he called 'the contradictions of the aggressive colonial war'. The invaders have to fan out and operate far from their bases. When they deploy, said Giap, 'their broken-up units become easy prey'. First harass the enemy, 'rotting' away his rear and reserves, forcing him to deploy troops to defend bases and perimeters.

The historical comparison to Vietnam was superficial, but in one key way it rang true. The US military was accustomed to running wars. This time it was being conducted by the hawkish Rumsfeld. The boss of the Pentagon could so easily have made the cast of *Dr Strangelove*. He served Richard Nixon as Nato ambassador and at 70 became a civilian warrior in the White House of George Bush. Rumsfeld is a believer in the case set out in Eliot

Cohen's influential book *Supreme Command*, which argued that politicians should impose their own military views on generals.

When, more than a year ago, Rumsfeld had received General Franks's first draft of the Iraq invasion plan, he sent it straight back, saying the plan was too troop-heavy. Later drafts went back and forth across Rumsfeld's desk ever since. His aim throughout had been to embed three key points into the plan: precision bombing, enhanced use of intelligence, and blitzkrieg-style armoured advances. But Rumsfeld left little to chance. He is both a big thinker and a micro-manager.

The last time there was this level of involvement in military affairs by a suit was 40 years ago, when Robert McNamara and his Kennedy-era whizzkids decided to take the battle to the North Vietnamese. Just like Rumsfeld, they were not content to lay down general policy. Just like Rumsfeld, they decided they knew better than the generals what forces would be needed to take on the Vietcong. More than any other single politician, arguably including Lyndon Johnson, McNamara took the blame for the Vietnam disaster. Rumsfeld was now looking like the Iraq conflict's McNamara. His second-guessing of the deployment orders in the months before the fighting started was being blamed by retired and serving officers alike for the thinly pro-tected 300-mile supply lines on which US troops were now depending.

Their message was clear. Whatever happened now, this had be-come 'Rumsfeld's war'. If Saddam's regime suddenly collapsed, his superstar status from the Afghan war, when he proved the doubters wrong, would only be enhanced. If it was to slide into a gruelling slog, as coalition casualties climbed into the hundreds, there was no doubt he would take the blame. Fiercely worded criticisms littered the press as unnamed former and acting officers were quoted complaining about Rumsfeld's interfering ways. According to a senior Pentagon planner quoted in the *New Yorker*, Rumsfeld was the decision-maker 'at every turn' of the extended argument about invasion plans.

Just as soldiers' nerves were edgy and there was rising concern about the pace of the war, the military support in Washington for the Secretary for Defence was notable for its paucity. The White House had to step in: 'The President has tremendous faith in Secretary Rumsfeld.' More troops were to be sent to the Gulf, but they were not reinforcements, said the Pentagon.

Rumsfeld's gamble, in fact, was modelled on the German blitzkrieg of France in 1940, when Panzer divisions simply rolled on without pause until they hit the sea. France surrendered in 44 days. In Iraq, US forces would not stop until they reached Baghdad. Operation Desert Storm was a ponderous advance where American armour trundled at about 10 mph with divisions of US troops supported by up to 9 brigades of artillery. In Operation Iraqi Freedom the 3rd Infantry Division set out with just one. Air power would patrol the tail of the convoy. That was the theory, and the retired generals 'embedded' in television studios did not think it could work. Rumsfeld did not care.

That the battle for Iraq was not going to plan was plain for all to see. Yet wars rarely go precisely to plan. Television shots of cheering Kosovans, British soldiers patrolling streets in Sierra Leone and the implosion of the Taliban meant the public had become unused to the way wars are fought. People had become innoculated against the death and disorder battles bring.

But the true horror of this war did come to the world's attention – largely through the reporter's notebook and the camera lens. Far from the debate over whose fault it was that American supply lines were stretched, or whether American jets deliberately targeted civilians, or whether Iraqis were acting with valour or treachery when defending their country, was the unspoken truth: that war not only kills, it degrades.

To understand how far the noble aims and gestures of the invading forces had been undermined, the *Washington Post* reporter William Branigin, embedded with US soldiers of Bravo company, posted a remarkable report from near Karbala on March 31, recounting the shooting of women and children by American soldiers on 'a warm, hazy day' in central Iraq:

As the blue Toyota came barrelling towards an intersection held by troops of the army's 3rd Infantry Division, Captain Ronny Johnson grew increasingly alarmed. From his position at the intersection he was heard radioing to one of his forward platoons of Bradley armoured vehicles to alert it to a potential threat. 'Fire a warning shot,' he ordered as the vehicle kept coming. Then, with increasing urgency, he told the platoon to shoot a machine gun round into its radiator. 'Stop fucking around!' Johnson yelled into the radio when he still saw no action being taken. Finally, he screamed: 'Stop him, Red 1, stop him!' That order was immediately followed by the loud reports of cannon fire from one or more of the Bradleys. About half a dozen shots were heard in all. 'Cease fire!' Johnson yelled over the radio. Then, as he peered into his binoculars from the intersection on Highway 9, he roared at the platoon leader: 'You just fucking killed a family because you didn't fire a warning shot soon enough!'

Fifteen Iraqis were in the the Toyota, which was packed with their possessions. Ten of them, including five children who appeared to be under five years old, were killed on the spot. Branigin quoted Sergeant Mario Manzano, 26, a medic with Bravo company, as saying: 'It was the most horrible thing I've ever seen, and I hope I never see it again.'

8 Holy war

It is interesting to note how frequently the phrase 'forging a nation' is used, because most nations are forgeries.
                                   Avi Shlaim, historian, March 2003

The going was getting tougher, the American bombing wilder and the civilian death toll was rising precipitously. After 12 days of fighting, soldiers from towns and cities in the West still did not have control of any big urban centres in Iraq.

There could be no quelling a population of 24 million without taking charge of the cities and towns where two-thirds of Iraqis lived. There had been no big breakthroughs – on the battlefield or off it. There had been no defections of senior politicians from Saddam Hussein's Ba'ath Party or military commanders from the Iraqi army. There were, despite intelligence information at 10 sites, no sign of chemical or biological weapons of mass destruction, the reason quoted by Washington and London for attacking Iraq. The rhetoric of war left more smoke in its wake than a Challenger tank rumbling through the desert, and coalition claims of an easy victory now looked as empty as the sandy plains the American and British troops controlled.

Doubts about the campaign were being aired to reporters – even in Central Command's futuristic press centre at Camp as-Sayliya, Qatar. Two weeks into the war, military commanders were wandering about the Hollywood-style set at Coalition Forces Headquarters admitting to the world's press that the American understanding of the Arab world was too limited. This meant that US Central Command had not yet figured out a way to convince the Iraqis that US troops were liberators, not occupiers. In one of the most low-key assessments of the war, a high-ranking US officer told the *Guardian*'s Rory McCarthy that it would be unrealistic to expect Baghdad to fall within days.

The Americans had just had the realisation: the Arabs were different. 'There is a big cultural difference between the US and the Arab world. That makes it hard,' said the experienced officer, who had been closely involved in the planning of the war. 'We Americans are not very good at judging what a totalitarian regime is like, looks like and acts like. There is an information psychology front that we are trying to push, but we are probably not as sophisticated about it as we would want to be.' These were not the words of an officer on the verge of victory.

The psychology of the war as seen from Qatar seemed to revolve around the Saddam cult of personality and the grip this extended over the people of Iraq. There was no mistaking the brutality of the regime. The Iraqi President had been a demonic social engineer, building a pervasive apparatus of surveillance and coercion and staffing it with men from the Sunni and Tikriti minorities, from the marginalised tribes, both Sunni and Shia, of the countryside, and from the urban lower middle class. He was never content with mere loyalty: it must always be cemented by crime to ensure there was no easy way back into the ordinary community for his servants.

The system encouraged not only the crimes inherent in its operation – arbitrary arrest, imprisonment and torture – but also freelance crimes, such as extortion and rape. Life was pure, untrammelled terror. Saddam ruled and gassed the Kurds. A few months after coming to power, he launched, with western encouragement, what turned out to be the longest war of the 20th century against his neighbour, Iran, which was three and a half times the size and four times as populous.

Saddam needed to weld together a severely fragmented country, constructed by Britain out of three ex-Ottoman pro-vinces. He used terrror to do so. Iraq lacked the national bonds of ethnicity or religion. The Kurds in the north aspired to poli-tical independence in Kurdistan. They were non-semitic, with their own language. The Kurds were Sunni Muslims, but they were not Arabs. The Shia of the south, who made up most of the population, were bereft of power which traditionally rested in the hands of the Sunni minority, of which Saddam was a non-praticising member. The Shia and Kurds felt the frequent blows of the torture chamber that was Saddam's Iraq.

American war planners in Qatar had ignored both Saddam's ubiquity and the complexity of life under a dictatorship. This exposed a flaw in the right-wing belief that if you simply offered people freedom they would rush to grasp it. Planners ignored the dangerous calculations inherent in everyday Iraqi life, the shadings of collaboration, which only the luckiest or strongest could wholly avoid, and the degradation of all under a tyranny. Until Saddam fell from power in a visible way, there would be no uprising from the Iraqis this time, no cries of thank you, no tears of joy – no matter how much the Anglo-American soldiers wished for it. Decades of terror had enslaved the Iraqi mind; and the Americans had discovered that nothing would free Iraqis until their President had gone.

Yet there were signs that the British and US troops were winning, by the slow and methodical grinding down Iraqi resistance. The armoured thrusts, known as thunder runs, into small towns and cities were becoming increasingly effective in knocking out groups of fighters. The dropping of bigger bombs from the skies drained Iraqi morale and destroyed war materials. American forces were certainly more violent in executing the strategy; the British version was more finessed but just as effective.

On 31 March the US Marines 5th Regiment overran an area an hour's drive from Baghdad, known in Arabic as Bridge district, after a leap out of the desert into Babil province, on the edges of the Iraqi heartland, close to the site of ancient Babylon. Here the invasion was looking more hopeful for US forces. An American reconnaissance unit in light vehicles met little resistance when it plunged into what was supposedly solid Iraqi-held territory. Lieutenant Colonel Stacy Claridy, commander of the battalion, said it had come under fire from anti-aircraft cannon for about two hours, after which the Iraqis fled.

The Americans were not being welcomed with open arms, but neither were there signs of resistance or civilian hostility as they approached the capital. Iraqis showed the same mixture of deference and diffidence, fear and enthusiasm that they had displayed ever since troops invaded. It was here that Hamza, a middle-class Iraqi, came out of the dusty streets to speak to reporters. He had a baccalaureate in English and a diploma in public health, and had fled Baghdad to his old home village to escape the bombing. 'We don't think this is a good way for the Americans to do what they want to do,' he said, looking over at the tanks with their gun barrels pointing down the streets of the village. 'There are many ways to do what they want to do.'

Hamza was reluctant to criticise Saddam and his regime. It was not clear to the *Guardian*'s James Meek whether he genuinely felt Saddam was an acceptable leader or whether he feared informers. Iraqis appeared to be sitting on the fence. 'Fifty-fifty,' was Hamza's response when asked what he thought of the invasion. 'If the consequences are as Bush promised, very good, but if the Americans stay, the consequences will be very bad.'

US military medics, accompanied by a marines' foot patrol, began offering basic treatment to local people. They treated a boy, the son of a veteran of the 1991 Gulf War taken prisoner by the US, who had fallen off a wall and broken his arm. Hamza said it was good that the medics had come. The invasion had caused deaths, he said. A few days earlier a helicopter gunship had shot and killed a local man who had been carrying a machine gun. He had shot at the helicopter, but he had the gun because he was involved in a blood feud and had shot at the helicopter in a moment of anger. 'The difference between an armed helicopter and a small bullet coming out of a gun is a big difference,' Hamza said. 'The pilot behaved like a cowboy.'

The marines were now pushing up against the territory supposedly defended by the dreaded Republican Guard, yet there was no sign of them, and their menace was constantly receding. US marines were now a little over an hour's tank drive from Baghdad. There were reports, from the US army in Najaf and Kerbala and from Kut, downstream of Nassiriya, of an enemy that melted away just as the coalition troops were arriving.

The next day convoys of US marines snaked their way towards Baghdad. The convoy, as usual, travelled almost without
lights. The dark, purposeful stream of heavily armed vehicles
passed Iraqi towns blazing with lights. The local population
stayed indoors, cooking, watching television, and sleeping, but
they must have heard the rumble of the convoy as it passed. Nobody came out, much less fired shots. It was as if the two worlds,
America and Iraq, were ignoring each other, even though they
were supposed to be at war.

Perhaps precision attacks by smart bombs and guided missiles were taking their toll on Iraqi troops by disorienting them.
The bombing also devastated the morale of Iraqi troops on the
ground. Was there anybody left to command Iraq's guerrilla
forces, given the pounding they had received? It now looked as
if coalition troops were pushing forward against the most eph-
emeral resistance. US troops were momentarily caught off-guard
because the Iraqis appeared to have nothing else to offer, apart
from their guerrilla tactics of shoot and flee.

Curiously, the Iraqis did not blow up a single one of the numerous bridges US and British forces had to take. US Central
Command said troops had also seized control of a dam on Lake
al-Milh near Baghdad. There had been fears that the Iraqis would
try to destroy the dam to flood the American forces. Events were
moving so rapidly that it was difficult to see whether this lightning advance to Baghdad was a brief respite in battle or the
result of some sudden, silent implosion of Saddam's regime. The
lightning advance meant oilfields and infrastructure could not
be set on fire or blown up by Saddam's soldiers, which would
have considerably slowed the coalition's progress.

Light resistance did not mean there were no casualties. It is
just that most were Iraqis. In a battle in early April, the US
marines attacked company-sized units – 100 to 200 men – of
Saddam's troops as they drove towards the Tigris. An Iraqi
checkpoint on a bridge over the Saddam Canal, west of the
river, was scorched where it had been hit by US fire. The bodies
of Iraqi soldiers lay scattered and bloody by the roadside. The

apparent indifference some American troops showed to this death and destruction neither helped their cause as liberators nor endeared them to the Arab world, aghast at this new form of bloody imperialism.

The mood of Captain Ted Card, commander of a company of US marines on the road to Numaniya, a town south-east of Baghdad, summed up what many American troops were telling reporters. His company had been shot at that morning, in a desultory way, from a gigantic munitions storage base nearby, even though the base had been battered by B-52 strikes. 'We were a little bit surprised to get some fire, but we fired back. It only lasted five minutes,' Capt Card said. 'These guys are cowards. None of them fight. This is boring. I'm surprised I'm not in Baghdad already.'

There were moments of real drama for the folks back home. The news that US special forces had rescued Jessica Lynch, a 19-year-old private held in an Iraqi hospital by Saddam's troops in Nassiriya, was a dramatic representation of life as art. Blurred green images, seen through the lens of night-fighting equipment, were beamed across the world. Amid the fuzz, the viewers witnessed something new: the first war movie being made as the script was being written.

The rescue cushioned hopes in the United States that Operation Iraqi Freedom could and would be a short, neat war under the desert sky. *Saving Private Lynch* was a heroic event, no doubt. But in among the magazine front covers, hundreds of news pages, thousands of column inches and millions of words spoken, read or written, how many noticed the faceless, nameless conscripts and innocent victims who left families and homes in Iraq bereft and heartbroken? It was a good question and one those opposed to the war felt was never answered in battle.

From the fertile crescent in the south of the country to the Syrian Orthodox monasteries of the north, Iraq was not just another country but part of many peoples' past. The land between the Tigris and Euphrates rivers is the cradle of civilisation. So it was no surprise that the 19-mile stretch of dry land between

Razzaza Lake and the Euphrates was cast as the Battle of Baby-lon by headline writers in America and Britain. During this fight the modern world crashed onto ancient sites for the first confron-tation between US ground forces and the Republican Guard. 'It is the first ground contact in the real sense of the word,' a military source in Qatar said. The outcome was never in doubt.

In this country of holy sites and holy wars, nothing compared to Najaf and Kerbala. To the south of Baghdad, this pair of towns are the most revered cities for the majority Shia population in Iraq. Kerbala is the site of the battle where Hussein, the son of the Shia Imam Ali Ibn Abu Talib, was massacred by the Sunnis 1,300 years ago in a conflict that divides Islam to this day. A sense of Ali's importance can be gauged by the fact that he was a cousin and son-in-law of the Prophet Mohammed and is considered the first Shia Imam. His son was Hussein III. Both are considered martyrs; hence the importance of martyrdom within the Shia world community. It was their deaths that gave birth to the Shia sect in Islam. Hussein's mausoleum is like the Vatican, Gethsemane and the Wailing Wall rolled into one. The cities are sites of annual pilgrimage for thousands of Shia and became the focus of the uprising against Saddam in 1991.

But it was in the holy city of Najaf that spiritual discourse suddenly found a voice in a war that the coalition said had nothing to do with religion. Najaf, which in Arabic means 'a high land', lies 100 miles south of Baghdad on a desert plateau and ranks only after Mecca and Medina in importance for the world's 120 million Shia Muslims. During this phase of the bomb-ing, B-52s were circling the city, emptying their payloads on to the Medina Division of the Republican Guard, one of Saddam's elite battle units. They know about slaughter in Najaf, now sur-rounded by tanks of the US Seventh Cavalry, Custer's old devil-may-care outfit. Ali was murdered at the gates of Najaf.

It was at this point that US Central Command claimed Iraqi forces had occupied the holiest Shia shrine in Iraq, the golden-domed mosque where Ali is buried, and were firing on Ameri-can troops encircling Najaf. US forces would not be returning fire, said the coalition, against Saddam's Fedayeen fighters. Baghdad's Minister of Information, Mohammed Saeed al-Sahaf, with typical robustness, retorted that it was the coalition forces, not Saddam's, that were desecrating the mosques. 'After we repelled them to the desert, they hit the mosques. It is obvious they are doing this to destroy these shrines,' he said.

This was not just another battle on the road to Baghdad, but a pivotal moment in the progress of the war. The Shia population of Iraq would never back the coalition while their holy cities were in danger. Until this moment, no statement was made to assure the Shia, who make up 60 oper cent of Iraq's population, that the coalition respected the religious significance of Najaf, but rather the reverse: Central Command had been referring to it in military briefings like any other city.

But it was in Najaf that US correspondents reported the most enthusiastic welcome yet from local people as US troops entered the city. Rick Atkinson of the *Washington Post*, embedded with the 101st Airborne Division, reported that thousands of Iraqis came to greet them as they approached Ali's tomb.

In the midst of the fighting, a US patrol approached Ali's tomb attempting to contact local clerics, but were met instead by a crowd. Lieutenant Colonel Chris Hughes, a battalion commander in the 1st Brigade, said: 'The crowd got bigger and bigger, so we pulled back out. But it was like the liberation of Paris.'

A day later and the first shaft of sunlight for the coalition penetrated the clouds of conflict. Television pictures showed a convoy of US troops being warmly greeted as they moved through dusty, narrow streets. It was perhaps the first time that American forces had been so openly received, raising the spirits of military planners who had hoped for this type of welcome throughout the country.

There was better news to come. Grand Ayatollah Ali Sistani told Shia Muslims not to hinder the invasion force. The supreme religious authority of the Hawza al-Ilmiyya theological school in Najaf, who had been put under house arrest by Saddam, called on Iraqis to stop fighting around the tomb of Ali. Donald Rumsfeld welcomed the ruling, describing the ayatollah as 'courageous'. Winning over Iraqi hearts would need much more than this, but it was an important victory far from the battlefield.

The fight was being taken to the Iraqis – but where were they? For the first time in the battle, with troops closing in on the capital, Saddam did not read out his own speech. Instead his Information Minister mouthed his master's words, calling for a jihad. 'Those who are martyred will be rewarded in heaven,' said Mohammed Saeed al-Sahaf, on April Fool's Day, somewhere in Baghdad. On two previous occasions Saddam had appeared on Iraqi television himself. It may not have been much, but for British and American politicians it was the sound of another nail being hammered into the coffin of the Ba'athist regime.

The airwaves and newspapers were full of annihilation and antiquity. Iraqi guardsmen had been told to make a stand at Babylon, seat of Mesopotamian civilisation, but were blasted away. When a marine force crossed the Tigris at the town of Kut they expected the worst. But, after days of intense bombardment – including the dropping of two massive 15,000 lb 'daisy-cutter' fuel-air bombs – the Baghdad division of the Republican Guard was smashed to smithereens. US mechanised and airborne forces probing the Iraqi defences reported coming across corpses in uniforms of the Hammurabi and Nebuchadnezzar divisions, both named after ancient Babylonian kings in whose steps, we were told, Saddam believed he was treading. The signs were that the Iraqi army was disintegrating.

Amatzia Baram, Professor of History of the Middle East at the University of Haifa, wrote: 'By keeping his best army divisions outside Baghdad, confronting the allied forces with very little ground-to-air protection, Saddam in fact sentenced them to death.' Central Command could barely find enough blood-curdling cries to describe their successes. 'The dagger is clearly

pointed at the heart of the regime,' was the attempt by Brigadier
General Vince Brooks from Command headquarters.

The bombs were now falling on Baghdad like autumn rain.
For many there was no escaping the shards of steel, the bits of
bombs and the crashing of masonry hit by a missile. The blast
spewed shrapnel and glass into a Red Crescent maternity hospital. Three people were killed and scores injured. Even so,
Iraqis displayed no signs of weakening. America's choice of
civilian targets had deepened their anger and erased the faint
hope that US forces would be welcomed into Baghdad. 'Let
them go and liberate the Palestinians. We are not afraid of them,'
was how one woman in a Baghdad suburb put it to Suzanne
Goldenberg.

Maybe resolve had been bolstered by freshly released pictures
of the Iraqi leader talking to his generals. Maybe the people of
Baghdad did not believe that the Americans would come. If
Washington and London sounded hopeful that the end was in
sight, so did the Iraqis. The modern half of the city, home to the
presidential palaces and other official buildings, was crawling
with armed Ba'ath Party militia. They spent the day expanding
sandbag posts and turning them into more formidable defences. There were outpourings of orchestrated anger, of stage-
managed defiance but also a visceral hatred for what America
was doing.

But for all the noisy triumphalism from both sides, what resounded was the silence of the dead. On the outskirts of Baghdad, desolation and adversity pitted the faces of ordinary Iraqis.
Conflict was a curse and there was little sign, as American
bombers took wing above, that it would be lifted soon. These
untold stories were what the war were really about. Far from
rhetoric and the real-time television coverage, people were dying
unnoticed and uncared for. One strike on the edge of Baghdad
in early April destroyed two homes of an extended family of 12
people. The raid destroyed the local school.

There, reported Goldenberg, in Sueb, 22 miles from the centre
of Baghdad and just beyond the ring of burning crude oil that

marked the outer reaches of the capital, a battle that had gone largely unseen had been raging for days. The last five days had seen intense, round-the-clock bombardments, forcing locals to flee to makeshift underground shelters or to relatives elsewhere in the city. This easily forgotten neighbourhood, part village, part spillover suburb, a dumping ground for Shias too poor to afford homes in Baghdad proper, found itself in an unwanted – and lethal – position of strategic importance. 'There are bombings – missiles and airplanes – all day long, and all night,' said Walid Hathem, whose home was replaced by a giant crater a few hours before dawn one day. 'It's continuous.'

The problem was that the poor found themselves in a target-rich environment. On the far side of Sueb village, Saddam's farmhouse rose from a grove of palm trees, and a radar installation marked the start of the military zone of Radwaniyah, a few miles down the road. America's bombardments brought almost daily casualties.

Tragedy struck Sueb when US missiles killed six members of one family and five others living in the same road. Twelve houses were destroyed in the blast, hastily built one-storey structures crumpled into the earth. Taliya Ali Mohammed, whose house was strewn with shattered glass, said: 'The people living in this area are the very poorest people. It really is so cruel that we are being hit.'

The children in Sueb cried themselves to sleep. And the missiles still rained down. One flew into two homes as the owners and their families watched. All they had in the world was gone, apart from a kerosene cooker and a television set. 'When the missiles came in, everything shook,' said Yas Khudayar, who was left homeless and had to share a tunnel space of barely two square metres with his wife and 5 children. 'We expected to be dead any minute.' Next door, at Suad Abdur Rahman's house, the floors were carpeted with broken glass and chunks of plaster. Overhead fans were plucked from the ceilings like flowers. 'Just look at what those Americans have done,' she said. 'We hate them now more than ever. What have we done? Why should our children suffer? Saddam Hussein has not hurt us. He hasn't been a nuisance to us.'

This was not what the Anglo-American forces wanted to hear. American troops were now within 30 miles of Baghdad, only days away from the bloodiest fighting – and ultimate prize – of this conflict. There was no doubt that the outcome of the war would be decided by the capture of the obscene symbols of Saddam's presence in the capital and perhaps his death, but US forces must first conquer the periphery. Sueb and the other suburbs which had sprung up as population growth outstripped available land in Baghdad, lay directly in the Americans' path. These roads would soon hear the rumble of American tanks as US troops drew ever closer to the columns of thick, oily smoke surrounding the city.

From the advancing columns, Iraq looked and felt like hell on earth. The land stank of burning. The town of Aziziya, 40 miles from the capital, was marked by thick clouds of grey smoke. Once as lively as any other in the Middle East, it was now pocked by the flames flickering in the heart of scorched trucks and tanks. This was all that was left of the ugliness of the swift and nasty battle waged there to push the Marine Corps to the threshold of Baghdad. The *Guardian*'s James Meek, embedded with troops, saw a row of scorched shops, a truck still burning in front of a restaurant and figures silhouetted against the leaping flames on the roof of a building as people jumped hither and thither to try to put the fire out.

Civilian traffic with headlights on moved through the dark streets. A civilian ambulance, red lights flashing, was trying to negotiate a US marine checkpoint on the main road skirting Aziziya. Beyond the town, an Iraqi tank transporter, complete with tank, was on fire where it had slewed into a ditch after being hit. War was mad, but life went on.

The marines were only bothered about getting to Baghdad. They wanted to get past Aziziya safely, without actually taking it. That meant hostile forces in the town had to be neutralised. So when Iraqi forces mingled their troops and equipment with the civilian population, civilians inevitably got caught in the crossfire. There were claims from Aziziyans that civilians, including women and children, had been killed as they tried to leave. Others said the Americans had used cluster bombs.

The unobscured fact was that there had been waste of human life and little redemption. The US soldiers were not yet helping people with drugs or hospital treatment or repairs or law and order, because the Americans were not entering the city, leaving whatever dubious conjunction of desperate Ba'ath Party hacks, looters and elders remained to organise relief.

The clutter of battle, the dazed Iraqis, the opaqueness of military battle plans all permeated the atmosphere like a thick miasma. From the conflicting information given by local people in interviews with the *Guardian*, it appeared that the town had been subject to preliminary attack by planes, helicopters and artillery. The marines then sent tanks through, followed by battalions of infantry whose aim was simply to get past the town and head on towards Baghdad without getting hurt. If they were fired on, they fired back, even if it meant firing into nominally civilian areas. There were no questions asked later about lives lost or who was guilty or blameless.

But nothing, apart from the fact that death had visited the town, appeared to be clear. Abdel Karim, a local man who spoke with genuine anger, said 50 civilians had been killed in the fighting, including women and children, and 50 wounded. He said all the dead had been buried but could not say exactly where. 'They sent bombs like silver rain,' he said. In the background, a huge oil storage tank gushed flames and black smoke. 'These are innocent people. They are not fighting.'

Another resident, who would not give his name, said, after the mob of dozens had drifted away, that Karim was speaking to curry favour with the Iraqi authorities, and most of the dead and wounded were members of the Republican Guard or local Ba'ath Party fighters.

Asked why he would not give his name, he said: 'I am afraid nothing will happen to my friend, and we will be slaughtered.'

By 'my friend' he meant Saddam Hussein. 'We are not angry with the Americans. For 35 years the Ba'athists have been killing us, suffocating us. Even if the Americans killed me the sacrifice would be worth it. The army and Ba'ath people go into hospitals and schools and put themselves in the middle of the civilians. Over 100 of the Republican Guard and Ba'ath were killed last night. The ones they buried are military but they wear the dish-dash [civilian tunic].'

Another man spoke of the agony of being caught between two opposing forces. 'Don't bomb us any more, we have children,' he said. 'We are afraid he will use chemical weapons, and we don't have masks.' 'He' referred to the President. In all the con-fusion, fear and loathing, war had claimed another victim: the soul of the Iraqi people.

The marines raced past Aziziya and towards Baghdad along Highway 7. It was insane: a column of Humvees charging down the wrong side of the dual carriageway, half on, half off, over-taking and being overtaken by tracked amphibious vehicles going in the same direction. Tanks sped along at 40 mph – ex-tremely fast for a tracked vehicle. Brick-sized chunks of rubber from the vehicles' tracks flew into the air and bounced off the tarmac, and the noise of diesel and gas turbines going at full power was deafening. The US marines had Baghdad fever.

Like a bizarre scene from a Mad Max movie, thousands of civilian Iraqis, in cars, pick-up trucks, coaches and trucks, were mixed up in the marines' drive forward. They were heading in both directions along Highway 7 between Kut and Baghdad. They waved, smiled, and shouted fragments of English like: 'Thank you!' and 'Good, good!' For reporters implanted with US troops it was hard to tell whether their apparent happiness was genuine or expedient or a mixture of both.

People who have lived under a totalitarian regime for dec-ades learn how to tell those in power what they think they want to hear, and if marines liked smiles and waves, it cost nothing to give them. Was this liberation? Freedom to do, say, think what one wanted without fear of an unseen executioner acting on the whim of a faraway, tyrannical ruler? At that moment, it did not seem to matter. Many of the greetings, recorded James Meek, particularly from the young and the old, seemed genuinely warm, tinged with the excitement of novelty. For some of the young men, the well-fed ones with short army haircuts, it may have been partly relief that they were still alive. These scenes may have been the clue to the question of where the enemy was. The marines had obviously bloodied their main conventional opponent, the Nida Division of the Republican Guard, on the way to Baghdad. But had the unit, feared across the Middle East, been maimed or killed?

Lieutenant Colonel Sam Strotman, a senior marine officer, standing on a rise overlooking the smoke from Aziziya, thought he had a good answer. 'You can see what happened to the lead trace of the Nida Division when they met the 2nd Tank [Battalion of the Marines],' he said. 'There are two groups of people – the people being forced to fight and the people who really wanted to fight, and I think the second number is extremely small.' He said the Republican Guards were caught in a dilemma: they could stay in place and be attacked by ground forces, or they could move and be destroyed by air forces.

An unconventional attack, or a carefully planned trap for converging US forces, resulting in thousands of deaths, would quickly erase thoughts of capitulation of Iraqi soldiers and the break-up of Saddam's regime. Such a reverse was what made the marines jumpy. One day, just past Aziziya, with temperatures rising to 35° C (95° F) in the shade, the marines heard the call of 'Gas! Gas! Gas!' Both times it was a false alarm, but for half an hour the troops sweltered in their tight-fitting rubber masks and thick nuclear, biological and chemical protection suits.

The other unconventional weapon would be to hold the population of Baghdad hostage and move the remaining core of loyal troops into the city. War is difficult to construe as good. But it could have been much worse. Iraq's crumbling towns and cities had been blasted and smashed by the coalition but its roads and bridges had not been mined by Saddam. There had also been no attacks on Britain, America or Israel. No chemical or biological weapons – the reason for going to war – had been used.

Some of these scenarios could still occur; but others had been foreclosed by the success of the Anglo-American advance. Some 300 miles in 4 days was impressive. But it was not over yet. If the marines could do so much damage to towns such as Aziziya, which they were not even trying to take, it was terrible to think of what would happen if they had to storm Baghdad.

9 Far from over

The worst policy is to attack cities.
Sun Tzu, Chinese military strategist, 500 BC

In Baghdad, the bombing continued and the lights went out. There was no audible explosion, no discernible change in the early evening bombardments, but in an instant, after 15 nights of bombing, an entire city of 5 million people was plunged into an awful, endless night.

The row of orange lights along the western bank of the Tigris, marking the perimeters of Saddam Hussein's official domain, lingered a few moments after that initial shock to Baghdad's electricity grid, which had struck at about 8 p.m. They soon died too, encasing the city in a darkness relieved only by the head-lights of passing cars. Hospitals were without power. There was no clear idea how people would manage without the power that water pumps and water purification plants needed. American commanders denied they had dropped a 'blackout bomb' on Baghdad to knock out the power supply, vital for civilian life, so that special forces could enter the capital unnoticed.

For Baghdadis the attack had arrived. The *Guardian*'s Suzanne Goldenberg was caught on the southern edges of the city, where urban chaos gives way to the plains of the Tigris. She reported few signs of resistance. Dozens of militia from the Ba'ath Party were on the streets, but none of the signs of mobilisation app-eared to live up to expectations of an epic battle.

The wall thrown around Baghdad was not made of steel, or even muscle and sinew. If the Iraqi people could see that this was the beginning of the end, then it was over for Saddam. The first significant battle for Baghdad took place at the city's air-port: Saddam International. Thanks to 12 years of sanctions, its tarmac and terminals were the most underused in the world.

But now it was the scene of heavy fighting, said the Americans. The US 3rd Infantry's front line swept into the area and took control of one of the most potent symbols of Saddam's ambitions in a huge victory for the coalition. They even renamed the airport Baghdad International.

It helped that the event was being recorded by Bob Schmidt, an American television reporter with the ABC network. Speaking from a runway, he said troops had captured the airport with tanks and a few armoured cars. They had met little resistance and opposition had come from 'scattered firing by Iraqi foot-soldiers and men in pick-ups'. On the other side of the world, at Camp Lejeune base in North Carolina, President Bush was, uncharacteristically, clear: 'The vice is closing, and the days of the brutal regime are coming to an end.' Donald Rumsfeld could barely conceal his delight and claimed US forces were 'closer to the centre of the Iraqi capital than many American commuters are from their downtown offices'.

In those confused moments, it was hard to say whether this was news or propaganda. No single report could capture the entire military operation that was taking place a little more than 10 miles from Baghdad. Mohammed Saeed al-Sahaf, Iraq's Information Minister, flatly denied all reports of US progress. 'They are not even 100 miles' from Baghdad, he said. 'They are not anywhere. They are like a snake moving in the desert. They have no foothold in Iraq. Their lies are endless.' This suspension of belief in events that were plainly occurring was to become a trademark of Sahaf's spin.

As the two sides gave starkly opposing assessments, the dead continued to pile up. As many as 80 Iraqis, some of them civilians, were reported to have been killed at the village of Furat, near the airport, in what witnesses described as a US rocket attack. Nadim Ladki, a Reuters correspondent, said: 'We saw a pile of dead bodies at one of the four hospitals where the victims were taken. Most of them appeared to be military.' There were also tense moments for US troops in Najaf, where a mob had blocked them from moving towards the gold-domed mosque containing the tomb of Imam Ali. Local clerics had to intervene to protect the troops and defuse the explosive situation.

The thought was forming that American troops were being lured into a city-sized trap. From the very beginning US and British military planners said that Saddam would try to suck the invading troops into his capital. Iraq's military doctrine, noted Air Marshal Brian Burridge, commander of the British forces in Iraq, was based on the Soviet model of defence in depth. Saddam, he said, 'is going for a Stalingrad siege. He wants to entice us into urban warfare.'

On the face of it, that kind of asymmetric guerrilla warfare was the only way to fight a modern, well-equipped army. Street-by-street fighting could lead to heavy casualties on both sides. It was a prospect US commanders and their soldiers could not have relished. Unexpected resistance in other Iraqi towns, including Basra and Nassiriya, did not augur well. There was no doubt that American forces had been caught off-guard by the ferocity of the resistance.

The war between the American superpower and the dilapidated state of Iraq had lasted little more than a fortnight. The attack, once seen as bogged down and sluggish, was now at the gates of Baghdad. US and British military tacticians rarely tire of invoking the name of Sun Tzu , the ancient Chinese philosopher of war, credited with laying the groundwork for everything from 'decapitation strikes' to the policy of 'shock and awe'. But it was another aphorism of Sun Tzu's that rang in the ears of the commanders: 'The worst policy is to attack cities.'

From Stalingrad, Manila and Seoul to Beirut, Grozny and Mogadishu, the history of what the US marines call Mout (military operations on urbanised terrain) and the British call Fibua (fighting in built-up areas) is one of massive civilian and military casualties with incendiary effects on public opinion back home.

The modern city is a battleground that allows weak defenders to hold out against overwhelming force. Despite a 2–1 advantage in artillery and 4–1 superiority in tanks, Hitler's Panzers lost their famed mobility inside Stalingrad, and the Germans were defeated in four months of street fighting. America was haunted by Vietnam. In 1968, US forces were bidding to retake the city of Hue from North Vietnamese forces, and troops became embroiled in some of the most intense street fighting of the war. After three weeks, air strikes and artillery shelling were eventually used to repel the North Vietnamese force, but not before an estimated 10,000 people had been killed.

Since the end of the Cold War, the application of overwhelming US military force had had only had one conclusion. The first Gulf War lasted just over 40 days, Kosovo nearly 80 days, and Afghanistan no more than 60 days. However, a prolonged and bloody denouement would be too high a price to pay for this war. In this sense, Baghdad was the key to unlocking Iraq.

The fear, too, was that desperate Iraqi forces, with nothing more to lose, might let loose the so far missing stocks of chemical or biological weapons. Even before the fighting had begun, Tariq Aziz, Iraq's deputy Prime Minister, warned that taking the war to Iraq's cities would exact a heavy price from the invaders. He said: 'People say to me you are not the Vietnamese. You have no jungles and swamps to hide in. I reply let our cities be our swamps and our buildings be our jungles.'

It might have been bravado, but the grisly reality of war is discounted at one's peril. As the Americans swooped onto Baghdad airport, 3 US special forces soldiers and 2 Iraqis were killed when a car bomb exploded at a checkpoint in central Iraq. A pregnant Iraqi woman stepped out of the car as it approached the checkpoint and, according to US Central Command, began 'screaming in fear'. Moments later the car exploded, killing 3 soldiers, the pregnant woman and the driver. Two American soldiers were injured.

The Iraqi government news agency later put out a report saying that two Iraqi women had carried out a suicide attack on US forces. A day after that, Al-Jazeera broadcast videos of two Iraqi women vowing to carry out suicide attacks. Each showed a woman standing in front of the Iraqi flag with an assault rifle in her left hand and her right hand resting on a copy of the Koran. One of the women, who identified herself as Wadad Jamil Jassem, said: 'I have devoted myself [to] jihad for the sake of God, and against the American, British and Israeli infidels, and to defend the soil of our precious and dear country.' The other woman said she was 'martyrdom-seeker Nour Qaddour al-Shanbari' and swore to 'take revenge on the enemies of the [Islamic] nation, Americans, imperialists, Zionists'.

The message was that Iraqis were prepared to resist occupation by taking their own lives. Sahaf threatened more of the same should American boots land on Baghdad's streets. 'We will commit a non-conventional act on them, not necessarily military,' he said. 'We will do something that will be a great example for these mercenaries.' Asked if the government had plans to use weapons of mass destruction, he said: 'No, not at all. But we will conduct a kind of martyrdom operation.'

But after swearing for 16 days that they would fight to the death to defend their country from foreign invaders, Iraqis at last found the enemy upon them – and its arrival was devastatingly swift. Residents were seen fleeing, and on the outskirts of the city American tanks ran the gauntlet of small arms fire. It was unclear how far Baghdad's writ ran with US forces advancing from the west, the south and the east.

After a dreadful night of total darkness when the entire electricity grid shut down, and the devastating loss of the city's airport, Baghdad awoke to its first clear skies in a fortnight. Significantly the burning ring of crude oil around the city had died out. But while the choking smokescreen had lifted, there was terrible confusion. Where were the Americans, people asked, and where were the Iraqi troops who had sworn to resist them?

Daybreak brought more dead and more wounded, with heavy casualties from the outlying western areas of Baghdad and the airport. Jamal Abd Hassan, the director of al-Yarmouk, the city's biggest casualty centre, said the hospital had received 185 injured and 42 dead in 24 hours. Most appeared to be soldiers, although the doctor said a family of six had also been killed by cluster bombs. 'Last night it was carnage,' he said. 'Too many dead and too many wounded.'

Omar al-Hadidi's military career was cut short during an Iraqi attempt to retake the airport. The young Republican Guard officer was shot through his abdomen. A veteran of the fighting from Najaf, he said his unit had been constantly on the move until it shifted up to Baghdad to prepare for the defence of the capital. 'We received our orders to advance and defend the airport, and that is what we did,' he said from his bed at al-Yarmouk hospital. He described an intense 90-minute battle, with Republican Guards and militiamen sustaining heavy casualties from American jet fighters.

Other Iraqis had strayed within range of America's ground forces as they advanced from the desert towards the western outskirts of Baghdad. Mohammed al-Marsumi, a lorry driver, was on a regular run when he drove straight into a column of American tanks blasting their way towards the city. He took shrapnel in the leg. 'I saw houses totally destroyed, with pieces of children flying in the air,' he said. He saw no sign of Iraqi troops, except for a unit of the 10th Republican Guard retreating towards the city in army trucks. 'They have been wiped out in that area,' he said. 'There is no sign of resistance.'

In the western neighbourhood of al-Ameriya, armed cadres from the Ba'ath Party guarded virtually every street corner. Companies of up to 10 men huddled beneath overpasses or manned sandbag posts along the roads, waiting for the Americans to arrive. 'All the weapons that were in other places in Iraq are right around Baghdad now,' Qassem Ali, an electrician and party member, told Suzanne Goldenberg. 'Now there is going to be a fight.'

Even so, there was an atmosphere of recklessness around Baghdad, with Iraqis speaking more frankly about the possibility of defeat than since the crisis began. While Saddam's grip on the loyalists of his Ba'ath Party appeared secure, ordinary Iraqis appeared to view the fall of the airport as an omen.

Vehicles headed out of Baghdad with suitcases piled on roof racks and car boots stuffed so full of household goods that they would not close. Many residential areas in the centre of the city had been cleared after the fall of the airport.There were the first signs that defeat was upon the city. 'Militarily, we are the losers, it's already obvious,' said Bassem Mohammed, an electrician. 'Naturally, the airport was a huge loss, and now people know that they are coming to the city, and that they are overwhelmingly stronger than us.'

Outside the Iraqi capital, the apparent collapse of the Republican Guard was matched by the visible collapse of popular Iraqi belief in the possibility of Saddam's survival. As the marines' 1st Division poured towards Baghdad along the Highway 7 dual carriageway, preceded by a rolling storm of artillery shells, cluster bombs and missiles, Iraqis by the roadside – predominantly young men – cheered, waved and gave the thumbs-up sign.

Until now, their enthusiasm for the invaders could have been interpreted as caution in the face of an unknown occupier. But there was no doubt any more. In the minds of those roadside wavers the argument had been settled. Saddam was finished, and they were glad. For the first time so close to the capital, Iraqis could be seen mocking the images of their President hanging at key points along the dusty roadside – Saddam the suited statesman, Saddam the Bedouin, Saddam the general. One youth picked up a stone and hurled it at a mural of the dictator.

The marines had put days, if not weeks, into their invasion timeline for taking the Republican Guard to pieces on the way to Baghdad. Instead, they ended at the edge of Saddam City, the mainly Shia neighbourhood at the east of the capital, in a time that could be counted in days and hours. The guard had been atomised. For years, the story of the Republican Guard has been told as an epic in waiting, a tale of an elite, well-equipped, motivated force, loyal to Saddam, outgunned by the US, no doubt, but ready to force America to fight and slog and shed blood if it tried to take Baghdad. In the cold light of the fine Baghdad morning of 4 April, in a furrowed field by a shelled school building not far from the capital, the reality could be seen and heard.

Three members of the Republican Guard's feared Medina Division sat hunched and miserable among a larger group of prisoners. Their uniforms were newer, they seemed marginally more aware of what was going on around them, but otherwise they were every bit as beaten and pitiable as the thousands of regular army soldiers captured by the US marines in their rapid march to Baghdad. The trio admitted they were guardsmen only after an Arabic translator working for the marines noticed they had torn off the shoulder patches that identified their units. From one soldier's shoulder, red threads protruded where he had ripped the badge off in a hurry.

It had been widely assumed that the guards had been subjected to nightly bombing raids but, according to Dawi Hussein Mohammed, it had taken just two hours of air attacks on his unit, the 10th Brigade of the Medina Division, to rip it apart physically and psychologically. The brigade had been stationed close to civilian areas in the town of Daura, south of Baghdad, trying to use the trees as cover for armoured vehicles. Mohammed said: 'The Americans started bombing at 9 a.m. They destroyed tanks and other armoured vehicles and a bridge was bombed. The bombing came as a surprise. It shook the people very hard. With these cluster bombs they hit buses and cars. Some people went under the bridge, then they came and blew up the bridge too.

'I went to a trench when the bombs started. I was in the trench and over me was death.' Twenty-five tanks were destroyed and two fuel tankers, he said. He jumped into his truck and fled with his two comrades. They went through Baghdad and were heading south to where their families were when they were captured. 'The 10th all ran away to Baghdad,' he said.

Another prisoner, a private, Muslim Mahdi, said he had heard that US forces would treat Republican Guards harshly, so he had torn off his shoulder patches. They were still in uniform, but were already making their transition to civilian life. 'It's a relief,' he said of his capture, of the collapse of the guard, of the end of the regime. 'It's like a weight off my chest.'

Yet Mohammed spoke of how difficult it would be for Iraqis of his generation – they are all in their early 20s – to think themselves out of the tyranny inside their heads. Asked what he thought about Saddam, he said: 'He's my father, he's my President. We didn't understand him properly. We grew up with him around so we don't know anyone else but him.'

A few hours later on 4 April, Saddam, or someone who looked like him, went on a walkabout in a downtown Baghdad neighbourhood. Television pictures showed him in uniform, looking relaxed and beaming at the attention of his people. The film was clearly recent: the clouds of smoke from oil fires that had been hanging over the city for several days could be seen, and the President was shown inspecting what appeared to be bomb damage. He was greeted by people in the street, some of whom looked genuinely surprised and pleased to see him. During the impromptu stroll, the crowd around him grew from a handful to 100 or more. Most were cheering, and some could be seen waving rifles in the air. Others kissed him on his cheeks or hands, and at one point he held up a small child. This was pure political theatre from the dictator.

The American soldiers were undeterred by the propaganda. US troops entered Baghdad for the first time on the 17th day of the war, 5 April, in a symbolic move designed to show Iraqi forces that opposition to the coalition's superior firepower was futile. A force of 25 Abrams tanks and 12 Bradley fighting vehicles rumbled through the suburb of Dawra.

The dramatic events were captured live on television by an American Fox News crew who travelled with the tanks. Their pictures showed apparent suicide bombers in cars trying to ram the tanks. US machine-gunners unleashed a hail of bullets at the cars, killing the occupants. The incursion was not an attempt to capture and hold sections of the city but 'a clear statement of the ability of coalition forces to move into Baghdad at the time and place of their choosing', said US Major General Gene Renuart at a news conference in Qatar. 'This fight is far from over.'

What was missing from the press conference was how much thought had been given to the 7 Iraqis, including 3 children, who had died when US marines opened fire on two vehicles that had failed to stop at a road block south of Baghdad a day earlier. News of the shooting had seeped out, but it was military success that was visible, not the bodies of innocents concealed under the mound of press releases and facts from Qatar.

The human face of suffering was terrible. The cost of victory would not be worth it for Omar, the 15-year-old orphaned by US marines. He discovered the price of war. His father. His mother. Two sisters. A brother. And an uncle. All dead. That was the terrible reality when the vehicle he was riding in failed to stop at a US checkpoint near Baghdad. Even the marines wept in sympathy.

Was it worth it? For Omar, left alone in an Iraq that was being remade, his shirt and trousers saturated with his parents' blood, the answer was no. For Corpsman Thomas Smith, a few days short of his 22nd birthday, exhausted and unbelieving after a day and night of mayhem that had seen three marines killed, himself almost among them, the answer was yes. For the senior Iraqi commander, dead in the dirt at the side of the road next to the white Toyota in which he had tried to escape, the answer would never be known. The second hand on his watch was still ticking, but the hour and minute hands had stopped at 2 a.m.

If George Bush, Donald Rumsfeld and Saddam Hussein have anything in common, it is that the lives of Omar, Smith and the Iraqi officer are petty cash in their grand accounting of the balance of war. They would not smell the dead rotting in the heat along the route of the marines' final charge to the gates of Baghdad; there was no way to make them look Omar in the eye as he stared through his tears at the embarrassed foreigners who shot his mother and father.

The boy did not know whether to be enraged or engulfed in sobbing, so he was both. He would always be haunted by what happened at a crossroads five miles east of Baghdad. His family was travelling out of Baghdad in a bus and truck, which, the marines say, refused to stop when challenged – in English – and accelerated when warning shots were fired. Fearful that they were being attacked by suicide bombers, the marines shot to immobilise the vehicles. Result? Besides Omar's father and mother, two of his sisters, one brother and an uncle were killed. The children were aged 3, 6 and 10. Aleya, Omar's aunt, was close to hysterics. 'People cry for one dead person. Who am I going to cry for?' she screamed through her weeping.

In the end the corpses, including one the marines had begun to bury, were carried by the Iraqis and the marines to the back of the truck for the family to take away and inter. When Aleya went with a medic to change the dressing on the badly shot face of Omar's baby brother, Ali, she confided that she had seen one of the marines weep in sympathy at the family's grief.

The driver of one of the civilian vehicles claimed in an interview with the *Observer* that they did stop. But Corporal Adam Clark, one of the marines manning the checkpoint, said: 'We gave them warning shots. A lot of them. And they didn't stop. That first truck right there just about ran over our forward troops. It's not a good day when you carry dead people out of vehicles. What can you do?' Another marine, Lance Corporal Eric Jewell, said: 'We didn't know what was in that bus. It may sound bad, but I'd rather see more of them dead than any of my friends . . . Everyone understands the word "Stop," right?'

Nearby, a military compound had been reduced to smoking black ash. Thousands of brass cartridge cases glinted on the road where armoured vehicles had dumped the waste of the night's fighting. These were the units – thousands of infantry, tank crews and supporting arms making up what the marines call the 5th Regimental Combat Team (5RCT) – which had run the gauntlet of Iraqi ambushes along Highway 7 north to Baghdad.

Omar and his family were victims of this fighting. The endless cycle of violence that war initiates and only peace can stop meant that soldiers from both sides were gripped by a tiredness and insanity that only those in battle can recount. Corpsman Thomas Smith, a marine medic from New York, sat in the driving seat of his ambulance, still stunned by the experience of the previous 24 hours. He had just finished scrubbing the blood out of the back. 'We must have taken about 20 casualties last night,' he said. 'The whole floor was covered in blood. There were guys vomiting blood. There was blood on the seats. All the stretchers were full of blood. There's one stretcher we had to put down here where the marines won't see it because we can't get the blood off.'

Smith, the ambulance driver and the unit's doctor were driving north towards Baghdad in a convoy when they ran into what officers variously described as one long ambush and six separate Iraqi 'killing zones'. There was a torrent of fire from rocket-propelled grenades, anti-tank launchers and small arms. Normally Iraqi ambushes waited until heavily armoured vehicles such as tanks had gone past before targeting the thin-skinned vehicles, such as trucks and Humvees. This time, however, they hit the external fuel tank of an M1 tank, and the crew bailed out. The tank could still be seen on the road, a charred wreck distinguishable only by its shape from the numerous burnt-out Iraqi tanks, a reminder that even the most fearsome US armour is not invulnerable.

Smith found himself in the middle of a bloody firefight. He was hit in the chest but his flak jacket saved him from injury. The torn fabric over the damaged protective plate where the bullet bounced off could be clearly seen. Rockets and bullets were flying across the road in both directions. 'I didn't think we were going to make it,' he said. 'Thank God for the Cobras [helicopter gunships]. They came in and took everything out with their missiles. It was a nice little fireworks show.'

Lieutenant Colonel Mike Oehl, a tank battalion commander, said he had lost 3 men, with 9 injured. 'I think we quelled most of it, but it was a pretty substantial ambush. Every time you lose somebody it's disappointing, but when you consider there are maybe 900 in a battalion, we've lost 3.'

Close by, a Humvee with a bullet hole through its windscreen and shot-out tyres was being towed away. The running board was thick with dried blood, the same nasty colour as the blood of Omar's parents. A marine lieutenant died during the attack on the vehicle. He was standing up through the hatch in the roof when he was shot in the head.

Sergeant Dwight Gray, a 30-year-old reservist in his unit, said it had been the dead officer's first mission after he was brought in to replace a lieutenant injured earlier. Like other marines, he was not stopping to mourn yet. 'It's part of the game – you've got to keep your head and stay focused,' he said. 'What I tell my troops is we'll deal with that when it's over. Right now I'd rather not know who's lost, who's died.'

10 Deep south

Will they bring us flowers tomorrow?

Anonymous Iraqi, April 2003

Before America's mechanised noose began to tighten around Baghdad, Basra was encircled by a chain of British squaddies. The troops sitting on the outskirts were perfecting raid and aid tactics, striking when the opportunity presented itself while trying to provide humanitarian assistance. Decades of experience in Northern Ireland had taught the British army that guerrilla warfare could only be worn down by open moves to win trust. Outside Basra, where CNN had shown pictures of women scooping water from puddles, the British army wanted to show that it sympathised with the besieged and that it was the snipers and saboteurs, not the civilians, who were their targets.

After two weeks in Iraq, British soldiers had the run of the countryside around Basra. Zubayr, one of the first towns the soldiers quelled, was not quite theirs, but it was certainly not Saddam's any more. Lieutenant Colonel Mike Riddell-Webster, commanding officer of the Black Watch, tam o'shanter perched on his head, pistol secured in its holster on his belt, symbolised this as he strode ahead through its crowded marketplace in the town centre. The day before, the street was thought to be too dangerous to drive down in a soft-skinned Land Rover, but the commanding officer had decided that enough was enough. The order had gone out that the Black Watch was going to patrol the streets of Zubayr on foot. The dozen or so officers and infantrymen chosen to accompany him on the first sortie were told that they could keep their helmets on if they wished, but he would be donning his distinctive red tartan hat. It was a quintessentially British moment recorded in a pooled dispatch from the *Scotsman*'s Gethin Chamberlain.

At 8 a.m. the town was already teeming with people, pouring in from all around in battered trucks laden with tomatoes and carts towed by donkeys, when out of the gate strode the British officers, Lt Col Riddell-Webster in the lead, chatting earnestly to the man by his side, divisional staff officer Lt Col Roger Warren, a fluent Arabic speaker. Those gathered round the trucks of tomatoes looked up, bemused, as the men approached, but the British did not break their stride. Hand outstretched, Lt Col Riddell-Webster greeted the first wary Iraqis on the edge of the gathering. The crowd parted and then engulfed the men.

Lt Col Warren addressed the crowd. They were not there to hurt anyone, he told them, they were there to help the people of the town. The crowd found its voice, talking all at once and pointing to their mouths. Water was the most important thing. It is coming soon, Lt Col Riddell-Webster assured them. The men talked at him again. The electricity was broken, they said. A team of engineers was on its way to fix it, the British officer replied. He walked past bags of grain, rice and lentils, piles of vegetables, bundles of herbs, jars of spices, and bottles of fizzy drinks. 'They have plenty of food,' the British officer said. 'Water is everything now. We are going to win or lose this by getting them water.'

The British had started to make discoveries about the apparatus of fear run by Saddam. Soldiers uncovered what appeared to be evidence of torture at a police station in Abu al-Kacib, a suburb of Basra. They found dozens of ID cards, thought to belong to dead Iraqi men, in the Chief of Police's desk, and were told by local people that Saddam's internal security service, the Mukhabarat, had operated from the station. Spatters of blood stained the walls. Electric shock torture was carried out in one of the rooms: there was a live lead and two rubber tyres to insulate the torturer's feet. There was no doubting the terror of the Ba'athist regime and the lifting of ordinary Iraqis' hearts at the sight of a hated place being desecrated.

In an attempt to reassure local people that their intentions were benign, troops handed out leaflets at the edge of the city.

'This time we won't abandon you,' the sheets read in Arabic, referring to the failure in 1991 to back an uprising that America and Britain had encouraged. The reverse contained the lines: 'People of Basra, we are here to liberate the people of Iraq. Our enemy is the regime and not the people. We need your help to identify the enemy to rebuild Iraq. English speakers please come forward. We will stay as long as it takes.'

The squaddies tried another tactic in the battle for hearts and minds: football. Just as British units had secured the confidence of the people of Kabul over a leather ball, so the men of Juliet Company, 42 Commando, Royal Marines, swapped their weapons and helmets for T-shirts and trainers in the dusty streets of Khor az-Zubahir to line up against the local first team, whose captain turned out in an immaculate Arsenal strip. The marines lost 9–3 but won the trust of local Iraqis.

In other startling ways, the coalition was making progress. Saddam was an ogre and tyrant but his was the only recognisable name. So the coalition was relieved to come across the sulphurously named Chemical Ali. To western ears, the name Ali Hassan al-Majid had not stood out. But in Iraq only the name of Saddam himself was more terrifying. Saddam's monstrous cousin and right-hand man was unquestioning in his obedience to the Ba'athist regime – and will for ever be linked with the village of Halabja. It was Ali who ordered the killing of 5,000 Kurdish civilians there with a mixture of nerve gas and mustard gas. To the name of Halabja should be added other villages: Guptapa, Bota and Karadagh. All felt the wrath of Ali's chemicals in the military operation known as al-Anfal.

But the fear had now gone. British forces stumbled on his home in a flat landscape of muddy fields and farmhouses. With its yellow columns and date palms, it stood out for miles, an island of ostentatious wealth in a sea of poverty, and a symbol of dominance and power. Or at least it used to be. As soon as the war began, Ali had abandoned his palace. Looters had stripped it of its finery and wealth. Even the fittings had gone from the walls, the windows were empty of glass and the air conditioning units had disappeared. There was not a scrap of furniture left. One looter, Hassan, stood in the heat outside with his beaten-up Chevrolet, its boot bulging with timber and glass from the palace. He chuckled as he saw the squad of British soldiers approaching. 'Ali Chemical! Ali Chemical!' he shouted, pointing at the palace. Hassan and his like owned this land now.

The Shia of southern Iraq, like the Kurds of the north, had reason to hate Ali. After their failed 1991 uprising, Ali co-ordinated the crushing of their revolt, levelling rebel villages with tanks, even crushing the graves of Shia saints. At his command dozens of Shia clerics were hanged from the rafters of their own mosques. A month before the war Ali was made commander of the military in the south. To make his mark he shot an opposition supporter dead in the streets of Basra.

But it was not Ali's fate to go on trial for war crimes. He was believed to have died the way he lived – by the bomb. On Saturday 6 April, an air strike was called after an SAS surveillance team noticed Majid among a group of men entering a three-storey building in the city. Harrier ground-attack aircraft dropped two bombs. The first one failed to detonate. Ali had only nine seconds to flee the building before the second bomb exploded. When the dust settled there was nothing left of Chemical Ali.

As his spirit left the city, the British decided it was time to move in. For almost three weeks the British forces surrounding Basra were, the military said, 'fixing it'. This did not mean they were already engaged in repairing buildings damaged in battle. Rather, they had sealed off the perimeters to neutralise any Iraqi troops still inside the town without having to risk engaging them in potentially costly street fighting, so that the main advance could continue north towards Baghdad.

As US forces began the final assault on Baghdad the British decided to make their move in the south as well. Columns of British troops poured into Basra, destroying its Ba'ath Party headquarters. The centre of the attack was a college four miles from the edge of the city. Supported by attack helicopters and jets, around 15 Warrior armoured personnel carriers led the assault on the city's College of Literature, defended by Ba'ath Party loyalists with small arms and rocket-propelled grenades. Three British soldiers were killed in the attack.

Saddam's rule finally ran out in Basra at an anonymous roundabout with a few official-looking buildings and lined on one side by a canal. It was there at lunchtime on 7 April that the men of 3 Para, walking in double file through the centre of the city – said to be close to the site of the Garden of Eden – met up with the tanks of the Scots Dragoon Guards. The invading troops had descended on the junction from opposite directions, cutting the city in two. Troops moving into the more affluent centre of the city reported that their reception was 'extremely benign' and that they were encountering virtually no resistance. Instead of facing attack from all sides, soldiers from the Black Watch battle group were able to concentrate on finding somewhere to consolidate and affirm their control of the city.

As for the paratroopers, they were at first objects of cautious curiosity, but as they passed through the city they were mobbed by children, shopkeepers and crying women. The paras walked through the city all day long, passing through suburbs, wrecked industrial areas, shops and areas of poor housing. They seemed weighed down in the scorching heat by their equipment, each fourth man carrying on his shoulders the bulky tube of an anti-tank missile propped on a rucksack. At each sidestreet, at each break in the walls that lined the dusty highways, the soldiers jogged across or took up firing positions, placing their weapons on the dilapidated buildings. Occasionally they came across signs of war – the body of a Fedayeen fighter who had sprung from behind the low boundary wall of the university complex and died trying to engage a British Warrior with a rocket-propelled grenade. But as the paratroopers walked on, past frescos and murals of Saddam, painted on doorways or set in bridges above the central canal, they were scarcely able to believe that they had walked so far and yet not fired a shot or been fired on.

'The Black Watch had the same eerie experience,' said Major Douggie Hay, whose D Company had been brought into the fighting the day before when it became clear that resistance was crumbling. The entire situation was surreal. After weeks of nibbling away at the edges, testing the strength of the defences, they had simply strolled in. 'I was surprised. I thought there would be more opposition, although it is clearly not over yet,' he said.

Among those sweeping through the city, there was a palpable sense of disappointment that this citadel that had held out for so long could be quite so ordinary. In the end, it seemed, nobody had really wanted to stay to fight. On the streets people were going about their business, sometimes pausing to wave at the soldiers, others not even turning round to see the tanks rolling past. There were a lot of sports facilities, with their large floodlights by far the tallest structures around, and some ornate public and private buildings, but there was also plenty of evidence of a population living in abject poverty.

In an ominous warning to Saddam, many local people seemed genuinely happy to see the army rolling past, laughing and joking even as they were frisked at the checkpoints into and out of the city. A jubilant crowd of about 100 Iraqis surrounded two British tanks sitting side by side near a mural of Saddam and started cheering the soldiers inside and giving the thumbs-up sign. Soldiers were handed pink carnations and yellow flowers. Abdul Karim, an English teacher, was wandering through the city late in the day. Standing opposite a burning building, painted with the inevitable portrait of Saddam, he said it was used as a food warehouse by the Ba'ath Party and that it had been looted and set on fire. He said he had a BA in English. 'It's great, it's great,' he said with an expansive gesture. 'The Fedayeen have gone. They left on Saturday and Sunday. It is fantastic.' If anyone were to ask where did it all go right, the British could claim it was here in Basra.

Even on the day of the advance into the city, British troops were reporting that local people had been coming forward to point out the hiding places and names of militia members. Local people had likened the Fedayeen to hired thugs who would be criminals if they were not involved in the state.

But not everybody wanted to stay to meet the new soldiers. Cars filled with families and trucks loaded with merchandise – mattresses, boxes of generators, televisions and refrigerators – had been leaving the city all day. 'The situation is not good. There is no water in the city. All the citizens are very thirsty,' said one man. 'On television and radio, they promised to give us water, but all we have is air,' he said, holding his one-year-old daughter in his arms.

But at US Central Command in Qatar there was no talk of dwindling water supplies, only of success. Air Marshal Brian Burridge, Commander of the British forces in the Gulf, called the march into Basra 'historic'. Group Captain Al Lockwood, the British forces spokesman, said the troops had gone in for a purpose: to 'reassure the people of Basra we're there and we're coming to liberate the city'.

The British assault on the southern city drew plaudits not only at home but also from the Americans. 'The British occupation of Basra was the pilot project for the US assault on Baghdad, using tank and armour thrusts to get control of a city without taking it apart house by house,' an aide to Donald Rumsfeld was quoted as saying in the *International Herald Tribune*. The report went on to eulogise the British tactic of 'thunder runs' – noisy, swaggering tank thrusts several times a day along the city's main thoroughfares designed to convince its inhabitants that Saddam's forces were on the run. The soft hats approach was also praised. 'Basically, Americans think in terms of instilling fear all around them while British fighters have an additional reflex of trying to win trust too, and trying to remain accessible to people who want to change sides,' a somewhat smug British policymaker was quoted as saying.

Day after day the public were being fed stories about how the British were better. Better at not killing their own side: most of the 'blue on blue' deaths were caused by Americans. Better at not killing innocent Iraqi civilians: it was US troops who failed to fire warning shots and so killed those women and children at a checkpoint. Better at winning over hearts and minds: the

Americans wore intimidating sunglasses and stayed inside their armoured vehicles, while the British took off their helmets at the first opportunity, donned picturesque regimental tam o'shanters and strode boldly into the middle of Iraqi crowds, handing out their own chocolate rations. From Umm Qasr to the suburbs of Basra, it was the British forces who had been distributing aid and working to get the water flowing again while the American vengeance machine thundered north.

Yet the British were apparently better at killing, too, whether it was 'a clean shot to the head', as one reporter cheerfully described an Iraqi's death, or the dirty, dangerous business of street fighting, picked up by British regiments over the years in Northern Ireland.

Rumsfeld, who had earlier suggested the British contribution might not matter much in the coming war, was by now said to feel the British troops in Basra had been superb, while American generals were apparently indulging in 'soul-searching' about their troops' performance. The British were also better, apparently, at history and culture. Lieutenant Colonel Tim Collins, of the 1st Battalion of the Royal Irish, provided the spine-tingling talk about Iraq being an ancient land where the invading armies should tread lightly, and said men who killed unnecessarily would have 'the mark of Cain' on them forever.

The British were, it seemed, a nation led by wise diplomats, whose armies were commanded by poets steeped in Shakespeare and staffed by feral monsters – yet monsters who abruptly turned into sentimental aid workers at the drop of a helmet. It might have been true that British troops – sergeants and corporals who played vital roles as senior officers – were better trained and readier to empathise with local people than US ones; but Britain as a country was letting itself off very lightly, forgetting its own colonial role in the modern tragedy of Iraqi history, and that, whatever the private Arabist sympathies of some in the Foreign Office, Britain had gone along, every inch of the way, with Washington's plan for the Middle East. The implication from some of the coverage was that, in the midst of a dirty war, the British could walk through the inferno in white suits, untouched and unsullied. In fact, Britain was in it up to its elbows.

The troops may have been behaving professionally and well, but it was British missiles and British pilots too, who rained down death on Iraqi cities. It was British tanks and British soldiers too, who were fighting, street by street, through impoverished districts of bewildered and innocent people. It was a British war, as well as an American one, that was bringing still greater hunger, thirst, fear and death to people who had little enough to start with. The anger of the Arab world did not distinguish between Britons and the Americans, and the British were fooling themselves if they thought it did.

Conquest on canvas: US Soldiers in Sadam's palace (AP/John Moore)

11 The end

*O people of Baghdad, remember that for 26 generations you
have suffered under strange tyrants, who have endeavoured
to set one Arab house against another in order that they
may profit by your dissensions. This policy is abhorrent to
Great Britain and the Allies for there can be neither peace
nor prosperity, where there is enmity and misgovernment.*
                        Stanley Maude, British general, March 1917

Barely three days after the devastating loss of Baghdad airport
to the American army, the Iraqi authorities seemed to recover
their nerve, and reasserted their iron grip on the city. The Ba'ath
Party establishment imposed a curfew, evacuated families from
the suburbs that were about to turn into war zones, and moved
concrete blocks across main arteries to deny access to an invading force. As the crackle of anti-aircraft and machine-gun fire
moved closer to the centre of Baghdad, it was clear that the battle
was drawing nearer.

It was also clear that a rout was taking place in slow motion.
The airport had fallen to the sound of gunfire but little else. A
few hours later, US forces launched a dramatic three-hour foray
into Baghdad. The battle was unrecorded, but the signs were
that the outer defences had crumbled. Lining a motorway on
the southern extremities of Baghdad, dotted with the blackened
carcasses of Iraqi army vehicles, were the gruesome souvenirs
of the American army's brief jaunt through the suburbs. The US
excursion ended in clashes that brought such heavy casualties
that for the first time since the war began the hospitals lost
count. 'We just couldn't keep up,' the director of Baghdad's main
casualty ward said. America's Brigadier General Vince Brooks,
speaking in Qatar, referred to Iraqi deaths euphemistically as the
'physical destruction of human beings'.

There were Iraqis who would witness the city's last stand, but the population had thinned considerably since America first threatened to bring war to Iraq. Many if not most of Baghdad's 5 million residents remained without electricity and water, following the loss of power. The suburb of Daura, like the others on the edge of Baghdad, had become a dead zone. The streets were empty and homes deserted. The residents of entire districts had packed their belongings and fled, belatedly joining an exodus that began in February and was almost complete as American armour landed on Baghdad airport.

There were few abandoned homes that had not been taken over by Iraqi soldiers or armed cadres from the Ba'ath Party, increasing the peril to those lonely families who had stayed. 'In our whole street, we are the only ones left,' said Suad Abdul Rehman. 'We didn't have a car to go earlier, and now there are no taxis. Everything is closed down. Everyone has gone except us.'

Her husband, Dhiya Khalid Hammoudi, watched the Americans roar in the previous morning. He saw a column of 25 tanks and armoured vehicles drive along the motorway skirting Daura for about a mile. The column paused at the vegetable market, mowing down two more Iraqi army pick-up trucks. 'They came in just to find out, just to feel what the situation is like,' he said.

In the battle to take Baghdad America was winning, easily. The problem was that there was no hiding place for civilians in the capital. Doctors, too, were voicing concerns that they would be overwhelmed as the wounded and the dying swamped the city's hospitals. The writ of Saddam was shrinking, but in its place was the bedlam of battle. The fighting meant the Red Cross and other aid agencies could not make it across Baghdad. No ambulances meant no fresh supplies and water. There were not enough anaesthetics, warned the Red Cross. The World Health Organisation also reported a shortage of equipment to deal with burns, shrapnel wounds and spinal injuries, and described the situation in the hospitals as 'critical'.

The US forces controlled the highways in and out of the city. Saddam's forces were either laying down their arms or dying in a hail of bullets. The Americans were slowly but surely battering Baghdad and Saddam into submission. On the outskirts of the capital a C130 military transport plane landed at the renamed Baghdad International, demonstrable proof that Iraq's capital was slipping from Arab hand. So confident was George Bush that Saddam's last stand would be a short one, that the controversial leader of one of Iraq's main opposition groups, Ahmad Chalabi, head of the Iraqi National Congress (INC), was secretly flown by the US military to Nassiriya for talks on how to run a post-Saddam Iraq.

The fighting was not over, but the endgame was unfolding. Those defending Iraq from the invaders continued to defy the evidence that the hostilities would end soon. Two American marine pilots died when their AH-1W Super Cobra attack helicopter crashed in central Iraq near the city of Kut. An accident, not enemy fire, was the explanation from America's military high command. Soldiers from the US 82nd Airborne Division forces, manning a checkpoint at Sanawah, near Najaf, destroyed a minibus packed with gas cylinders, suspecting it to be a suicide attack.

Just to the south of Baghdad, American soldiers were on the way to taking the Shia holy city of Kerbala. The streets there were littered with Iraqi corpses as Saddam's fighting units, who put up a guerrilla resistance from rooftops and alleyways, were overwhelmed, swept aside by terrifying technology.

In the confusion, disorder and disorganisation of war, there is also madness. An icy draft of the Cold War blew through the conflict when a convoy of Russian diplomats, including the Ambassador to Iraq, came under fire as they were trying to leave Iraq. Several people were wounded as the officials tried to flee to the Syrian border. A statement from US Central Command said: 'Initial field reports reveal that no coalition forces were operating in the area of the incident.' It said the shooting was believed to have taken place in an area controlled by the Iraqi government. But Russian reporters with the convoy said it had been caught in the crossfire between Iraqi and US forces.

Relations between the superpower and its once greatest rival, already tense because of Russia's opposition to what many Muscovites saw as American imperial aggression, fell off a cliff.

There had been intense gun battles inside Baghdad for 48 hours. Iraqi soldiers were attacking in small groups of between 20 and 40 lightly protected vehicles, mostly pick-up trucks loaded with machine guns. They were no match for America's heavy Abrams tanks and Bradley fighting vehicles. The sheer uneven nature of the battle appalled. As many as 3,000 Iraqi soldiers were believed to have been killed since the airport was taken. Only two American soldiers were thought to have died. It was a turkey shoot and there was no sign that Baghdad's population was ready to thank the Americans for it.

The sum of all the Anglo-American advances was now so great that it was difficult to see what the defenders could do apart from spilling the very last drop of blood. The end was near, but it had not arrived. Instead the shambles of the Iraqi regime slowly and visibly fell to the ground. Its decomposition started at around 8 a.m. on 7 April when an unholy din erupted on the edges of the Tigris: tank and mortar fire from the Americans, and the thin staccato of machine guns and AK47s from the Iraqis.

Days after their first false claim that they had entered the centre of Baghdad, the Americans at last arrived. The outlines of four armoured vehicles hove into view, making their way north along the embankment. It was just about possible to see a scurrying motion lower down the riverbank: Iraqi troops running for their foxholes. Some, it later transpired, dived into the river in panic. Others turned up on the eastern shore in their underpants. An oil tanker burst into flames, the one note of colour on a grey, hazy morning. Shortly before 9 a.m. there was another fireball as the corner of the New President Palace, amidst the crackling of ammunition, was consumed in flames.

Just over two hours later, the Iraqi authorities tried to demonstrate their continued mastery over the west bank of the Tigris and the official buildings and palaces concentrated in the bend in the river that was Saddam's power centre. Journalists were herded on to buses and taken across the river, with much trepidation. After trundling through the deserted streets of western Baghdad, the buses crossed the river to the Information Ministry, which had been briefly visited by an American tank during the excursion around Baghdad. A few Iraqi troops laughed and waved from their sandbags.

The buses proceeded up the road, arriving at the junction that leads to the towering Rashid Hotel, when two shots rang out, confirming its capture the day before by US forces and its transformation into a sniper's position. Seven minutes after the tour of Iraqi-controlled Baghdad had started, the buses were in retreat. By lunchtime renewed sounds of battle wafted across the Tigris from the palace and south-western areas of Baghdad beyond. Iraqi fighters and Ba'ath Party militia patrolled the streets, or huddled beneath highway overpasses, out of sight of American aircraft. Two truckloads of troops crossed the river to the west, preparing to shore up defences. The soldiers cheered. A few took up the ritual chant: 'With our blood and our spirit, we will sacrifice for Saddam.'

No one knew then that the 19th day of war was to be a day of tragedy, farce and life as art. In eastern Baghdad there was a firefight where reporters described seeing a number of pedestrians, including an old man with a cane, confused and then shot by the marines. There was Iraq's information minister, Mohammed Saeed al-Sahaf, who in jovial tones popped up to declare that the 'infidels' were facing 'slaughter'. Standing on the roof of the Palestine Hotel, Sahaf ignored the sight of Iraqi troops running for cover on the other side of the Tigris river to declare: 'Baghdad is safe. The battle is still going on. Their infidels are committing suicide by the hundreds on the gates of Baghdad. Don't believe those liars. As our leader Saddam Hussein said, "God is grilling their stomachs in hell." '

Unperturbed by the sound of sirens and gunfire, Sahaf adjusted his trademark black beret to continue with his diatribe. 'We besieged them and we killed most of them. We will finish them soon. My feelings? As usual, we will slaughter them all. Their tombs will be here in Iraq. They have no control even on themselves. Don't believe them. Those invaders will be slaughtered.'

This was a surreal performance that denied the presence of dozens of US armoured vehicles several hundred metres away, across the river. Sky Television showed the Information Minister speaking live on a split screen juxtaposed with equally live images of American tanks across the Tigris. US light armour rolled across Baghdad's main military parade ground, near the al-Rashid hotel, and blew up a 40 ft statue of Saddam in Baghdad's Zawra Park. But the greatest prize was the presidential palace. Television pictures showed US soldiers strolling through its cavernous marble halls and examining the gold taps in the bathrooms.

A full eight hours after an audacious US army raid on the very heart of Saddam's regime, a lavish riverside estate so terrifying to behold that Iraqi drivers would beg visitors not even to point their fingers in its vicinity, the people of Baghdad had yet to absorb the message of America's excursion. Baghdad was theirs to enter at will. Saddam's palace was their playground. Yet the population of the capital was in denial, not wanting to process the sights and sounds of defeat. The coalition forces were winning on the streets, but not yet in the minds of ordinary Iraqis. Only once they had accepted that the regime no longer existed in the collective psyche could the coalition hope to finally call an end to hostilities.

Just how the war was being paid for was clear in the casualty wards of Baghdad's al-Kindi Hospital. There the wounded were streaming in every few minutes: fighters with blood spurting from their boots, a middle-aged woman screaming as she was pulled out of a battered red Datsun. One fighter was brought in with horrifically blackened face and arms, right hand raised as if in a salute, and chest scored by thin red gashes. By late afternoon the elderly women in blue smocks who rushed to meet each ambulance or battered civilian vehicle were clearly exhausted. The gurneys were encrusted with blood and feeding flies. This was the real, untelevised performance of war. Dirty, obscene and rarely ever fought by the men who declare it.

Two pictures stood out. Both were iconic and told different stories about the day's fighting. Both are unforgettable and will occupy our minds long after the names of Basra and Najaf fall from our memories. One was the photograph of 12-year-old Ali Ismail Abbas, with no arms and a scorched body. His lips are pursed and his eyes filled with pain. The image captured enough of the terror for people to cope with – just as the little naked napalmed Vietnamese girl running in terror and agony down a rice paddy road 35 years ago expressed the horror of another, earlier American war.

The other photograph is not about desolation but triumph. Used on the front page of the *Guardian* on 8 April, it showed six US soldiers lounging insolently in a seized presidential palace. A machine gun and helmet are prominently placed in the picture and another soldier is drawing heavily on a cigarette. This was life as art. The photograph by AP's John Moore was an extraordinary homage, inadvertent or not, to Anton von Werner's famous 1894 painting of a scene from the Franco-Prussian war, 'A Billet Outside Paris'. As Professor Jonathan Osmond pointed out: 'The iconography of conquest, occupation and possession is the same: uniformed soldiers in dirty boots in a panelled room, sitting and smoking in pseudo-baroque armchairs. In each case the owner has fled. War art has produced another defining image.'

Baghdad was now being conquered, block by block. But the removal of Saddam was going to be the only way to convince the Iraqi people that his regime had collapsed. The Pentagon found an opportunity. High above Iraq's western desert on 7 April a US B-2 Stealth bomber was refuelling in mid-air on its way to a scheduled series of air strikes when it received urgent orders. They came in the form of a new set of target co-ordinates, but an air traffic controller made it clear what they meant: Kill Saddam Hussein. 'Those were the words that were used. "This is the big one," ' Lieutenant Colonel Fred Swan, the bomber's weapons officer, recalled in a telephone interview later. As far as Lt Col Swan was concerned, it was business as usual. 'I did not know who was there. I really didn't care,' he said. 'We've got to get the bombs on target. We've got 10 minutes to do it. We've got to make a lot of things happen to make that happen. So you just fall totally into execute mode and kill the target.'

What is clear is that 12 minutes after that radio conversation, at about 3 p.m. Baghdad time, Lt Col Swan's bombs left a 60 ft crater in the ground where a restaurant once stood in the capital's prosperous al-Mansour district. For nearly three weeks CIA and MI6 intelligence about Saddam's movements appeared to have dried up and special forces were not getting anywhere on the ground. Then, on Monday 7 April, came reports of a new sighting of Saddam. At least 40 senior officials were understood to be meeting Saddam and his sons, Uday and Qusay, in a bunker at the back of the building connected to a restaurant in the al-Mansour district of Baghdad.

The Iraqi leadership, according to the intelligence the Pentagon had received, had decided the game was up and gathered to discuss an escape route out of the city. The extent to which America could pinpoint both the location and conversations of Saddam suggested that US forces had completely infiltrated the city. Reporters were assured that the Iraqi President and his sons had been seen walking into the restaurant and a voice sounding like Saddam's had been overheard. The level of detail provided, if true, was an indication of how much America could know and how quickly it could act.

For all the awe, however, the shock was that Saddam was not killed. The intelligence had simply been wrong. British intelligence sources agreed that Saddam had survived the attack. 'He was probably not in the building when it was bombed,' a well-placed source said. It was supposed to be precise, but even that was questioned by reporters who visited the smoking hole left by the four 2,000 lb 'bunker-busting' bombs. One claimed that at least one restaurant was intact, with only its windows blown in. Three adjacent houses were reduced to rubble.

Unless Saddam was found, the war lacked a distinct, definable finish. Instead, the Pentagon started talking of a 'rolling victory'. 'There won't be a single point,' was the answer Rumsfeld gave journalists who asked when would it all end. But Baghdad was looking like, to use a term favoured by the American neo-conservatives, a 'cakewalk'. Truckloads of Iraqi fighters – a few regular soldiers among the militia – had dared a dawn counter-attack on the compound of Saddam's palace and were mown down by American fire from the ground and the air. As thick black smoke swirled out of at least six separate pyres, and amid a barrage of mortar and artillery fire, the US forces moved northwards. They roared past the grounds of the palace to offices of the Republican Guard, the force under the command of Saddam's second son and heir, Qusay, which had been pounded on an almost nightly basis for two weeks.

As it had from the outset of the war, America enjoyed absolute control over the skies. Fighter planes prowled low overhead, attacking the eastern, southern and northern suburbs. In one surreal moment two rockets travelled the length of Sadoon Street, flying at about 20 metres. The Planning Ministry and the Information Ministry, both symbols of Ba'ath political power, were on fire after being strafed by low-flying American planes.

There were other less heralded results of US progress through Saddam's dominions. Unsaid was that this was an advance that obliterated at the same time as it claimed to liberate. What could one make, then, of the fact that the Medical City group of four hospitals, one of Baghdad's most modern facilities, was without power or water and only six of its 27 operating theatres were able to work? The water station near the hospital had been hit. Or that if the Red Cross had not managed to deliver 5,400 one-litre bags of drinking water to Baghdad's parched Karama and Mansour Hospitals more would have died from poor sanitation than perished on the battlefield?

In two adjoining stalls of the casualty ward of Kindi Hospital, the main trauma centre of eastern Baghdad, a girl, long black plait held off her forehead by a red alice-band, was laid out beside her little brother. Their mother lay across the aisle, beige dress soaked in blood from hem to armpits. Another brother slumped on the floor, unaware that he was sitting in his mother's blood. A neighbour told the *Guardian*'s Suzanne Goldenberg the girl was called Noor Sabah and was 12 years old, though she looked smaller next to the doctors who surged into the examining cubicle. Her brother, Abdel Khader, who began the day neatly dressed in dark trousers and a check shirt, was 4 or 5. When the small corpses were loaded on to the same trolley to take them to the morgue, even the nurses were reduced to tears.

The elderly female orderlies who were constantly lugging blood-encrusted trolleys back and forth to the ambulances and battered cars that pulled up at the gates wailed until they were hoarse, and thumped their pain out on the walls. The doctors turned to watch the small bodies pass, the best they could offer by way of a ceremony, and abandoned the mother, Wael Sabah, on her trolley. 'She's fatal,' said one. The doctors could do no more than watch her die.

For Goldenberg, who had reported from conflicts around the world for a decade, history would be haunted by Baghdad's unremembered dead.

Death's embrace gave the bodies intimacies they never knew in life. Strangers, bloodied and blackened, wrapped their arms around others, hugging them close. A man's hand rose disembodied from the bottom of the heap of corpses to rest on the belly of a man near the top. A blue stone in his ring glinted as an Iraqi orderly opened the door of the morgue, admitting daylight and the sound of a man's sobs to the cold silence within. These were mere fragments in a larger picture of killing, flight, and destruction inflicted on the sprawling city. And it grew more unbearable by the minute.

By mid-morning the centre of the Iraqi capital had in effect been split in two. The western bank of the Tigris, with its modern neighbourhoods and broad, tank-friendly roads, was under American control. On the eastern side of the river, shabbier now, but still the repository of Arab history as the site of medieval Baghdad, Iraqi soldiers and militia sealed off three bridges that cross the heart of the city with concrete blocks and lorries.

Even on the eastern banks of the river, the city came to a halt, with little evidence of the presence of the millions of Iraqis who normally live there, beyond the accumulating piles of rubbish in the largely deserted streets. Teashops and cigarette kiosks, the last preserves of commerce in a shocked and battered city, were shut. The militia who swarmed the area only a few days ago, toting their assault rifles and rocket-propelled grenades over their shoulders, had melted away. The army trucks that had sheltered beneath palm trees and highway overpasses vanished, as did the heavy gun emplacements. The only sign of motion came from the dreary trickle of civilians heading for safety. They had withstood the bombardments for more than a fortnight, and had been without electricity and phones for nearly a week, and they could take no more. They packed up whatever they could carry and made their way out of the city on foot.

Nothing in the Americans' path was safe. That was the message the troops sent out. And in Baghdad it included the messengers carrying it to a global audience. At 7 a.m. Al-Jazeera cameraman Tarek Ayoub, a 35-year-old resident of Jordan, was killed by two rockets fired on the local bureau of the Arab satellite network, cutting him down live on camera. In the tense arena of battle, mistakes occur, but it seemed an unfortunate and avoidable attack given the coalition's claims that it had the technology to take out its enemies and little else. It was also troubling that Al-Jazeera had been hit, as its coverage of the war had set the tone for the Arab world. The channel was frequently critical of US and British forces and spent hours highlighting the number of Iraqi civilians killed. Soon after the bombing Al-Jazeera said it would pull out of Iraq and US forces could count the loss of its voice among the victims of war.

An American tank also fired on a multi-storey hotel at least a mile away, the Palestine, home to the contingent of foreign journalists. Reuters cameraman Taras Protsyuk, 35, was killed

and Jose Couso, 37, a cameraman for the Spanish television channel Tele 5, was wounded in the same attack and later died in
hospital. Three members of the Reuters team in Baghdad were
also hurt. The American military command were quick to defend
their actions: 'Commanders on the ground reported that coalition
forces received significant enemy fire from the Palestine Hotel
and consistent with the inherent right of self-defence coalition
forces returned fire.'

The trouble was that the world's press pack, encamped at the
hotel, did not see it that way. Sky's correspondent, David Chater,
said he was on a balcony at the hotel immediately before the
shell exploded. 'I never heard a single shot coming from any of
the area around here, certainly not from the hotel,' he said.
Chater said he saw a US tank pointing its gun muzzle directly at
the hotel and turned away just before the blast. 'I noticed one of
the tanks had its barrel pointed up at the building. We went
inside and there was an almighty crash. That tank shell, if it was
indeed an American tank shell, was aimed directly at this hotel
and directly at journalists. This wasn't an accident, it seems to
be a very accurate shot.'

It was here on the eastern side of Baghdad that marines were
clearing away Iraqi resistance. The intangible fleeing fighters,
still loyal to Saddam despite his disappearance from the airwaves, were facing a final grim reckoning in the dusty yellow-
brick alleyways of eastern Baghdad. Ranged against the Iraqi
militia and the remnants of the Republican Guard was the fighting strength of the 1st Marine Division, a force of about 20,000
men. The marines had been inside the Iraqi capital, starting east
and moving west, emptying the city with ease, block by block.

There was some real resistance. In the marines' 1st Regimental Combat Team, one of three brigade-sized units carrying
out the westward sweep of Baghdad, a soldier was killed in a firefight. There were also 3 casualties, one serious, when a company
came up against what an officer described as a fortified strong
point, firing machine guns and rocket-propelled grenades,
north of the Tigris and east of Saddam City.

The intention appeared to be to squeeze Saddam's regime between the marines heading west and the US army heading east. As civilians fled, hid and looted ahead of and behind the marines, the mysterious opposition diehards variously fought back and fled. It was between Al Amin – a vision of litter-strewn bleakness and homes built of haphazardly bevelled clay, where almost every house flies the black and green banners of the Shia faith – and a date grove that the marines pitched their tents.

Before the marines arrived, Saddam loyalists had rounded up a handful of local men and proceeded to torture them, accusing them of aiding the Americans. When the US troops came, the torturers fled. Despite the show of strength there were few voices signalling that hope was being carried on American shoulders. One of the men, Salem Ali, showed where his hands had been cut open when they were roughly bound with wire. His back was red with beating, his face was cut on the cheekbones and on his chest was a fresh cigarette burn. 'Even if you [the British and Americans] are here for two years, I will still be afraid of Saddam,' he said.

A shortage of cigarettes was the soldiers' biggest complaint. Iraqis wise to the deficit were making a fortune. At a US marine encampment, constructed in two hours, Lance Corporal Jason Booker, from Kentucky, had given away his army knife to an Iraqi in exchange for two cigarettes. 'It sucks,' he said. 'We cleared a whole bunch of buildings in the city today. If the people are home, they [marine commanders] like you to knock first. They don't want you to tear the whole place down. We got a bit of small arms fire at first. A little bit. They would jump out, brr! brr! and shoot, and then jump back in.' On questioning, he admitted that 'they' was an exaggeration. A single man with a Kalashnikov had shot at them once. 'We heard 2 shots, we let off 150 back,' he said.

For their troubles, the marines were still viewed with suspicion and a wariness that bordered on hostility. The departure of the Ba'ath Party and the arrival of the US troops meant a creeping lawlessness. Streets in the suburbs seemed half derelict at first, but only a few families had left. Women and children stayed indoors and the men came out to talk and loot and offer tea. Mahdi Sultan, 75, said: 'Saddam destroyed the Shia, and this is what caused us to be humble and go to the Americans and go like this,' giving a thumbs-up sign. 'If America came here for the Iraqi people, the Iraqi people can live exactly on the same living standards as the Gulf states. We don't want anything extreme. We just want our wealth.'

The war, if not over, was being won by the coalition forces without serious difficulty. The wide motorways of Baghdad and the ineffectiveness of shabby city defences had made the toil and task of US troops, bent on deposing Saddam and freeing his people, much more possible than impossible. But they were not in complete control of the city: there were too many sudden volcanic eruptions of gunfire, too much insanity where there was supposed to be calm. And discontent was bubbling through the city. 'Bush is a rich bully. The US has no legal right to be here. Probably Saddam would have sold chemical weapons to somebody someday and then the US would have been right to invade, but now this is the first free democratic country ever to occupy another without good reason,' said a heavily armed man standing by the roadside. He was a lance corporal in the US marines.

A mere three weeks after the war started, the regime of Saddam Hussein got the end it deserved. It was a slow collapse. Iraqi television, a symbol of the regime's defiance, disappeared from the airwaves in the morning. The secret police and minders of the hated Mukhabarat, the Ba'athist state's secret police, were nowhere to be found. On 9 April in Baghdad, the air palpably began to thin as the fear of more than 20 years slowly lifted. Iraqis began drifting towards Firdouz Square, towards a huge and commanding statue of Saddam, as the noisy grinding of gears announced the arrival of the American tanks.

This was the real heart of Baghdad, not the conglomeration of security buildings and palaces that were the preserve of the regime on the opposite shore and had been bombed for 3 weeks by the US military. The crowds seemed to know what was expected of them. A man went up to one of the marines, whose tanks controlled the circle and both sides of Sadoon Street, and asked for permission to destroy the statue. But it was still too heady an idea. 'You, you shoot it,' the Iraqi pleaded. The marine replied, with no apparent irony for the days of killing that preceded his arrival in Baghdad: 'No, no, I cannot shoot. There are too many innocent people around.'

So it was left to the Iraqis themselves. A scrawny man tore down the brass plate on the plinth while others set off to find a rope to pull down the statue. Sledgehammers appeared and a rope was thrown over Saddam's head. But the statue resisted the crowds tugging on the noose around its neck for two hours. It held steady above their heads, right arm pointing to the horizon.

As the world's television crews gathered to capture this extraordinary sight, an American armoured vehicle drew up. A marine ran up and threw the Stars and Stripes over Saddam's head. The flag had flown on the Pentagon on 11 September, and the US army had thoughtfully brought it along to Iraq for just such an electrifying spectacle. This obviously was not in the script and it was removed. Within minutes an Iraqi flag was in its place. It was the old flag, without the inscription in Saddam's own handwriting of 'Allahu Akbar' (God is most great) that had been added to the gaps between the stars after the last Gulf War. The US tank then pulled hard, cheered on by hundreds of Iraqis, and, at last, metal legs buckled at the knee, forcing Saddam to bow before his people, and the statue snapped in two, revealing a hollow core.

Finally American soldiers got the welcome they expected. And those who wanted war got their single, identifiable moment of liberation on a balmy afternoon, like a thousand April afternoons in Baghdad before it. Here on the eastern bank of the Tigris the world found out that the Iraqis hated Saddam more than the forces that had ousted him and his tyrannical regime.

Nemesis: the fall of Sadam (Reuters/Goran Tomasevic)

12 Burning and looting

If a country's civilisation is looted, its history ends.
  Raid Abdul Ridhar Mohammed, Iraqi archaeologist, April 2003

A vacuum appeared and something had to fill it. In Baghdad chaos did. Colonel John Toolan woke up on 9 April to lead thousands of men into battle across Baghdad, block by sniper-infested block, against a tricky foe. By mid-morning, although the city still snapped and crackled with the occasional burst of gunfire, he faced a situation more akin to the Los Angeles riots. In the US, a state governor would call out the national guard. The conquest of Iraq had run away from Col Toolan. Iraqis – looting, cheering, honking up and down the quickly congested highways of the capital in their sanctioned-out jalopies – had decided that they no longer believed in the invincibility of Saddam Hussein.

Standing amid the shattered glass and broken equipment of the United Nations weapons inspectors' compound, Col Toolan, a thoughtful older commander appointed to head the 1st marines' regimental combat team just a few days earlier, admitted that the shooting audible a few hundred metres away might have nothing to do with the fading conflict between US forces and remnants of the Saddam regime. 'It's not clearly snipers. Potentially it looks like some looting going on over there. Maybe people are seizing the chance to exploit the lack of public security,' he said.

In other words, the abandoned weapons and ammunition littering the city, from Kalashnikovs to guided missiles, were being picked up and possibly used by looters or those trying to defend their property. 'We still have a duty of public security, at the same time making sure we preserve our force,' said the colonel, expressing the unease of a commander who has found himself embarking on one mission – fighting a war – only to find himself obliged to take on another: fighting crime.

There was looting going on, all right. The marines arrived at the UN compound an hour after the looters. They chased them out, but they had already blown through the compound like a whirlwind, ripping the lights and windscreen wipers out of UN cars, smashing windows, pulling out drawers and emptying their contents on the floor, hobbling off with anything that was not nailed down.

'When I got here people were everywhere, breaking into cars, trying to get these vehicles out of here,' Corporal Jason Matthews said. 'We swept through and yelled at everyone to get out. We didn't really have to push anybody but we sometimes had to fix bayonets to show we were serious.' One UN weapons inspector's car was being used by Iraqis to move weapons: six Kalashnikov rifles. The culprits bolted.

The colonel left the compound and sped through the city streets to meet some of his tank commanders. En route he passed a factory that had been taken over by marines, who were standing in the gap of a broken wall, talking to Iraqis wanting to get in. 'In areas we've taken, try to keep the looting . . .' the colonel trailed off, but everyone understood what he meant. Try to keep the looting down, if you can. The colonel jumped back in his Humvee and was off again. The traffic was thickening and the marines began to get stuck. Iraqis standing out of car windows and sunroofs at all angles, began tooting, crying: 'Good, good, good, Mr Bush!' and waving their white flags as if they were flags of victory and they had just won the World Cup.

Col Toolan arrived at a vacant lot where marine tanks and armoured amphibious vehicles were parked. The officers spread out their maps on the bonnet of a Humvee and described the movement of tanks as if the war were still in full spate. But they all knew it was not. The Republican Guard HQ that the marines were due to attack had been abandoned. Its occupants had fled. 'The resistance has changed,' the colonel mused. 'It's getting less and less.' He turned to the cavalcade on the highway. 'I don't know if they're happy to see us,' he said. 'I think they're happy because they're carting away refrigerators and TVs.'

In Basra two days earlier, on 7 April, chaos was also the victor when British troops took the city. A day after the big guns of the British artillery fell silent, the rattle of gunfire continued to echo through the city's streets as looters ransacked official buildings and helped themselves to whatever they could find. British soldiers, still battling a few diehard militia, could do little but watch. It led to surreal scenes. At a further education college a few hundreds yards from the old city and the now ruined Ba'ath Party headquarters, William, a former English student at the college, was dragging a metal handcart behind him, keen to get his share of the loot at his alma mater. 'I need air-conditioning units,' he said. 'It gets very hot and we do not have any in the people's houses.'

Ahead of him streams of people were running into the college, leaping the metal fences surrounding it. They returned laden with furniture, ceiling fans, electric lights, even floorboards. A fire had started and smoke billowed through the roof. William, while keeping an eye on the looters, was happy to talk for a few minutes. 'Looting is bad, but I am going to get some. We have had nothing for so long that now we have to take what we can,' he said.

Along with thousands of others, William waved and gave the thumbs-up sign to every British tank and armoured vehicle that trundled by. It was not exactly the singing and dancing in the streets dreamed of by Whitehall spin doctors, but heartening none the less. 'I am very happy,' William said. 'Saddam Hussein is vanished. He was our nightmare and he is gone.'

With Saddam's fall, the poor rushed to the dictator's many homes – to steal back what had been stolen from them. Outside the President's Basra retreat, described by the *Daily Telegraph*'s Tim Butcher as 'part Alhambra, part Barratt home', it was no different. Poverty-stricken inhabitants gathered outside the palace, situated in the squalid suburbs, and appealed to British guards to step out of way and let the people of Iraq get their hands on the assumed treasures inside. 'There is gold in there, there is gold in there,' was a typical chant. 'Let us in, let us in,' was another.

What was inside, according to the pooled despatch, was everything a tyrant could wish for, from gold-plated loo brushes to ornate French lamp-posts entwined with ivy. There were Moorish screens carved from teak, giant marble-clad columns, vaulted ceilings and stained-glass windows. There was parquet flooring by the acre and sweeping staircases connecting ballroom to ballroom. Local people said the palace was less than 6 years old, built when Iraq was subject to strict trade sanctions and Saddam's regime regularly claimed its people were being starved by a US-led conspiracy.

Like so many of Iraq's presidential palaces, across the country from the mountains of Kurdistan in the north to the desert plains of the south, the Basra palace was more a folly than a residence. It had a sad, *Marie Celeste* air, with dust covering every flat surface and the 24-carat gold loo fittings, which suggested it had never been used. Like so much of Saddam's regime, the palace was designed to send a crude message to the Iraqi people: only one man in Iraq is powerful enough to afford such a palace.

Even as the British troops entered the palace, looters were wrecking the city's water supplies, fixed just days earlier by the Red Cross and the UK military. Establishing law and order was becoming more important for the British troops than mopping up the last shreds of the regime. As widespread looting continued in Basra, an army spokesman, Colonel Chris Vernon, told journalists: 'We're still trying to cement the security situation and then we will turn our attention to the law and order issue. We are trying to utilise what is left of the police force.'

In Baghdad, hospitals overwhelmed by casualties had been cut off after water supplies and electricity supplies were knocked out. The war had already claimed its first international aid worker. Vatche Arslanian, a 48-year-old Canadian employee, was shot in crossfire in Baghdad, a serious blow for the Red Cross, virtually the only agency still operating in Iraq after the coalition invasion.

Months before the first strike on Baghdad, experienced observers warned military commanders not to underestimate the scale of the humanitarian challenge. Clare Short, International Development Secretary, told MPs in February that with 60 per cent of the population living on government handouts under the UN-sponsored oil-for-food programme, coalition forces had to be ready to look after millions of vulnerable citizens once the regime collapsed. As the bombing started, the United Nations launched its largest-ever humanitarian appeal, calling for $2.2 bn, most of it earmarked for food. The director of the UN's World Food Programme said feeding Iraq would be the biggest aid effort ever undertaken.

The looting, burning, stealing and lawlessness were taking place in the middle of some of the largest concentrations of military equipment in the world. This was an irony few would laugh off – except Geoff Hoon, the Defence Secretary. Speaking a day after Saddam's statue fell, he quipped that Iraqi citizens were merely 'liberating items from the regime'. He told MPs that the scenes they were witnessing were just Iraqis 'redistributing that wealth among the Iraqi people'. Encouraged by laughter, he added: 'I regard such behaviour perhaps as good practice, but that is not to say we should not guard against more widespread civil disturbances.'

Iraq was sliding into anarchy. The day after television screens worldwide were filled with the toppling of Saddam's statue in Baghdad, the Red Cross warned that the looters in the city had ransacked a hospital. A spokeswoman in Geneva said that the al-Kindi Hospital near the city centre had been attacked by armed looters who stripped it of everything, including beds, electrical fittings and medical equipment. Nada Doumani said: 'Al-Kindi has been looted by an armed group. Security in the city is very bad and people are not daring to go to the hospitals. Small hospitals have closed their doors and big hospitals are inaccessible.'

Looters drove tractors, pick-up trucks and trailers, and even a large bus, to a villa belonging to Tariq Aziz, Saddam's Deputy Prime Minister, stealing everything from paintings to curtains and stripping the electrical wires from the main switchboard. His library was ransacked, although the looters left behind a book on geopolitics by Richard Nixon, the Mafia novels of *Godfather* author Mario Puzo – and the complete works of Saddam Hussein in Arabic.

In Baghdad, Lieutenant Colonel Michael Belcher of the US marines told his officers to try to quell the looting, but the task was proving overwhelming. 'There's so much. How do you stop it? I'm a security force. I can fight, I can keep the peace. But police work is not our forte.'

Some items looted were inexplicable, the unwieldy prizes of people who simply wanted to claim something, anything, from the disorder. One boy, in ripped rubber boots, was dragging a dilapidated electric ceiling fan down a Baghdad street. A man driving a small Volkswagen pointed to his own prize, a broken industrial air-conditioner, protruding from the car's boot. A group of men sat on a boulevard guarding a pile of office chairs. One man carried a mattress on his back, another an armload of fluorescent lightbulbs. A particularly industrious participant rigged a looted chair on his donkey cart and perched atop it to drive his rickety load along.

Several diplomatic buildings were burgled, including the German embassy, the French Cultural Centre and the Finnish Ambassador's House. The National Museum was looted. The National Library, Theatre and Central Bank were set ablaze. The only sign of resistance came from Saddam City, a poor, densely populated Shia Muslim neighbourhood, where residents set up roadblocks and confiscated loot, sending it to a local mosque. A suicide bomber set off a number of grenades at a US check-point, killing at least one marine. During the day three civilians were killed, and many injured, reportedly in crossfire or by the guns of nervous American soldiers. Among them was a 6-year-old girl, shot in the head.

In Basra, the locals were still raiding shops and government buildings. It was not freedom but anarchy. It might also be illegal. International law requires that occupying powers ensure the safety and needs of the civilian population in areas under their control. The United States appeared to forget such a basic rule of warfare, enshrined since 1949 in the Geneva Convention. It meant there could be no victory in the swirling debris of a riot.

Perhaps the most poignant act of looting was the destruction at the National Museum of Iraq in Baghdad. Its 50,000 artefacts, recording the history of the world for the past 7,000 years, disappeared in two days. Nothing had prepared anyone for its loss. Thousands of people poured in – while American troops, armed and dangerous, stood by and watched. There had been a guard at the Oil Ministry, but none for an equally precious, finite resource: the past.

Gone was a solid gold harp from the Sumerian era, which began about 3360 BC. Other looted antiquities included a sculptured head of a woman from Uruk, one of the great Sumerian cities, and a collection of gold necklaces, bracelets and earrings, also from the Sumerian dynasties and at least 4,000 years old. 'A country's identity, its value and civilisation resides in its history. If a country's civilisation is looted, as ours has been here, its history ends,' Raid Abdul Ridhar Mohammed, an archaeologist, told John F. Burns of the *New York Times*.

The turbulent post-Saddam whirlpool was also felt in the Shia holy city of Najaf. Terror stalked the town as a militia group smashed through the streets with impunity. A senior Shia cleric, who until two weeks earlier had lived in London and was an adviser to Tony Blair, was murdered in the city's main shrine, the Imam Ali mosque. Abdul Majid al-Khoei was the son of Iraq's most prominent clergyman, the late Grand Ayatollah Abul-Qasim al-Khoei. He was also close to the man who currently holds that title, Ayatollah Ali Sistani, whom US military authorities were wooing for support. He had arrived in the south on 3 April, having travelled with the British military. He was overjoyed to see the golden dome of the mosque again, but he was shocked by the terrible condition of the people. In the once beautiful countryside along the Euphrates east of Najaf, he remarked in a call home, the people were in abject poverty, the result of years of sanctions, repression, and now war. Abdul Majid al-Khoei and another cleric were hacked to death in the Imam Ali mosque while they were trying to get an agreement with a government-appointed official over control of the shrine. He died, martyred in the name of peace.

A failure to comprehend the character of the people whose land had been invaded was being exposed. The price of this shortcoming was death and disorder. Despite months of planning in Washington and London, it appeared that no attention had been paid to the intricate web of relationships that must support the birth of a new nation. Britain had not remembered the lessons of history. It was the British who created Iraq from the collapse of Ottoman Empire after the First World War. The League of Nations gave London the mandate over Iraq in 1920, and 12 years later Britain gave Iraq independence, installed a puppet regime and helped crush dissent until the revolution of 1958.

To help restore calm in Basra, the British troops enlisted a local sheikh who had approached military commanders. An offer of help in a time of crisis was gratefully received and he was asked to form a committee of local people to run the region. But Sheikh Muzahim Mustafa Kanan Tamimi was proving a controversial choice. It turned out he was a former brigadier general in Saddam's army and a one-time member of the Ba'ath Party. Several hundred protesters hurled stones at his home while he was meeting local dignitaries to discuss the situation. The crowd accused Tamimi and his tribe of collaborating with Saddam Hussein. The sheikh's supporters armed themselves and accused the protesters, members of a rival clan, of being Ba'ath Party sympathisers themselves. This was a strange kind of liberty.

Although Tamimi, 50, refused to discuss his past in detail with reporters, he confirmed that he had been a general in the Iraqi army and at one time was in the Ba'ath Party. Some of his relatives dismissed the notion that he was sympathetic to Saddam, and said his brother was a 'martyr' shot dead by the secret police in 1994. The crowd gathered outside Tamimi's house in Zubay disagreed. They chanted: 'No, no Ba'ath Party, yes, yes freedom.' A sign in Arabic said: 'No to any opportunities that will lead to a repetition of the Ba'ath Party.' Stones were thrown at the house and a window was smashed. Several of the men inside grabbed weapons and prepared to defend themselves.

Neither side probably had heard of the British Armed Forces Minister, Adam Ingram, and the crowd outside Tamimi's house probably would not have cared for his explanation: 'We have to work with people on the ground.' It was a 'fraught situation' and British forces might have to deal with 'compromised and tainted' Iraqis. 'These are not easy issues,' Ingram concluded. For Iraqis, this was a glimpse of the blindingly obvious.

A religious leader, Sayed Naim al-Musawi, tried to calm the crowd. He told them they were protesting outside the 'house of a martyr'. But he also expressed concern at Tamimi's appointment. He said of the British: 'We don't want them to tell us what to do. It's insulting to educated people that anyone from coalition forces would declare one of the sheikhs to be controlling our people.' He said the British had been tricked into believing Tamimi could impose order in Basra. 'People want someone who was not a member of the Ba'ath Party, who has no relation to the previous government,' he said. 'They want someone who has loyalty to the people of Iraq and not to the Ba'ath Party.'

13 Soldiering on

*We go to liberate, not to conquer ... Wipe them out if that is
what they choose. But if you are ferocious in battle, remember
to be magnanimous in victory.*
  Lt Col Tim Collins, 1st Battn, Royal Irish Regt, March 2003

Trooper Timmy Howland said he did not know where he was,
just that he was in Iraq. The stretch of water in front of him
could have been the Euphrates or the Tigris for all he knew. It
was, in fact, the Shatt al-Arab Canal and he was near Basra. The
day before, 9 April, had seen US troops sweep into Baghdad, but
for Trooper Howland of the Household Cavalry's D Squadron the
capital city might as well have been in another universe. 'I know
we are in Iraq, near some village. I just lost track ages ago,' he said.
'My mum wrote me a letter saying you must have been there because that's where 16 Air Assault Brigade has been, and I thought,
"Where the fuck is that?" ' Most of what he has seen of Iraq has
been through a little window, about 6 in x 3 in, in the back door
of a Spartan armoured reconnaissance vehicle. For weeks it was
a view only of clouds of dust kicked up by the tracks.
  There seem to be only two certainties when the British army
prepares to go to war: equipment will break and supplies will
run out. It was no different this time around, but it was not the
rifles that were seizing up in the heat and dust, and they didn't
run out of food or water. Instead their desert boots melted and
there was a severe shortage of toilet paper. It was all very British.
While the tabloids made much of the failings, with the *Daily
Mail*, in particular, using them as a stick with which to beat the
government, there was little sympathy from General Sir Mike
Jackson, the army's senior officer, during a visit to the Royal
Irish Regiment in a camp north of Kuwait city on 8 March, less
than two weeks before the war started. 'If anything, I'm a little

concerned it may be too comfortable,' he said, without the hint of a smirk on his face.

The British military build-up in the Gulf began stealthily and remained surrounded by a thicker screen of secrecy than the parallel, much larger US effort. Downing Street was still anxious to shield the public's eyes from the fact that British troops were very much preparing to fight, and not simply waiting in the desert to see what happened in the diplomatic arena.

By the beginning of March it was becoming pretty hard to disguise, even to the most casual observer, that most of the 25,000 British combat troops had arrived in Kuwait. In the spring, the desert east of Highway 80 would normally be thick with the tents of picnicking Kuwaiti families and Bedouin herdspeople. But they had all been moved south, and a new tribe had arrived – the British, and the number of their tents was beyond counting.

British trucks, tank transporters and Land Rovers were grumbling north and south. Most still sported their green European camouflage, with How's My Driving? written in German on the mudflaps. A company of British combat soldiers, some wearing the shoulder flash of 16 Air Assault Brigade, sped north in convoy, exhausted from their journey to the emirate. In helmets and goggles, most with checked Arab scarves round their necks, they slept against each other in the back of trucks like toppled skittles. Their Land Rovers, crowned with black machine guns, had been painted to be invisible in the desert, and would have been if the desert was the colour of custard and not a blinding near-white in the afternoon sun.

In the sprawling camps, signposted according to London districts (Holloway Road, Hammersmith), the British were in the same strange limbo as the Americans, brought from the UK or Germany direct to the desert, where for weeks they saw no civilians or any reminder of civilian life, no buildings and virtually no vegetation. The next time the troops expected to see civilians they would be Iraqis, and that anticipation hung over their tents.

In the murky, sandy waters of the Gulf the sailors and Royal Marines with the amphibious task group were also itching to get on with the job. More than 30 ships had left the UK in January, and because of fears over security they had not been able to put in to port since. Their only view of the world for what seemed like months had been the flat, featureless horizon broken only occasionally by flames from a distant oil or gas well, and a heavy sand-filled sky.

The Sunday before the war began, Mark Anderson, the Captain of HMS *Marlborough*, a type-23 frigate that had spent the previous two months patrolling inside Iraqi territorial waters, called the crew together in the junior ratings dining hall, the only space inside the ship big enough to accommodate all the men. Back in the UK there may have been suggestions that a reversal in Parliament for Tony Blair could delay the conflict, but the Captain was in no doubt. 'We will be at war within seven days,' he announced to a sombre audience. 'I see nothing that will stop the United States from going down that route. Bush, Blair and Aznar are meeting in the Azores at the moment, and there is no doubt that is a council of war. Blair will go even without a second UN resolution. We are now on 36 hours' notice to move to commence liberation of Iraq and conflict.'

The ship made its final preparations. In the sick bay the surgeon carefully removed little silver packets of pills from a cardboard box and placed them beside what looked like oversized marker pens. A few hours later the crew of HMS *Marlborough* formed an orderly queue to pick up the final piece of kit they were to be issued in their preparations for war. The sailors were already wearing flameproof suits and carrying white cotton 'battle' bags, stuffed with chemical warfare clothing, respirators and anti-flash gloves and hoods. Extra ammunition was loaded into the guns, the water and airtight bulkhead doors were locked tight, secured with 12 stainless steel clips, while action snacks – plastic packs containing bars of chocolate and a drink – were hoarded in corners around the ship.

In the messes and officers' wardroom, where groups of men sat waiting for the off, all loose fittings, from the cushions to the bottles behind the bar, were firmly secured. Every eventuality was carefully thought through. Nothing was left to chance. But nobody wanted to think about the tablets or emergency injector pens the doctor prescribed. Having to use nerve agent antidote is something the sailors found it was best not to dwell on.

About 100 miles away in the northern Kuwaiti desert clumps of hair lay in a pile on the sand-covered wooden floor of a tent being used by D Squadron of the Household Cavalry. Beside the temporary barber's shop, where a soldier with a pair of hairclippers was shearing the heads of his comrades, Corporal David Simpson from Bramhall, near Stockport, was packing his kit for the last time. He had packed and repacked his bag six times in the last few days, but now there was nothing left to pare down. Two pairs of pants, four pairs of socks, a pair of trousers and a basic wash kit containing soap, a razor, toothbrush, toothpaste, and a small towel. Tucked away in a little pocket of his bag was one final item: a cigar. He said he was keeping it for 'the victory'.

As the clock ticked towards the moment the first coalition boots were due to land on Iraqi soil, across the desert commanding officers gathered their men together one last time. It was the moment Lieutenant Colonel Tim Collins, the man leading the battle group of the 1st Battalion of the Royal Irish, gave the now famous eulogy to his men. 'We go to liberate, not to conquer . . . Wipe them out if that is what they choose. But if you are ferocious in battle, remember to be magnanimous in victory,' he told his men.

The Royal Marines, who would be the first coalition troops on Iraqi soil through an airborne and amphibious assault on the Faw Peninsula, were also making their final preparations. As darkness fell on the evening before the war, a myriad of small fires glowed in their camps across the Kuwaiti desert. Letters from wives, girlfriends, parents, sons, and daughters were being fed into the flames and going up in smoke. Royal Marines never carry personal possessions into battle.

For Trooper Howland and the rest of the Household Cavalry's D Squadron, the war began with a charge over the border from

Kuwait, their job to help secure the precious oilfields in the south. From its headquarters in the western Hijara desert, an Iraqi brigade was meant to be there to meet them, its anti-tank weapons trained on the advancing coalition forces as they made their way north. The Iraqi plan had been to set alight the gas and oil separation plants, preventing the forward movement of Anglo-American troops in billows of choking smoke.

But instead of protecting or setting fire to the plants and the Rumaila oilfields, the 54 Iraqi soldiers and officers in the HQ capitulated. Leaving their weapons behind, they came out of the crumbling building and sat cross-legged with their hands on their heads in the middle of the rubble-strewn courtyard, waiting to give themselves up to whoever might come up the road. The haste with which the Iraqis quit their barracks was evident inside. Lentils and rice were piled on plates, ready to be eaten, sandals were under the beds and a shaving set was discarded mid-use in the colonel's bedroom.

During the night, clumps of men came up with their hands in the air, giving themselves up and waiting to be taken away. The lack of language skills showed as troops tried to get the Iraqis to head up to the road and make their way out of the front line. 'They don't understand anything and if they do they don't let on,' said Corporal Major Dai Rees.

HMS *Marlborough* had begun to make her way towards the mouth of the Kwhar Abd Allah river five hours after the first coalition troops began the invasion of Iraq. Her job was to lay down naval gunfire in support of 40 Commando as they landed on the Faw Peninsula. The crew might have spent weeks patrolling off the coast of Iraq, but they had never been as deep into Iraqi territorial waters as they ventured that morning. In complete darkness and as silent as the crew could make her run, *Marlborough* inched her way through a narrow channel, at times less than 15 feet of water beneath the keel, until the ship was within six miles of the Iraqi coast. She had been secured for action stations several hours earlier when the airtight and watertight doors had been locked shut, while the crew donned their anti-flash suits and gloves to go with their white fireproof 'romper' suits. Out on deck sailors wearing chemical warfare suits manned the guns.

When the Royal Navy goes to war it is a very gentlemanly affair. The enemy is a long way off, and there is a palpable sense of dislocation from the battlefield. There were four ships on the naval gun-line, and the crew of *Marlborough* desperately wanted to be the first Royal Navy vessel to fire a shot in anger since the Falklands, and to fire the most shells. When the first two fire missions fell to other ships, several officers on the bridge put their heads in their hands. On that first morning of the war, there was still a belief that all the Iraqi forces would throw up their hands and surrender at the first sight of a coalition soldier. The gunnery officer was expecting to fire a couple of shells at most and perhaps none at all. But he need not have worried.

The first round, fired at 7.20 a.m. exactly, landed 400 yards from the target. The artillery spotter on shore had purposefully called the strike short to give those in the bunker a chance to surrender. After the next three shots had been 'walked' progressively closer, and with still no sign of submission despite a misfire that had given those inside the bunker a few precious extra minutes, the spotter asked for the full force of the warship to be unleashed.

It took only 20 seconds for *Marlborough*'s main gun to fire 10 rounds at the Iraqi bunker complex six miles away. The shockwave of each high-explosive round exiting the barrel might have shaken the 3,500-tonne ship to the core, but it was nothing compared with the effect the shells had when they hit their target 25 seconds later. Moments after the final shell reached its destination the radio on the bridge crackled into life. 'End of mission, good shooting,' said the Royal Artillery spotter on the ground, who had ordered the strike on the bunker. 'Enemy positions thoroughly neutralised,' he added.

Exactly how many Iraqi casualties the salvo inflicted nobody on the ship knew, but those soldiers who survived the explosions and the cascade of white-hot razor-sharp shrapnel were in no doubt they did not want to go through the experience again. A few minutes later the artillery spotter was back on the radio. 'Possible white flags being raised,' he reported.

It was a sequence that was repeated several times over the next 48 hours. By the time it was over many of the sailors on board had gone the best part of three days with barely any sleep. But with the marines having secured a solid boothold on the peninsula and the first dramatic phase of the conflict coming to its conclusion, *Marlborough* was ordered south, back to the relative safety of the carrier group. Her war was in effect over. But for the men of the Household Cavalry their war was just beginning.

They heard the noise first, somewhere above the spring clouds that hung over RAF Brize Norton, safely far away. Then a shape broke through, and dark reality landed. At 12.10 p.m. precisely on 29 March, Flight 22073, the hulking black C-17 cargo aircraft carrying the bodies of Britain's first war dead, drew to a painfully slow halt on the runway of the Oxfordshire airbase. Flags were flying at half-mast, and the generals were waiting in full dress uniform. A hundred yards away, the families of the dead leaned on each other for support as they rose slowly to their feet to watch the coffins being brought from the aircraft and placed in black hearses.

Three chaplains, from the navy, air force and army, were the first to walk towards the plane. It was a poignantly small welcome party, utterly dwarfed by the shadow of the craft. The coffins, each draped in the Union flag, appeared tiny next to the C-17, normally used to carry tanks and armoured personnel carriers to war. The bodies wouldn't have taken up much space in the hold.

There was a moment of stillness broken only by birdsong, then the rear door of the terminal building opened and the Royal Marine band marched out in silence. It was followed by 70 pallbearers and 10 hearses. The six-strong groups of bearers emerged from the gloom of the aircraft hold with a coffin on

their shoulders and began the painfully slow, rigidly choreographed march – the march for which servicemen train but
hope never to put to use – to the waiting hearses. As each coffin
was brought out, the three chaplains said quiet prayers. The
band began to play Handel as the coffins emerged from the aircraft. The first eight belonged to the first casualties of the war.
They died within hours of the hostilities beginning when a US
Sea Knight helicopter crashed in the Kuwaiti desert nine miles
from the border with Iraq. There were no survivors among
the four American crew and eight Royal Marine commandos
on board.

Among the dead was Captain Philip Guy, who had been due
to return home from the Gulf immediately after the fatal mission to be with his wife for the birth of their second child. By the
time he was buried on 12 April Emily Catherine Guy was 10 days
old. Anyone who stays in the armed forces long enough will
inevitably have to perform the rotational duty of the Casualty
Notification Officer (CNO), the person sent to break news of
incapacitation, illness or injury (known as a 'Triple I') or death.
In the case of the army, CNOs are sent out by the 24-hour Casualty Response Unit at Upavon, Wiltshire. Since army families
don't all live within easy reach of regimental headquarters, the
CNO could be retired, or a member of the Territorial Army, or, in
extreme cases, from one of the other armed services. It takes a
couple of hours for news of a soldier killed in action to reach
home from the Gulf: Divisional Headquarters informs Joint
Force Logistic Headquarters, who, after doing some checks, send
a flash signal via the military's satellite communications system
to Upavon. This takes 9 to 15 minutes.

Personnel at Upavon look up the soldier on the wired army
manning index, which lists both emergency contacts and any
requests he or she might have made, such as hymns for the
funeral. Ministry of Defence protocol for breaking news of a
soldier's death to the next of kin has moved on from the days
when everybody involved was expected to maintain a stiff upper
lip. It is now unusual for the officer charged with the duty to

arrive at the house in uniform. A suit is thought to be less alarming for the family, unless they live in a barracks, where all army personnel wear uniform. It is never, as it sometimes used to be, done over the phone. More than one trip will be made, if necessary, to inform the parents and the partner.

At the end of 2002, for reasons of expediency, personnel chiefs also lifted the ban on waking families in the middle of the night. Before the era of 24-hour news this was thought to be unnecessarily traumatic, but now the knock on the door comes at any time. 'We don't compete with Sky News,' says a senior army personnel co-ordinator, 'since speed for us is subordinate to accuracy. The mobile phone is a marvellous bit of kit, but thoroughly dangerous for my notification chain.'

There is no script, no formal way to introduce the news, no preparatory role-playing. The CNOs – who may be accompanied by a clergyman – are advised to be as human as possible, while remaining detached, and to be ready for anything. Experienced CNOs say that most families go into immediate shock and take the news passively. Occasionally, however, there is anger: officers experienced in this duty warn juniors to be prepared to be expelled from the house. CNOs are not allowed to drive themselves to the location. When they return to HQ, they are made to sit down and talk their experience through.

'As the car turns into the road and stops, your whole stomach turns to bloody water,' says one experienced CNO, who notified several families of a death during the war with Iraq. 'You go to that front door and inside there's a television on and you can see it reflected through the window and all the normal trappings of suburban life in England are going on. And you know that you're just about to bombshell someone's life. It is an awful moment.'

Five days before the C-12 transport plane landed at Brize Norton it was the families of RAF Flight Lieutenants Dave Williams and Kevin Main whose lives were shattered by the dreaded knock on the door. For the CNOs charged with delivering the news it must have been a particularly difficult task. The

Tornado crew who arrived back in Britain on that spring day were not killed in an accident, or shot down by the enemy. Instead the pilot and navigator had fallen victim to that most cruelly ironic way to die in warfare: 'friendly fire'. A US Patriot missile battery shot down the Tornado over northern Kuwait as it was returning from a bombing sortie over Iraq on 23 March. The downing of the aircraft was met with incredulity by some of the British servicemen in the Gulf. 'Exactly how can you mistake a Tornado for a Scud?' one Royal Navy weapons officer said when the news broke. 'It can't be done. They fly completely different profiles. It beggars belief.'

The US has a stockpile of phrases to describe the all-too-common tragedy of allied forces being killed by people on their own side. 'Blue on blue', which made its debut in the war after the downing of the Tornado, comes from wargaming exercises where the goodies are blue and – in a hangover from Cold War days – the baddies are red.

Before the war even started, 'blue on blue' was considered to be one of the biggest dangers to coalition forces. In the 1991 Gulf War 24 per cent of Americans killed – 35 in total – and 15 per cent of those wounded fell victim to their own forces in 28 friendly fire incidents, while nine British soldiers were killed when a US jet attacked British armoured vehicles by mistake.

When the captain of HMS *Marlborough* had called the crew together to brief them on the then coming confict, friendly fire had been uppermost in his mind: '99.5 per cent of everything coming off that beach will be friendly,' he told the crew before the ship went into battle. Just because something did not respond on the radio did not mean it was hostile. It might just be damaged and trying to limp home. 'You have to be absolutely sure before you can open fire,' he said.

By the time the C-17 touched down at Brize Norton news was already breaking of another friendly fire incident the day before, on 28 March. Once again it involved US forces firing on British servicemen, but this time there were survivors to speak of the horror of coming under attack from your own side, and they did not hold back.

The one sound the men of the Household Cavalry said they would never forget was the guns. A cross between a moan and a roar, a fierce rattling of heavy rounds of 30 mm canon fire from two A-10 Thunderbolts flying low overhead. Aircraft that shouldn't have been in the British-controlled area in southern Iraq, 'cowboying' at just 500 feet and looking for something to have a crack at.

Two American pilots had turned their guns on a convoy of five British vehicles from the the regiment, killing one man just three days short of his 26th birthday, injuring four others, and wiping out two armoured reconnaissance vehicles. Two Iraqi civilians, waving a large white flag, were also killed. Coloured smoke signs were sent up to indicate that they were friendly troops but it didn't stop the attack. The planes came back a second time, injuring those who had managed to scramble out of their vehicles with only superficial wounds. The gunner, Corporal of Horse Matty Hull, was the victim of a direct hit into his gun turret. The men in the Scimitars were screaming over the radio to 'stop the friendly fire, we are being engaged by friendly fire' and 'pop smoke, pop smoke'. The forward air controller, the liaison with coalition air forces to bring in fire missions, was shouting 'check fire, check fire'. Frantic calls were made to 16 Air Assault Brigade headquarters to find out what was going on. But no one seemed to know.

The A-10s were about to take a third swing when they were told by the American air patroller working with the Household Cavalry to stop firing. Instead of providing air cover while helicopters came in to evacuate the casualties, they flew away. 'He had absolutely no regard for human life. I believe he was a cowboy,' is how Lance Corporal Steven Gerrard described the pilot who had killed his friend and colleague. 'There were four or five [planes] that I noticed earlier and this one had broken off and was on his own when he attacked us. He'd just gone out on a jolly.'

The two Scimitars of 2 Troop had been probing a dusty road, checking for landmines, enemy locations and assault batteries when they came under fire. For the rest of the squadron, ears pricked up as shouting came over the radio. At first it seemed like someone had just lost their rag. Then the full horror dawned. One of the vehicles had been hit, no two, and by 'friendly call signs'.

They stood still, stopping what they were doing. At first they thought it was one lad, then another. Whoever it was, it didn't ease the twist of knots that started knitting themselves in their stomachs. Later, they learned it was Matty. Amid the grief, their anger could not be contained. All of D Squadron's vehicles were clearly marked, with fluorescent panels on the roofs, flags and other markings. It was something the soldiers kept repeating. 'We spend all this money marking out our vehicles so this doesn't happen,' one said. 'If it was the heat of battle, shit happens. But it was clear daylight.'

Trooper Joe Woodgate, 19, the driver of the Scimitar in which Cpl Hull was killed, walked away with holes in his bulletproof vest and tears in his sleeves where shrapnel entered and exited without touching his arm. 'I was moving along and, for some reason, the wagon just stopped dead and these two massive sparks came flying into my cab. I turned round and the turret was just a well of fire behind me. There was fire everywhere. I tried to get out but my hatch was jammed. I was banging away at it for what seemed like a lifetime but was probably only a few seconds. As soon as I saw the fire, I thought, "Get the fuck out of here." I managed to get out and rolled on the floor. I didn't realise that it was the Americans that had hit us.

'I didn't know what was going on at that point. We were in this ditch and I still didn't realise it was Americans. I didn't realise that Matty was still in the turret. I thought Matty had got out as well but when I was pegging it off I thought where's Matty and I looked behind me and the fucking wagon was just a mess, man. It's weird because you are thinking, maybe if I had done things differently . . . I don't know why Matty couldn't get out. People said they remember hearing him on the radio but I don't remember a thing. In hindsight, you always think there's something else you could have done.'

In the final reckoning, five British servicemen died in the war as a result of friendly fire. Three died at the hands of the Americans and two crewmen of a Challenger tank were killed when their vehicle was fired on by another British tank during a night operation. But to the soldiers on the ground and the public at home it felt like many more. The word 'cowboy' struck a chord. It seemed to sum up at least the perceived difference between the US and British forces. While the Americans were riding around in their tanks blowing up everything in sight, the British were patrolling the streets of southern Iraq in their berets and tam o'shanters.

But tragedies don't stop wars, and the men of D Squadron had no choice but to pick themselves up and get on with the job. Outgunned and outsized in their small Scimitar armoured reconnaissance vehicles by Iraqi T-55 tanks as well as outnumbered, D Squadron – now down to 100 men from 105 – had been fighting 600 Iraqi soldiers in order to push forward across the western Hijarah desert towards the Euphrates. They had been limiting the Iraqi troops' freedom of movement and stopping them from withdrawing north of the Euphrates to regroup.

The squadron had been so far forward that they were beyond the range of the supportive guns of 7 Para Royal Horse Artillery, fighting it out with troops using guerrilla tactics, men in pick-up trucks and on motorbikes in civilian clothes, who were trying to spot their position and call in artillery. The thuds of incoming guns had become everyday life for the squadron, so much so that they had begun to give the Iraqis marks out of 10 for their accuracy. In just 2 days, 8 T-55 tanks, a number of armoured vehicles, 3 artillery positions, a rocket system, some dismounted patrols, an ammunition compound and at least 5 companies had been taken out. They had taken 20 prisoners.

Out in the field, in one of the vehicles, a soldier said: 'There's a lot of armour still out there. But they have taken a big hit over

the last couple of days. We think we have only scratched the surface and we will destroy them over the next couple of days. We
have some bigger guns coming in.' As he spoke he prepared to
engage a man running around on a motorbike with a rocket-
propelled grenade. 'The target has been neutralised, the motorbike
destroyed, the man with the RPG has either run away or is dead.'

His colleague, Bombardier Stephen Denby, said: 'There is
quite a lot of emotion when you are blowing people up but we
have to blow them up or they'll do it to us. After the other day,
losing one of our own guys, you sit down and think, "Hang on,
that's someone else's family losing someone over there and for
what? They don't even want to fight." '

But for the men of D Squadron things were set to get worse
before they were to get better. Just five days after the friendly fire
incident, the small unit lost another man when a vehicle over-
turned in a water-filled ditch, killing its gunner and seriously
injuring its commander. The driver, Wayne White, 18, managed
to clamber out of his hatch through the water and emerged
unhurt. He made frantic calls to the squadron ambulance at
temporary headquarters 8 miles away and dived back into the
channel to try to get his friends out. The commander was saved,
but the gunner became the 27th British soldier to die in Iraq since
the conflict began. He had a wife and a 4-year-old daughter.

Two days after the accident, and after 13 gruelling days on the
front line, the Household Cavalry pulled back to the grounds of
an old engineering works with three foul-smelling thunderbox
toilets, 'comfy bum' toilet paper, and two Formica cubicles
where the soldiers could hang up a shower bag and marvel at
the wonder of a proper wash in a solar shower. After days running around in the small overheated confines of their vehicles,
scraping up gravel hills and over Iraqi front lines, dodging incoming artillery at night and sleeping on the thick desert dust,
it seemed like luxury.

They called it Slipper City because the soldiers could kick off
their boots, air their trench feet and relax a little. Some even
made ersatz flip-flops by cutting soles from the sponge used to

pack ammunition and threading them with string. The Squadron Quartermaster, Reg Carney, had tried to obtain fresh rations
rather than the usual boil-in-the-bags, but his forages around
the various camps failed.

After two weeks in hard battle when the vehicles regularly
broke down – five conked out in one day – it was also a time to
try to fine-tune the hiccups. A lack of parts and supplies meant
the ad hoc repairs were done using everything available, from
paperclips to string. The biggest problem was air filters, which
were all too scarce, and those in place got clogged with sand and
dust. Then there were the difficulties with running gear and rear
idlers. Because of a change 5 years ago from what was regarded
as an overstock of parts to a policy colloquially known as 'just
enough, just in time', it seemed there was not enough and it was
never on time.

The Household Cavalry was at the top of the brigade supply
chain for its parts demands, and while its colonel in Windsor sat
hassling people on the phone, the stuff was still not coming
through. The Scimitars, Spartans and Sultans used by the regiment were designed in 1968 as a means of moving between rubber plantations in Borneo. Inside, the living space measured
about 6 ft x 4 ft, but typically much of it was taken up with a pile
of doss bags and rollmats for the 5 people who lived out of the
vehicle, and half-a-dozen large tins, each containing high-
explosive mortar rounds.

Piled up beside them in one of D Squadron's vehicles were
four SA-80 rifles, a 31 mm mortar and an Iraqi AK-47 – complete
with a serial number on the butt – which was taken from a prisoner of war. Usually there would also be an anti-tank weapon
inside, but they were allowed to store it on the roof when there
was no sign of Iraqi soldiers. The men bitched about their
vehicles all the time but admitted that, while they had a certain
vulnerability, they did have a great affection for them, compar-
ing themselves and the wagons to a hermit crab and its shell.

The vehicles, though, were not the only problem. Trooper
Ben Scollick, holding up a threadbare pair of desert combat

trousers with a gaping hole in the backside, took out a House-wife, a military repair kit, and began to attempt to sew them back together. 'I'll be in the Falklands before I get a new pair,' he joked.

Three days later the Household Cavalry was engaged in its own little bit of regime change symbolism. The men pulled down a picture of Saddam Hussein from the memorial building in the centre of the town of Ad Dayr, west of Basra in southern Iraq, and the locals trampled all over it.

The sheikhs of Ad Dayr had come to the outlying village of Qaryat Nas to greet Brigadier Jacko Page in their best clothes, their grubby jellabas covered with black robes trimmed with gold, their headdresses immaculate. They patted the small, be-spectacled commander on the back, shouting, 'Salaam, salaam.' They said that just days before, soldiers from the Iraqi 6th Arm-oured Brigade had hightailed it out of town, along with mem-bers of the Ba'ath Party, after they burned the headquarters of their stronghold in the south-east. Not a shot was fired as the British entered the town.

As they fingered their prayer beads, the head men asked for help in securing the town, finding missing family members and providing food and water. Crowded by people, the brigadier told them: 'The first priority is security. What we don't want to see is people carrying weapons, or it will cause trouble.' The oldest man, who had been told on the telephone that the British had arrived, came to the village to meet them. 'Just give us a chance and we will clean up,' he said.

As they watched the scenes unfold from their vehicles, there was a palpable change in the soldiers' mood. After three weeks of living either on the desert floor or in the middle of a dried-up marsh, contact with welcoming civilians was a rare delight. Finally they began to feel like the army of liberation they had been told they would be.

Outside, in another village, Corporal Mick Flynn had found his armoured vehicle mobbed. Asked over the radio if he needed assistance, he laughed: 'We are with the kind of lord mayor of this village. He says he welcomes us and the Americans and he says he wants the head of the British army to come and speak to him.' For the time being, he had to make do with Corporal Flynn.

Freedom at last: Kurdish forces take first major city in Northern Iraq
(AP/Kevin Frayer)

14 Unfinished business

Fighting is better than idleness.

Kurdish proverb

By the time Asif Mohammed turned up for work three days after Baghdad's fall, the ancient contents of Mosul's museum had vanished. The looters knew what they were looking for – and in less than 10 minutes had walked off with several million dollars worth of Parthian sculpture. The 2,000-year-old statue of King Saqnatroq II, one of Iraq's forgotten monarchs, had disappeared from its cabinet. Several mythical birds and an Athenian goddess were missing. 'Iraq has a great history,' Mohammed, the museum's curator, pointed out, 'and it's just been wrecked.'

When George Bush announced the start of war three weeks earlier he had promised to respect not only Iraq's citizens but also the country's 'great civilisation'. Much of it had now vanished or was in pieces. 'I want to know whether the Americans accept this,' Mohammed demanded. As Mosul descended into a hellish post-Saddam chaos – worse than that seen in Baghdad or Basra – there were no American troops to ask.

The Pentagon had originally intended to send its most advanced fighting force, the technologically awesome 4th Infantry Division, into northern Iraq. But in early March, as its tanks waited in cargo ships off the balmy Turkish coast, the Turkish Parliament refused permission for 62,000 US troops to enter Turkish territory. The Parliament's vote stunned Washington, which had arrogantly assumed that the Turks, after some wobbling, would eventually accede to Donald Rumsfeld's imperious request. The upshot was that two weeks before embarking on a war in Iraq, the United States had no northern front.

This was to have many unforeseen consequences, not only on Asif Mohammed's vanished Parthian statues, but also on the inflammable ethnic situation between the Kurds and the Turks. Since the last Gulf War, the Kurds of northern Iraq had enjoyed considerable autonomy. After the doomed uprisings of 1991, the Iraqi army had counter-attacked. Millions of Kurdish refugees poured out of their traditional home in Iraq's Zargos Mountains into neighbouring Turkey and Iran.

It was John Major, the then British Prime Minister, who came to the rescue, suggesting that British and American warplanes could establish a 'no-fly zone' in northern Iraq. The plan worked and the refugees went home. In the ensuing 12 years the Kurds created their own prosperous de facto state, Kurdistan, free from Baghdad's control, and based around two pleasant provincial capitals, Irbil and Sulaimaniyah. Kurdistan looked and felt like a middle-income nation with modern hotels, internet cafés and freely available Amstel beer. It had all the accoutrements of a modern democracy: a parliament, two rival prime ministers, even a Kurdish Dwarf Society.

The only problem was Turkey. With a large, restive Kurdish population of its own, Turkey was determined to prevent the Kurds of northern Iraq seizing any more territory as the Anglo-American war against Saddam Hussein unfolded. The Kurds, 25 million of them, had been historically split across Turkey, Iran, Iraq and Syria. The last thing Turkey wanted was a nascent Kurdish state on its doorstep. But by refusing to let American troops in just as war started, Ankara had shot itself in both feet. In the end, though, the Pentagon did not begin its northern campaign in either of the region's two main cities, Kirkuk and Mosul, home to Iraq's biggest oil deposits. Instead it commenced hostilities in an obscure enclave of mountains and shimmering green pastures next to the Iranian border and the town of Halabja.

It was here, in north-eastern Iraq, that a radical Islamist group, Ansar al-Islam, had established its headquarters around the village of Biyara. For the past two years, bearded Ansar guerrillas had been involved in an acrimonious war with the main Kurdish party that controlled the rest of the area, the staunchly pro-American Patriotic Union of Kurdistan (PUK). There had been a lot of killing on both sides. The conflict would have remained obscure were it not for the fact that the Bush administration had convinced itself that Ansar's fighters, most of them Kurds, but including Arab veterans of the jihad in Afghanistan, were linked to Osama bin Laden and his al-Qaida network.

Four days after the war in Iraq broke out, the battle started. Dozens of American missiles ripped into Ansar's main military garrison in the shabby village of Serget. In January 2003 Colin Powell described the garrison – with optimistic hyperbole – as a 'terrorist chemicals and poison factory'. Realising what would most likely happen next, Ansar invited a group of foreign correspondents to visit their previously forbidden heartland, including the *Guardian*'s Luke Harding. 'We are just a group of simple Muslims trying to do our duty,' Mohammed Hassan, Ansar's bearded PR man, told him, as journalists stumbled around the site. The garrison revealed a hidden TV studio, a radio station – Radio Jihad – and several empty boxes of explosives, used by the presenter. But there didn't appear to be any poisons.

What happened next was an intriguing model of US-Kurdish military co-operation that would be repeated elsewhere as Saddam's empire in the north crumbled. Small teams of US special forces had slipped into northern Iraq several weeks earlier. Working closely with Kurdish PUK fighters – known as Peshmerga, a legendary bunch whose name means 'those who do not fear death' – the Americans set about blasting Ansar into tiny pieces.

Unfortunately not all American bombs appeared to hit the right target. The last thing that Omar Mohammed Saeed heard, for example, was the sound of a cruise missile plunging through the roof of his dormitory. It was 12.30 a.m. on 22 March, day two of the war, and he and his comrades had been asleep. Saeed was a member of Komala, a tiny mainstream Islamic group that had the misfortune to be based in a neighbouring village to Serget. The bomb reduced Komala's military headquarters into a tomb of pulverised concrete and metal. Saeed stood no chance. After the attack, which killed 33 Komala fighters, his nephew, Sadar

Mohammed, said: 'This makes us love Saddam Hussein rather than America.'

Ansar's response to the US attack was swift and characteristically savage. That afternoon an Ansar suicide bomber blew up his explosives-filled taxi near a PUK checkpoint, killing the Australian cameraman Paul Moran, 39, who had been filming nearby. Moran was one of the first journalists to die covering the war in Iraq.

Later that evening, meanwhile, the first US military plane to reach northern Iraq touched down in darkness at Bakrajo airstrip, 10 miles west of Sulaimaniyah, prompting locals to complain of 'strange noises' in the night. The plane carried several hundred US special forces troops and military personnel. Soon afterwards, the Pentagon indulged in a piece of TV-friendly theatre when 1,000 paratroopers from the US 173rd Airborne Brigade tumbled out of the sky near Irbil in one of the biggest US airdrops since the second world war.

The next day the American networks showed dramatic footage of the soldiers 'securing' Harir Airport, and digging foxholes in the middle of a lush green valley. The TV presenters seemed blissfully unaware that this was not enemy territory but was controlled by a bunch of pro-Washington Kurdish politicians who had despaired of the American military ever turning up. 'Better late than never,' one Kurdish leader said.

It wasn't quite the northern front that Donald Rumsfeld had envisaged, but the US did finally have boots on the ground. Over the next five days American warplanes launched a series of devastating raids all across the 140-mile front line dividing Saddam-controlled territory from Iraqi Kurdistan. Kifri, Chamchamal and Kalak resounded with explosions as American bombs pulverised Iraqi soldiers encamped in pathetic bunkers on the high ridges nearby.

It wasn't clear how many Iraqi troops were being killed. But Saddam's unhappy conscript army was finally coming up against the awesome firepower of the world's only military superpower, and it can't have been much fun. By 27 March, day seven of the war, the Iraqi army decided it had had enough – and abruptly retreated from the front-line town of Chamchamal back towards Kirkuk. It was the first in a series of mysterious tactical withdrawals. At the time it was not clear whether this was weakness on Saddam's part or a piece of majestic emperor-like confidence that the doomed American army could be lured into Iraq's cities and then crushed, like a large but clumsy beetle. Either way, the Kurdish Peshmerga wasted little time in occupying territory vacated by their Iraqi enemies.

The same evening Kurdish soldiers advanced 20km down the road, across an eerily deserted landscape of green hills dotted with pine trees and brilliant red poppies. They also liberated their first chunk of Saddam's Iraq – a small concrete bunker. A few kilometres further on they discovered an abandoned Iraqi army camp with a chemical unit, but with no chemical weapons. Few Kurds were in doubt as to what this all meant. 'It's a victory for the Kurds. This regime has been attacking us and killing us for more than 30 years,' said Mam Rostam, a top Kurdish commander, in charge of the advance. 'Thousands of our people have died or been killed by chemical weapons. Five thousand Kurdish villages have been flattened. I'm very excited and very happy.'

The American military was stumbling on a truth bizarrely ignored by coalition planners: that the quickest way to win the war in Iraq was to allow Iraqis – in this case Iraq's Saddam-hating Kurds – to do it for themselves. True, the Peshmerga's inexorable forward drift towards Kirkuk was causing panic in Turkey. But the Kurds were proving themselves an efficient and disciplined fighting force. The previous month a crowd watching a football match in Irbil against a team from Baghdad had broken into a long chant of 'Fuck the Turks'. The same sentiment, though more politely expressed, was wafting through the corridors of the Pentagon and State Department after Turkey's earlier snub.

The following day, 28 March, the long-awaited ground offensive against Ansar began at dawn in a fiery stream of tracer bullets and million-dollar missiles. American AC130 gunships and strike jets attacked the caves and rock bunkers where Ansar fighters, Tora Bora-style, had been hiding. Entire mountainsides flamed orange. Hundreds of PUK fighters then sprinted across the grassy slopes, tossing aside fears of anti-personnel mines, and poured into Ansar's villages. The Ansar fighters resisted for about an hour. Then they vanished up into the snowline and the border with Iran.

By the end of the day 120 Ansar fighters were dead, as well as 20 Peshmerga. The group had been completely routed. It was the first triumph of America's war in Iraq. But for Ashraf Sadak and other villagers living in Islamist Biyara it turned out next day that liberation was a mixed blessing. A 2,000 lb American bomb landed directly on his house, reducing to rubble the three rooms where he and his family lived. The missile also destroyed the mosque next door, gouging large chunks out of its Oxford-blue dome. 'There is nothing left. It's all been destroyed,' Sadak said, standing above a row of shops that had also been flattened. 'If America bought me a new house I would feel a bit better about this.'

The women of Biyara, however, were clearly pleased that George Bush had got rid of the guerrillas. 'Living here was like being in a prison,' Astari Ali Mohammed, 53, said, as she picked over the ruins of her house, also destroyed by a US missile. 'I had to wear a *chador* even when sweeping my front porch. And they wouldn't let me sleep on my roof in the summer. They told me it was immoral. This is a great day. I don't care that my house has been destroyed. We have got rid of Ansar al-Islam. My daughters can now come and visit me here freely.'

As American forces began closing in on Baghdad, up in the north US warplanes settled into a routine of round-the-clock bombing. Much of this was accurate, and had demolished, for example, the huge Iraqi Khalid bin Waleed military base in Kirkuk. Some of it was not. On 6 April, day 18 of the war, two F-16 planes above the front line east of Mosul spotted what they thought was an Iraqi tank, glimmering ahead of them on the plain. The pilot dropped a bomb not on a piece of military hardware, it turned out, but on a Kurdish convoy containing Peshmerga, US special forces and the BBC's John Simpson.

It was the worst friendly fire incident of the war. At least 18 people were killed with many others critically injured, including the brother of Massoud Barzani, leader of the Kurdish Democratic Party (KDP), which administered the western half of the Kurdish enclave and was a crucial ally of the United States. The BBC's translator Kamran Mohammed had his legs blown off, and died shortly afterwards. The rest of the BBC team escaped with only minor injuries.

Simpson later revealed that he had found a lump of shrapnel embedded in his flakjacket. 'Well, it's a bit of a disaster,' he said immediately afterwards, with forgivable understatement. 'It was an American plane that dropped the bomb right beside us. I saw it land about 10 ft, 12 ft away, I think. This is just a scene from hell here. All the vehicles are on fire. There are bodies burning around me, there are bodies lying around, there are bits of bodies on the ground. This is a really bad own goal by the Americans.'

The incident left Iraq's pro-American Kurds badly shaken. The entire top ranks of the KDP, including Barzani, descended on the hospital in Irbil where 45 wounded were being treated. The embarrassed US military flew Barzani's brother Wajih, who had a piece of shrapnel stuck in his brain, to Germany for emergency surgery. The grim confusion at the scene was vividly captured when an American medic tried to treat Simpson as he telephoned the bad news back to London. 'Shut up. I'm broadcasting,' he told him.

The episode marked the end of a disastrous week for the BBC. A few days earlier the distinguished Iranian BBC cameraman Kaveh Gulstani died after accidentally stepping on a landmine on another northern front line, in the town of Kifri. The BBC producer travelling with him, Stuart Hughes, also stepped on a mine. He would later lose his foot.

Of all of the ethnic groups in Iraq it was the Kurds who suffered most during Saddam Hussein's three decades in power. In 1987–88 Saddam sent his cousin and trusted aide General Ali

Hassan al-Majid, 'Chemical Ali', to sort them out. In the ensuing Anfal campaign Majid killed thousands of Kurdish civilians, using both chemical weapons and more conventional methods of slaughter. He dropped poison gas on Halabja, killing 5,000 people, carried out similar attacks on 200 other villages and towns in Kurdistan and transported entire communities to Iraq's south-western desert, where they were bulldozed into mass graves. The Kurds claim 200,000 people perished. It was hardly surprising that the whole of northern Iraq celebrated the news that Chemical Ali had been killed in an airstrike in Basra on 7 April, two days before the fall of Baghdad.

For Saeed Abdullah it had been a long wait. His 12-year-old daughter, Galwezh, and 17-year-old son, Najmadin, both died in Halabja in March 1988 in a cloud of chemical gas. 'I'm extremely happy,' he said, as it sunk in that the moment of revenge had finally arrived. 'We feel that justice has been done at last. My only regret is that he wasn't captured alive. I would have liked to have seen him tied to a donkey so that people could spit at him.' Kurdish women, putting flowers on the graves of their loved ones, held picnics in the afternoon sunshine in Halabja's cemetery.

Soon after US marines pulled down Saddam's statue in Baghdad, opposite the Palestine hotel, the Kurds began what turned out to be a 24-hour street party. Most Iraqis, it was swiftly emerging, did not support their President and were delighted at his demise. The hero as far as ordinary Kurds were concerned was America's President. Baban Mohammed, one of thousands celebrating on the streets of Sulaimaniyah, summed up the mood: 'We love Bush. We love Blair. I'm happy. Everybody in Kurdistan is happy. Thank you. Thank you.'

The Kurds had never really shed their fear that Saddam might one day come back and kill them again. With the fall of Baghdad, the fear disappeared. 'We have waited a very long time for this,' Mohammed explained, as cars tooted their way past crowds of ecstatic Kurdish men dancing with their arms wrapped round each other. 'We have been afraid for so long. We have not been able to sleep. Now we can,' he said.

Even the most optimistic Downing Street spin doctor or Pentagon hawk could not have anticipated scenes quite like these three weeks into the military campaign. Soon after the celebrations erupted, a group of US special forces, wearing military uniforms and wraparound sunglasses, emerged from their base just down the road and drove straight into the melee. The Kurds mobbed them, kissing their cheeks and jumping on to the bonnet of their white Land Rovers.

Over the next 24 hours relations between Washington and the Kurds were to reach an illicit climax. Earlier, US generals had made it clear that the Kurdish Peshmerga would not be allowed to seize Kirkuk, now a mere 10 km away from the new front line with Iraqi troops. The city, Iraq's fourth biggest, is predominantly Kurdish, but with a significant Turkish-speaking Turcomen population. It is also home to Iraq's largest oilfield, the hugely lucrative Bawa Gurgur refinery, originally established by the British in the 1920s, but now managed by the Iraqi Oil Company.

Since briefly capturing Kirkuk in the 1991 uprisings the Kurds had been determined to get the city back. For them it was unfinished business. Many Kurds had also been evicted from Kirkuk under Saddam's ruthless Arabisation policy, which saw Arab settlers from the south given Kurdish homes. The Turks, however, felt they had been cheated out of Kirkuk 85 years ago when the British and French created modern Iraq from the ruins of the Turkish Ottoman Empire. Any Kurdish invasion of Kirkuk would amount to a *casus belli* as far as Ankara was concerned – or that, at least, was the theory.

The morning after Baghdad's fall the Iraqi army defending Kirkuk seemed oblivious to what had happened 150 miles further south. They lobbed artillery shells as usual at Kurdish troops sitting with US special forces on the opposite ridge. But at about 11 a.m. the shelling mysteriously stopped. Just over an hour later, Kurdish Peshmerga, armed with Kalashnikovs and rocket launchers, began streaming towards the city in an over-excited cavalcade of battered Toyota pick-up trucks and taxis.

It was clear that the Peshmerga had swept aside the diplomatic niceties and were invading Kirkuk after all.

There was a brief hiatus. Iraqi troops had blocked the road with a huge wall of earth. The Peshmerga soon found a way round it – and pressed on. By 2 p.m. they had liberated Kirkuk, almost by accident and with no Iraqi resistance. 'We're delighted,' said Abdullah Ali, a 55-year-old retired civil servant, as a group of youths tried to pull down a stature of Saddam Hussein in a parody of the scene in Baghdad the previous day. 'The last three weeks have been hell.'

This was Turkey's nightmare scenario. The two Kurdish parties had already made it clear they had no intention of declaring their own independent Kurdish state, and merely wanted federal autonomy within a new post-Saddam Iraq. None the less, the Kurdish invasion of Kirkuk could only have been done with the connivance of Washington, a fact that only added to Turkey's painful humiliation. The Turks demanded that the Peshmerga immediately pull out of Kirkuk and again threatened to send Turkish tanks into northern Iraq. Inside the city, meanwhile, the Americans were nowhere to be seen. Nor was the Iraqi army. It had melted away long before the Peshmerga turned up.

In Kirkuk, as elsewhere in Iraq, liberation was being followed by looting. But unlike in the south, the liberators and the looters were the same people – in this case the victorious Peshmerga. Three Kurdish fighters tried to drive off from the oilfield in a fork-lift truck. Another group set off with the entire contents of a villa, including several air-conditioning units and a bicycle. When asked why he was stealing, he said: 'It's for my house.' But don't these things belong to somebody, he was asked. 'They belong to Iraq and I'm Iraqi,' he replied.

By 5 p.m. it became clear that the city was slipping into total anarchy. American forces still had not arrived. 'Everything is getting messy,' Harsham Wahab, a member of Kirkuk's Turcomen minority, complained as looters dipped into the technical college opposite his house. 'This isn't the kind of freedom we wanted. We are looking for proper freedom, where people don't try and steal our things.' The liberation of Kirkuk was turning into a PR disaster for the Kurdish parties, as they held an emergency meeting on how to stop it in Kirkuk's former Ba'ath Party head-quarters.

Nearby, on a traffic roundabout, another statue of Iraq's once mighty ruler lay in an Ozymandian heap, its broken legs hidden in the long grass. The following day, 11 April, similar scenes took place in Mosul, a culturally venerable, much larger city of a million people on the banks of the Tigris river. The Iraqi govern-ment had abandoned Mosul late the previous night. American special forces had briefly entered Mosul's eastern suburbs with groups of Peshmerga overnight, but then left again. By midday on the day of Mosul's liberation, as Kalashnikov fire echoed around Mosul's looted central bank, they still had not come back. A huge crowd was trying to help itself to large piles of Iraqi dinar. Fights were breaking out. Kurdish fighters were shooting wildly into the air. Nearby, looters were busy ransacking Mosul's former seat of power, its imposing government building, send-ing glass cascading into the street. Across the city fires burned from ruined government offices.

'I beg you to stop these terrible things,' implored Mufti Moh-ammed, one of Mosul's leading Sunni clerics, as dozens of wor-shippers, furious at the self-destruction of their city, poured out of his mosque following Friday prayers. 'If some kind of order is not restored in the next 24 hours we're going to take things into our own hands. We will start up our own armed groups to keep the peace,' he threatened.

While the Pentagon had spent months planning the military campaign in Iraq, it was clear that virtually no time had been devoted to the more nebulous question of how to how to keep order once Saddam was gone. Donald Rumsfeld, when asked what he planned to do to curb growing civil chaos across Iraq, merely shrugged and blamed the media for exaggerating the scale of the problem.

In Mosul, however, it would have been difficult to exaggerate. Mosul has traditionally been one of Iraq's most ethnically mixed cities. Arabs, Arabs, Syriac people, Armenians, Kurds, Turcomens, Christians and Yezidis – an esoteric sect who refuse to wear blue – all call Mosul home. As in Kirkuk, it was Kurdish fighters who ended up liberating Mosul, to an enthusiastic welcome from the city's Kurds, but a more muted one from everybody else.

The KDP fighters had been given orders to defend several key buildings. They arrived too late to save Mosul Museum and its priceless Parthian and Assyrian antiquities. But they did manage to secure the natural history museum a short walk away. A Kurdish commander, Wahid Majid, proudly showed off the dusty toucans and pickled reptiles he had just saved from the mob. 'We have not allowed anybody to take anything. We were told to defend the museum and other important establishments.' Had he seen the Americans? 'They were here earlier but they were unable to control the situation so they left,' he said.

On the other bank of the Tigris, a short drive past an abandoned riverside amusement park, looters spent the day demolishing Mosul's only five-star hotel, the ziggurat-shaped Nineveh International. It was perhaps a legitimate target: an entire wing had been reserved for senior members of the Ba'ath Party. Young Arab men set about removing the hotel's bedding and furniture. They attached rope to chairs, and were dangling them one by one down the hotel's glitzy 100 ft atrium. 'It is our money,' 17-year-old Hassan Ali explained. 'This hotel has been built with money from Iraq's oil. The oil belongs to us. That's why we are looting.'

To begin with, the mass collective stealing in northern Iraq was good-humoured and democratic, with different groups taking part. But within a day of liberation Arabs and Kurds had started killing each other. The beginnings of what looked like ethnic collapse were setting in.

Two days after the fall of Mosul coalition forces in north-central Iraq were engaged in what would turn out to be the last battle of the war. Some 250 light armoured vehicles had raced north from Baghdad and were now pushing into the southern outskirts of

Tikrit, Saddam Hussein's home town. He had been born in the small village of Owja, just outside Tikrit, 66 years earlier. Back then Owja was a collection of mud huts. Tikrit itself was little more than a shabby smuggling town on the banks of the Tigris.

Over the past 30 years, Iraq's ruler had transformed Tikrit, building new roads, mosques, a football stadium and a giant memorial to his late mother, Subha. Tikritis now occupied key positions in Saddam's rapidly shrinking empire – in the Ba'ath Party, the military and the secret police. Once Tikrit had fallen, coalition generals reasoned, a stake would have been driven through the regime's heart. Saddam would not come back from the dead.

And so on Sunday, 13 April, US marines began advancing into Tikrit, encountering minimal resistance. They destroyed 5 Iraqi tanks on their way in and killed at least 15 Iraqi solders. But the feared Republican Guard was not to be found. In the sky, the attack was terrifying and relentless. American F18s reduced what was left of Iraq's once mighty army to smouldering dust.

Inside the town, meanwhile, most of the Sunni Muslim tribes, famous for their loyalty to Saddam, were preparing to betray him. Some 25 out of 28 tribal chiefs wanted to surrender to coalition forces, it emerged. Only 3 reportedly refused, including the head of Saddam's own al-Bu Nasir tribe. Many of the Arabs who lived in newly liberated villages just outside Tikrit also made it clear that they did not support Saddam any more either. 'We are very happy that Saddam is gone. We will co-operate with the British and the Americans,' said Najim Abdullah Ahmed, from Terashad, 20 miles north-east of Tikrit. 'A lot of people from here have been taken away and tortured.'

The Iraqi army's retreat down the road from Kirkuk to Tikrit three days earlier was starkly visible. A truck carrying a 25 ft fin-tailed missile lay toppled on its side. The missile was still there. The driver had long fled. Inside his shattered cab there were vehicle-hire documents covered in blood. Further on towards Tikrit giant boxes of ammunition lay abandoned in the desert. Someone had left a pair of boots by the side of the road.

Just before dawn the following day, 14 April, the US armoured vehicles made their final push into Tikrit's central square, virtually unopposed. They swiftly captured Tikrit's main bridge – still standing despite two gaping holes left by US missiles. On the other side of the river, Kurdish forces advanced through the town's eastern suburbs. In the sky above, three bottle-green Cobra helicopter gunships circled above the shimmering blue Tigris, against the majestic backdrop of Saddam's presidential guest-house. It was a moment of sheer Hollywood, with more than a hint of *Apocalypse Now*. It took a while before anybody noticed that the war in Iraq had just ended. But if Tikrit's residents did not stage the final apocalyptic *Götterdämmerung* that many had expected, nor did they exactly greet coalition forces with flowers.

The mood ranged from indifference to anger. 'The Americans are invaders,' said Abdul Raouf, 28, staring sullenly at the American armoured vehicles that had just turned up in Tikrit's main square. 'We love Saddam Hussein here. He was the only Arab leader who had the guts to stand up to Israel. He hit Israel with 39 rockets. The other Arab countries didn't support him. I don't think Saddam has behaved badly towards his own people. He is a brave man.' Seemingly oblivious to what had just happened, he added: 'Nobody can defeat him.' What would happen now that America had occupied Iraq? 'Iraq will be another Palestine,' he predicted.

The *Guardian*'s Luke Harding, as well as other journalists who covered the fall of Tikrit, noticed that the town was a Saddam Hussein theme park. Although the man himself was nowhere to be seen, Tikrit was the home of a thousand Saddams. Several Saddam portraits were visible in the streets – Saddams in linen suits, military uniforms and wearing Arab headdresses. There was a portrait of a paternal Saddam with his arm round Uday, his elder son, and Saddam liberating Jerusalem from the back of a white horse.

Few other Tikrit residents expressed much enthusiasm for their new American rulers. 'Why shouldn't we like Saddam?' asked Rassan Hassan, 38, as he wheeled his bike past a group of

US marines. 'Saddam didn't hit us with aeroplanes. He didn't kill our children with bombs. He didn't shut down our schools.' He said American planes had bombarded Tikrit for more than a week. There was now no electricity, no water and virtually nothing to eat. Everybody was fed up.

Several hours after the war ended, it became clear that Saddam didn't just have one palace in Tikrit but many. Marines began setting up a new HQ in the grounds of the presidential guesthouse, a vast neo-Babylonian mansion overlooking the river. As troops relaxed in the shade, Lieutenant Greg Starace explained: 'There was minimal resistance. We were here at first light. We came across a few pockets of 3 to 10 guys. They popped their heads up and loosed off. Soon, though, they were running away, or were no longer in a position to run away.' Lt Starace said his 1st Army Reconnaissance Corps had swiftly achieved all its objectives, destroying only a single 'technical' – a pick-up truck with a machine gun – that fired at them from across the river.

Not everybody, though, was unhappy with the arrival of US troops. At 7 a.m. that day a group of marines burst into Tikrit's jail. They rescued its only remaining prisoner, Khalid Jauhr, a 36-year-old Kurd. He said he had been captured four days earlier by the Saddam Fedayeen when he went to visit relatives in a nearby village. The Fedayeen tortured him and shot him in a leg. 'When the Americans turned up outside the door of my cell I was a very happy man,' he said. 'I thought I was going to die.'

Other Tikrit residents admitted that they had never liked Saddam very much but had been too scared to complain. 'We were compelled to love Saddam Hussein,' said Abdul Karim, a 34-year-old Arab, as a group of young men played football in a park across Tikrit's main boulevard, oblivious to the US warplanes flying overhead. 'He has done many bad things over the past 35 years. The worst thing is that we don't have any money. People think that Tikrit is some kind of paradise. In fact everybody is poor.'

Tikrit traditionally holds a lavish celebration to mark the President's official birthday on 28 April 1937. Even Abdul Raouf, a bitter critic of the US's invasion, conceded that the party would be cancelled in 2003. 'I don't think anything will happen,' he said. 'The game is over.'

'The Iraqis gave us no advice or suggestions. They just issued visas at the embassy and told us to go to Iraq. We took no guns with us.'

Unlike the Palestinian camps on the Israeli-occupied West Bank or in Gaza, where constant curfews, Israeli incursions, and deepening unemployment and poverty keep tension and hatred at fever pitch, the camps for Palestinians in Syria are normally calm. The town of close to 150,000 people where Issam lived has a bustling economy, but at least 1,000 Palestinians from Yarmuk volunteered for Iraq in the first two weeks of the war, according to Moutaz Yassin, a medical student with a part-time job in a library. They did not support Saddam Hussein but wanted to help Iraq's people.

The Palestinians in the doomed convoy to Baghdad were outnumbered by Arabs of other nationalities. 'On our bus there were Lebanese, Syrians, Jordanians, three Moroccans or Tunisians – I never found out exactly – and even one guy from the Comoros Islands,' Abdullah said. 'We saw an American Apache helicopter hovering. It was about 6.30 p.m. and there was a sandstorm. We were about to go under a bridge about 30 km west of Ramadi. The bridge was hit and started to buckle on one side. The back of our bus was also hit, then crushed as the bridge fell on it. The second bus managed to swerve and squeeze past us but the third one rammed into the back. About four people died on that bus.' He was not sure whether the pilot's target was the bridge, the buses, or both, but the helicopter made two attacks.

Almost nobody in the Arab world believed the invasion of Iraq had anything to do with weapons of mass destruction, nor did they give much credence to the humanitarian purpose often cited by Tony Blair of freeing the Iraqi people from tyranny. Not that there was much real support for Saddam, either, apart from a degree of admiration for his willingness to defy the United States regardless of cost.

For the vast majority of Arabs, two issues lay behind the war: oil and Israel. Ordinary Arabs interviewed in Damascus at the end of March – Syrians and members of the large exiled Iraqi

15 Arab anger

*Pity the nation whose sages are dumb with years and whose
strong men are yet in the cradle.*

Khalil Gibran, Lebanese poet, 1883–1931

Issam Hajjo did not tell his parents he had decided to join the
war until he was already on his way. Crammed into a bus with
volunteers from half-a-dozen Arab countries, the young Palestinian phoned home with the news that he and two cousins
were about to cross the Syrian border into Iraq. Six days of
silence followed, as his family watched the television news with
even greater intensity than before. Then one of his cousins
phoned: Issam had never reached Baghdad.

Less than five hours after calling his parents to say goodbye,
he had died on the road in a hail of fire from an American helicopter. Thirteen other unarmed men in the convoy of three buses
were killed, but the cousin escaped with minor wounds to his
head and ribs.

At the family's home in Yarmuk Palestinian refugee camp,
Syria, Issam's mother, sat with women friends and relatives in
a small upstairs room, beside herself with grief at the loss of her
first-born son. She wailed in desperation, her voice rising and
falling in time with recitations from the Koran that sounded from
a loudspeaker. Her son's body had not been brought home, adding to the family's sense of desolation. He was 23, unmarried,
and had just finished 30 months of compulsory service in the
Syrian army.

When Hajjo left for Iraq, he had little idea what he would be
asked to do, according to his cousin, Mohammed Abdullah.
They were not planning suicide bombing, or even necessarily to
carry arms to defend Iraq. 'We wanted to work in hospitals, or as
human shields, or as fighters, whatever was needed,' he said.

community – all agreed on the importance of oil. While the Palestinian intifada was resistance to old-fashioned colonialism, with its seizure and settlement of other people's land, they saw Iraqi resistance to the US-led invasion as a popular defence against a more modern phenomenon. Washington did not need to settle Iraqi land, but it did want military bases and control of its oil.

Some suggested a second motive: Washington's desire to strengthen Israel. One theory was that American hawks wanted to break Iraq into several statelets and then do the same with Saudi Arabia, thus confirming the Zionist state as the region's superpower. Others cited comments about Iran and Syria by Donald Rumsfeld as proof that war on Iraq was designed to frighten its neighbours, who just happened to be the leading radicals in the anti-Zionist camp.

Many already defined the war as an historic turning point that might have as profound an effect on the Arab psyche as 11 September had on Americans. Arabs had long been accustomed to seeing Israeli tanks running rampant. Now the puppetmaster, arrogant and unashamed, had sent his helicopter gunships and armoured vehicles to Arab soil.

Historically, the US had supported numerous coups in the Middle East and had used crises, such as the Iraqi invasion of Kuwait in 1990, to gain temporary bases and make them permanent. In Lebanon it once shelled an Arab capital and landed several hundred marines. But never before had it sent a vast army to change an Arab government. Even in Latin America, in two centuries of US hegemony, Washington had never dared to mount a full-scale invasion to overthrow a ruler in a major country. Its interventions in the Caribbean and Central America from 1898 to 1990 were against weak opponents in small states. Three years into the new millennium, the enormity of the shift and the impact of the spectacle on Arab television viewers could not be overestimated. Was it an image of the past or the future, they asked, a one-off throwback to Vietnam or a taste of things to come?

Blair sensed Arab suspicions about the fate of Iraq's oil when he persuaded President Bush at their Azores summit on the eve of war to produce a 'vision for Iraq' that pledged to protect the country's natural resources (they shrank from using the O-word) as a 'national asset of and for the Iraqi people'. But the small print was rather different, as could be expected from an administration run by oilmen. Leaks from the 'Future of Iraq' office in the State Department's showed that Washington was already planning to privatise the Iraqi economy and particularly the state-owned national oil company.

If Downing Street had a better grasp than Washington of the need not to appear to be occupying Iraq, it was equally misinformed about Iraqis' views of invasion. Both western governments confused hatred of Saddam with support for war. People living under Saddam's rule never gave opinions readily, but British and American officials might have done a better job of talking to Iraqis living in Jordan and Syria who were in close touch with their families in Iraq. Once the war got under way it was only natural to blame US and British troops for the chaos. Yet, even before the first bomb fell, most Iraqis were against 'liberation' by force.

Just before the bombing started, a *Guardian* journalist interviewed 20 Iraqis in Amman individually or in groups of two or three friends for on average an hour each. They included Sunni and Shia, property owners, artists, factory workers and several unemployed. Most were fierce critics of the Iraqi President, but on the overriding issue of whether Bush should launch a war, a majority was opposed. Nine were against, 4 were torn and only 7 were in favour. Once war was no longer a theoretical option but a reality affecting every Iraqi at home and abroad, patriotic feelings grew stronger.

Western governments apparently confined their research to people with a narrow vested interest. They financed exiled politicians who wanted a share in US-supplied power, but then talked to them as though they were independent. They listened to businessmen who were hoping to cash in when the US privatised the Iraqi economy. They were fascinated by nostalgic Hashemite monarchists.

Besides being more sensitive than Bush to Arab concerns about Iraqi oil, Blair was also well aware of their fears about the Israeli-Palestinian conflict. In the run-up to war with Iraq, the Arab leaders had repeatedly expressed their belief that the unfolding tragedy in Israel and the occupied territories was a far more immediate threat to regional security than the weapons that Saddam might or might not possess.

Blair's approach was to seek a trade-off: supporting the Americans over Iraq in return for Washington's promise of serious efforts towards Israeli-Palestinian peace once Iraq had been dealt with. This evoked memories from the early 1990s when the ending of war with Iraq was followed promptly, despite earlier denials that the two issues were linked, by the conference in Madrid that marked the start of the Oslo peace process. In the 1991 war, however, George Bush Sr had needed Arab support to fight Iraq; this time, his son was going to war largely without it. In 2003 also, the changed political climate, partly as a result of the 11 September attacks, had produced a US administration far less inclined towards patient negotiations and compromise.

Blair's hopes were pinned almost entirely on the 'road map' to peace which the United States, the European Union, the United Nations and Russia, known collectively as 'the quartet', had been working on for some months. Although several drafts of the document had been leaked, by the time war with Iraq broke out it had still not been formally published. Israel had proposed more than 100 amendments and it was unclear whether the map had yet reached its final form. In its leaked form, the 2,500-word document set out what it described as 'a performance-based and goal-driven road map, with clear phases aiming at progress under the auspices of the quartet'. The destination, it said, 'is a final and comprehensive settlement of the Israel-Palestinian conflict by 2005'.

Crucially, this would require from the Palestinian leadership, at the outset of phase one, 'an unequivocal statement reiterating Israel's right to exist in peace and security and calling for an immediate and unconditional ceasefire to end armed activity and all acts of violence against Israelis anywhere'. At the same time, Israel would have to issue an 'unequivocal statement affirming its commitment to the two-state vision of an independent, viable, sovereign Palestinian state living in peace and security alongside Israel'. Although there was much in the later stages of the plan that might lead to delay or derailment, to secure acceptance of a viable Palestinian state from the government of Ariel Sharon – if it occurred – could be seen as a significant step forward.

On the last Friday before war broke out, Blair summoned a press conference at Downing Street. Bush, he announced, had agreed that the road map would be 'published as soon as the Palestinian Prime Minister [Abu Mazen] takes office'. The move was clearly aimed at strengthening Blair's hand in the face of domestic opposition to the war and also at heading off complaints of double standards, particularly from the Arab world, in relation to Iraq and the Israeli-Palestinian conflict. 'The most important thing that we can do is to show even-handedness towards the Middle East,' Blair continued. 'We are right to focus on Saddam Hussein and his weapons of mass destruction, but we must put equal focus on the plight of the people whose lives are being devastated by lack of progress in the Middle East peace process.'

Downing Street had made a point of inviting Arab journalists to the press conference and they, rather than the British parliamentary press corps, were allowed to ask the first questions. But the Arabs were unimpressed. 'For Palestinians I think this comes too little too late . . . before an unpopular and imminent war,' the first questioner said. 'Why should anyone read the situation any differently now that there is a commitment from the international community?' 'Why the road map?' asked another. 'What happened to Prince Abdullah's peace initiative that was blessed by everybody?' And another: 'Surely you would expect a few people in the Middle East to be a little bit sceptical about the very timing of this initiative in relation to the Iraq issue?'

For Bush, putting the peace plan back on the agenda at that juncture amounted to little more than an attempt to help out his friend and loyal supporter on the other side of the Atlantic, and he did so reluctantly. It appeared to reverse his previous insistence that the Israeli-Palestinian issue must wait – at least until after the coming war.

A few minutes before Blair's announcement in Downing Street, Bush made a similar statement from the Rose Garden of the White House. But it contained some subtle differences. Unlike Blair, Bush noticeably did not use the word 'publish'. He simply said the road map would be 'given to the Palestinians and the Israelis'. He also indicated that instead of pushing the plan forward to implementation in its existing form, it would be left on the table for further discussion. 'Once this road map is delivered, we will expect and welcome contributions from Israel and the Palestinians to this document that will advance true peace,' Bush said. 'We will urge them to discuss the road map with one another.' A further little phrase, slipped into the statement, pushed the release of the document beyond the moment when a Palestinian Prime Minister took office, as envisaged by Blair. Instead, the US President tied it, much more vaguely, to the confirmation in office of a Palestinian Prime Minister 'in a position of real authority'.

Israel, meanwhile, was uneasy about linkage of the Iraqi and Palestinian issues but willing to let it happen for the time being as a face-saver for Blair, and for the Spanish Prime Minister, Jose Maria Aznar, who had been America's only other ally at the Azores summit. Writing in the liberal Israeli daily, *Ha'aretz*, the paper's diplomatic expert, Aluf Benn, explained: 'The more public opinion in their countries opposes the war in Iraq, the more Blair and Aznar grasp the Palestinian issue as a political life saver . . . They have to prove to their constituents in Europe that they care about ending the Israeli occupation of the territories, to win legitimacy for their occupation of Iraq.'

But while President Bush was publicly delivering the road map as a sop to his European allies, he was privately telling a different story to Sharon. According to *Ha'aretz*:

> The White House hurried to console Israel and was helped by the Prime Minister's office in Jerusalem, which will always avoid any show of confrontation with Washington and prefers to emphasise the co-ordination and agreement. Sharon's aides, who visited the US last week, came back convinced that it will be a long time before the political [peace] process is renewed.

Two days after the 'road map' announcements, an Israeli army bulldozer was busy destroying Palestinian homes in the Rafah refugee camp, Gaza. It is a form of collective punishment (regarded by many as illegal) that has gone on for years, and the demolished houses usually belong to the relatives of Palestinians accused by Israel of terrorism. Rachel Corrie, a 23-year-old American peace activist, who was protesting at the destruction, got in the way and was crushed to death.

'She was standing on top of a pile of earth,' said one of the activists, Richard Purssell, who was a few feet from her. 'The driver cannot have failed to see her. As the blade pushed the pile, the earth rose up. Rachel slid down the pile. It looks as if she got her foot caught. The driver didn't slow down; he just ran over her. Then he reversed the bulldozer back over her again.'

Other witnesses said the bulldozer had approached from several metres away and that Rachel, who was wearing a brightly coloured jacket, was waving and they were shouting at the driver to stop but he ignored them. She was one of 8 foreign volunteers, 4 from the US and 4 from Britain, with the International Solidarity Movement, who were seeking to block house demolitions.

The Israeli military described her death as a 'very regrettable accident'. An army spokesperson said: 'We are dealing with a group of protesters who are acting very irresponsibly, putting everyone in danger – the Palestinians, themselves and our forces – by intentionally placing themselves in a combat zone.' A military official said there was limited visibility, especially on the ground immediately in front of the vehicle, from the windows of the armoured bulldozers used by the army.

Four days later, a memorial service at the spot where Corrie died was broken up by Israeli forces. Joe Smith, a young activist from Kansas City, said about 100 people were gathered when the first armoured personnel carrier appeared. 'They started firing tear gas and blowing smoke, then they fired sound grenades. After a while it got hectic so we sat down. Then the tank came over and shot in the air,' he said. 'It scared a lot of Palestinians, especially the shooting made a lot of them run and the tear gas freaked people out. But most of us stayed.'

Tensions rose further when a convoy of vehicles passed the area – including the bulldozer that had killed Corrie. 'I don't think it was deliberate but it was pretty insensitive,' Joe Smith said. 'I think they had been destroying some buildings elsewhere and had to pass by to get back to their base.'

A subsequent Israeli inquiry cleared the military of blame but accused Corrie and other protesters of 'illegal, irresponsible and dangerous' behaviour. It said she had not been run over by the bulldozer but 'was struck by a hard object, most probably a slab of concrete, which moved or slid down while the mound of earth which she was standing behind was moved'. The Israeli army did, however, say it would change its procedures to prevent 'further accidents'.

Rachel Corrie was the first American protester to be killed in the occupied territories since the outbreak of the Palestinian uprising in September 2000. In more innocent times her death might have aroused anger in Washington, but with all eyes turned towards Iraq it was easily overlooked.

At 7.30 p.m. on 19 March, Colin Powell phoned Sharon to tell him that an attack on Baghdad was about to begin. The White House had promised the Israelis prior notice as one of several means of keeping them out of the war. The Israeli airforce went on immediate alert and fighter jets began patrolling above the main cities. Batteries of US-manned Patriot missiles were also readied, many around Tel Aviv, the target of most of the 39 Iraqi Scuds that hit Israel during the 1991 Gulf War. This time no Scuds hit Israel, although in the ensuing days at least 5 people died of suffocation from sealing their rooms against chemical or biological attacks.

The main fear on the Palestinian side was that Sharon would use the war as cover to push forward his own objectives in the occupied territories – objectives that would have been too controversial to pursue in normal times.

On the day that Rachel Corrie died, Sharon took his cabinet on a secret tour of 'the fence', a 230-mile wall, 20ft high and topped with barbed wire, that Israel had begun constructing to separate Palestinians from Israelis. When complete, it would extend the length of the West Bank, creeping deep inside Palestinian territory for long stretches. It would almost surround at least one, and probably two, cities. During the tour, Sharon informed his cabinet of plans for another stretch, running the length of the Jordan valley, which would totally encircle the West Bank Palestinians, in effect imprisoning them.

'This just confirms that the wall is not to separate the West Bank from Israelis, it's to separate Palestinians into their reservation,' said Michael Tarazi of the PLO's negotiations support unit. 'It means that the Israelis will take control of our border with Jordan and what remains of the best agricultural land we have. The wall near the green line has already taken a lot of our best land and now they are going to do the same with what remains in the Jordan valley.'

In the first week of April, after more than two years of legal and political wrangling, Sharon's office approved an unprecedented plan for Jewish settlers to move into a Palestinian district of Jerusalem. Almost immediately, Jewish families began moving into the new flats in the Ma'aleh Ha'zeitim settlement, beside the densely populated Arab district of Ras al-Amoud. They included a millionaire, Irving Moskowitz, and his son-in-law Ariel King, a far-right political activist.

It was the first time a Jewish settlement had been built in a Palestinian area of Jerusalem since Israel seized control of the entire city in 1967, and seemed designed to test the resolve of the US and Britain over the 'road map'. Bush's National Security Adviser, Condoleezza Rice, telephoned Sharon's office to warn that letting Jews move into the settlement could raise tension during the war on Iraq and further undermine the prospect of a political settlement, but to no avail.

Israel also irritated the US by revealing private assurances by Rice that the White House had approved a $10 bn package of loan guarantees and military aid before it was formally announced in Washington. The assurances, given only hours before Bush ordered the first attack on Iraq, were part of Washington's attempts to persuade Israel to stay out of the conflict, but their disclosure heightened Arab perceptions of American double standards.

Meanwhile, Sharon stepped up his battle with Blair for Bush's ear. The Israelis were particularly unnerved at the prospect of Blair stiffening American demands over illegal Jewish settlements and forcing the pace on the creation of an independent Palestinian state far beyond the emasculated dependency that Sharon had in mind. Among the amendments Israel had proposed to the road map was the dropping of any commitment to an 'independent' Palestinian state in favour of one with only some 'attributes of sovereignty'.

The British Ambassador, Sherard Cowper-Coles, summoned to the Foreign Ministry, received a protest at what Israel described as Blair's 'worrying and outrageous' comments linking the war in Iraq to a settlement of the Palestinian conflict, and at Jack Straw's accusations of western double standards over the enforcement of UN resolutions on Israel. Blair had remarked that the Israeli-Palestinian conflict was a primary cause of the rift between the Islamic world and the West, and that resolving it would be a British and American priority once the Iraq war was over. Straw, the Foreign Secretary, had said that there was 'real concern that the West has been guilty of double standards – on the one hand saying the United Nations Security Council resolutions on Iraq must be implemented, on the other hand sometimes appearing rather quixotic over the implementation of resolutions about Israel and Palestine'.

As Saddam's regime began to collapse, however, Sharon's attitude appeared to change. Possibly believing that Israel could now negotiate from a position of supreme strength, he conceded in an interview with *Ha'aretz* that there would be a Palestinian state 'eventually' – though was still some way off what the road map envisaged. He also talked of giving up some of the Jewish settlements. 'I know that we will have to part with some of these places,' he said. 'There will be a parting from places that are connected to the whole course of our history. As a Jew, this agonises me. I feel that the rational necessity to reach a settlement is overcoming my feelings.'

If Ariel Sharon had clear objectives to be achieved from a US-led war with Iraq, the same could not be said of Arab leaders. Ever since war became a real prospect they had been fearful of the damage it might wreak in the region. Amr Moussa, Secretary General of the Arab League, warned that it could 'open the gates of hell', but there was little that any of the Arabs could do beyond urging Saddam to comply as fully as possible with UN weapons inspections.

The main exceptions to the consensus in the Arab world were Qatar and Kuwait. Kuwaitis, mindful of their terrible experiences in 1990 when Iraq invaded, still feared their northern neighbour and remained totally dependent on American protection. But even in Kuwait there was some ambivalence about the wisdom of a war to overthrow Saddam. Kuwait, too, had Islamic militants who opposed the American presence. Their activities were usually played down, though in the run-up to the war several attacks occurred, directed at the US military and others associated with it.

Qatar, home of the outspoken satellite TV station, Al-Jazeera, had an outward appearance of radicalism but, with enormous oil and gas wealth and only a tiny population, it also needed a powerful protector. Since the emir, Sheikh Hamad bin Khalifa al-Thani, seized power from his father in a bloodless coup in 1995, he had gradually but steadily modernised the country. Women in Qatar have been allowed to drive cars and stand in municipal elections, while the rules on alcohol were also quietly relaxed. The bold new buildings and tree-lined avenues in Doha gave the capital a distinctly western appearance.

Islamic militants, meanwhile, had found it difficult to establish a foothold. Observers attributed this partly to the close-knit social structure, in which most Qataris belonged to one of half-a-dozen huge families, and to the resilience of the regime, which, unlike the Saudi royals, had no need to curry political support from the clergy. The average Qatari also had very little to feel militant about. While the money from oil and gas continued to roll in, the government provided extraordinarily generous welfare benefits, which extended even to paying for citizens' local phone calls.

The emir's strategy, according to those close to him, was based partly on his observation of the growing problems in Saudi Arabia, where he believed the royal family had left reform far too late. Qatar's readiness to support the Americans provoked some local debate, but the government balanced its stance with sympathy for Iraq. Just a year before the war it signed a trade agreement with Baghdad that was seen at the time as weakening sanctions. Some Qataris appeared comfortable with their country's position because, while helping the Americans, they argued that Qatar was not playing a front-line role in attacking Iraq.

As the situation deteriorated, the annual Arab summit, scheduled for the end of March, was hastily brought forward to the beginning of the month. It was perhaps a measure of the dire state of Arab politics on the eve of war that the most newsworthy part of the meeting turned out to be a public spat between the Libyan leader, Colonel Muammar Gadafy, and Crown Prince Abdullah of Saudi Arabia. Col Gadafy accused the Saudis of forming 'an alliance with the devil' (the United States) and the prince retorted by calling Col Gadafy 'an agent of colonisers'.

Predictably, the summit declared its 'complete rejection of an attack on Iraq . . . and the need to resolve the Iraqi crisis by peaceful means'. It also called on Arab states to refrain from 'participating in any military action that targets the security, safety and unity of Iraq or any other Arab country' – which Syria interpreted to mean that Kuwait and Qatar should not provide facilities for the Americans, though both of them ignored it. A call by Sheikh Zaid bin Sultan al-Nahayan, President of the United Arab Emirates, for the Iraqi leadership to step down and go into exile – which many Arab politicians privately regarded as the best way to avert war – was not even debated.

The impotence of the leaders was all too apparent to the Arab public. One of the placards at a demonstration in Cairo shortly before the war carried the words: 'Vive la France! Arab leaders go to hell!' Despite that, fears of immediate turmoil on the streets of Arab capitals did not materialise, partly because of the firm measures to control them, especially in Egypt.

On the first day of the invasion, thousands of protesters collected in Tahrir Square, in Cairo. 'It's like Hyde Park,' was a common refrain, expressed in exhilarated tones. The anti-riot police initially stayed their hand. Demonstrators peacefully occupied the square until the evening, chanting slogans, making speeches, and staging street theatre. But next day the beatings began, and continued. The government's message was loud and clear: 'You've had your one day. No more.'

Nevertheless, there was a mood of quiet satisfaction when, in the early stages of the war, the invasion forces appeared bogged down as they 'secured' and re-secured Umm Qasr, or whenever the Iraqis put up more resistance than expected against what, after all, was the most powerful and deadly military machine in history. 'Where is this shock and awe?' Egyptians would ask one another in the cafés where they gathered to watch Al-Jazeera and other satellite channels. Perhaps the most enthusiastically greeted piece of news was the shooting down of an American attack helicopter south of Baghdad – though few were under any illusion that Iraq could win the war.

For some, this invited comparisons with the great Arab humiliation of 1967 when, in just six days, Israeli forces overpowered the combined armies of Egypt, Jordan and Syria. But analogies with 1967 were wrong, according to Hani Shukrallah. 'In 1967 the expectations were enormous,' he said. 'We never imagined defeat, let alone a battle that was finished in six days with no resistance. This time, the surprise was the level of Iraqi resistance.'

The failure of the Arabs, collectively or through their governments, to resist the invasion in any meaningful way brought calls for individual or guerrilla action. Samir Ragab, editor of *Al Gomhuria*, an Egyptian daily, lamented that Baghdad's resistance was crumbling before the world's only superpower and called for guerrilla war against the invaders. 'The only solution lies in the armed struggle and martyrdom bombers until the aggressors are compelled to withdraw in disgrace,' he wrote in a column on 8 April. By that stage, Iraq was already boasting that 4,000 Arabs had arrived in the country ready to 'martyr' themselves.

A student volunteer from Cairo named Amer told Reuters: 'This is a war for oil and Zionism. We want to help Iraqis, not Saddam. I know I might die. I don't want to kill people but I will if I have to.' The religious-militant Palestinian group, Islamic Jihad, also announced that it had sent a first wave of suicide bombers to Baghdad 'to fulfil the holy duty of defending Arab and Muslim land'. Abu Imad al-Rifai, Islamic Jihad's Lebanon representative, said the would-be bombers had not come from the Palestinian territories but from several countries. He declined to say how many there were, but he added that more were on the way.

Whatever the truth of these claims, there was ample evidence during March that at least some people were volunteering. The Iraqi Embassy in Algeria said over 100 people – fathers as well as young women – had offered to go into battle against the US and British troops. In Lebanon, an Iraqi Embassy source claimed that more than 20 volunteers had left for Iraq, and hundreds more had applied for visas. Abd al-Aziz al-Qassem, an outspoken Saudi cleric, said he expected Saudi nationals to head for Iraq, too. 'I feel a great eagerness among young people to go to help Iraq because of anger at America when people see pictures of victims and destruction,' he said. In anticipation of this, the Saudi authorities reportedly declared some towns near the border with Iraq out of bounds.

The Egyptian President, Hosni Mubarak, was one Arab leader who constantly warned that the invasion of Iraq could have a radicalising effect throughout the region. 'When it is over, if it is over, this war will have horrible consequences,' he told his soldiers in the city of Suez. 'Instead of having one [Osama] bin Laden, we will have a hundred.'

Bin Laden himself, if still alive, chose to keep a surprisingly low profile throughout the war, though one audiotape purporting to carry his voice did surface early in April. 'Do not be afraid of their tanks and armoured personnel carriers. These are artificial things,' the voice said. 'If you start suicide attacks you will see the fear of Americans all over the world.'

By the time Saddam's regime collapsed, though, the foreign resistance fighters had little to show for their efforts. Several explosions during the war were attributed to suicide bombers, though doubt has since been cast on that. On the day that American forces swept into Baghdad, a small group of volunteers was seen near the Palestine Hotel, pleading with taxi drivers to take them back to Syria.

In Kuwait, an American army sergeant – a convert to Islam who had changed his name to Asan Akbar – was arrested for allegedly throwing grenades into tents at a camp, killing one person and injuring at least 12. It was tempting to presume a religious motivation, but press reports in the US portrayed him as a social misfit, and an army spokesman said he had 'what some might call an attitude problem'. Later, at another military base in Kuwait, an Egyptian migrant worker drove a truck into a group of American soldiers, injuring several.

To Islamic militants, however, the war in Iraq is only just beginning. The parallel they draw is with the Soviet invasion of Afghanistan in the 1980s, which not only led to the collapse of a superpower but gave birth to al-Qaida. Whether history repeats itself in Iraq may depend on how long the American and British forces stay, and whether, over time, they come to be perceived as liberators or as occupiers. Equally, it is too early to know if the opposing vision will be proven right: of an Iraqi people freed from tyranny who eagerly embrace democracy and thereby become a catalyst that will change the Middle East for the better.

16 War games

We have the power to knock any society out of the 20th century.
Robert McNamara, US Secretary of Defence, 1961-68

It probably was not at the front of their minds, but when US and British forces crashed across the Kuwaiti border into Iraq as darkness fell on 20 March, they were embarking not just on a controversial war to disarm Saddam, topple his regime and deliver liberty to a grateful population. This mission was much more important than all that: they were the guinea pigs in an experiment orchestrated by the US Defence Secretary, Donald Rumsfeld, and the civilian leadership of the Pentagon to test a new theory of hi-tech 21st-century warfare informed largely by the writings of a legendary Chinese tactician around 2,500 years ago.

'If I am able to determine the enemy's dispositions while, at the same time, I conceal my own, then I can concentrate my forces and his must be divided,' Sun Tzu advised. 'And if I concentrate while he divides, I can use my entire strength to attack a fraction of his. If I am able to use many to strike few, those I deal with will fall into hopeless straits.' The Rumsfeld word for it was 'transformation'.

If one person won the war it was Rumsfeld. He is now more Sun King than Sun Tzu in Washington circles. With Iraq and Afghanistan under his belt, he has proved that the American military machine could be changed from fighting states that harbour communism to fighting states that could threaten terrorism. In recent American history he resembles perhaps the most memorable Defence Secretary to date: John F. Kennedy's Robert McNamara, who led America into the quagmire of Vietnam. Like McNamara, Rumsfeld mesmerised the world with American power. Like McNamara, he was a former business executive who brought Harvard Business School to the Pentagon. But unlike McNamara, Rumsfeld won.

True, this confrontation was always going to be a mismatch. The Iraq forces looked formidable in terms of numbers: an estimated 389,000 troops, 2,600 tanks and a small air force of about 300 planes. But the reality was that its equipment was antiquated and its troops poorly trained. Anthony Cordesmann, of the Centre of Strategic and International Studies in Washington, told the *Guardian* that the equipment was 'at best mid-1980s technology and combat-worn, and much of it is obsolescent'. Baghdad could muster bazookas, Kalashnikovs, a few hundred mobile rocket launchers, a couple of thousand tanks bereft of spare parts and a fleet of fighter-jets that could barely take off, let alone engage in a dogfight with the Americans.

The 'coalition of the willing', meanwhile, could summon up 120,000 American combat troops, 25,000 British ones and 2,000 Australian soldiers. At its disposal were B-52s, Stealth bombers, F16s, Tornados, 300 attack helicopters, 920 tanks and 750 armoured vehicles. In the Gulf, where the options for an adversary to use terrorism are limited, the battle fleet faced no serious military opposition. On the waves were 6 large battle groups – 5 from America and 1, HMS *Ark Royal*, from Britain. Three US aircraft carriers alone can fire at 2,100 targets a day and the fleet offered 1,500 cruise missile platforms.

But for Rumsfeld and his modernising allies in the Pentagon, this conflict was not about old-fashioned force of strength. It was about doing away with the traditional American way of grinding out a victory by pulverising the enemy from the air, then hitting them with division after lumbering division of heavy armour. The battle plan for Gulf War II would rely on a combination of smaller, more agile ground forces, surgical air power and special forces taking out targets deep behind enemy lines.

Rumsfeld was sending into battle America's overwhelming edge in technology, employing real-time digital communications, surveillance systems and precision targeting that more than compensated for lack of troops on the ground. The influence of this theory on Operation Plan 1003, the blueprint for the invasion of Iraq, was obvious. Although Rumsfeld had relented to the demands of General Tommy Franks, head of Central Command, for 250,000 combat and support troops, he made sure that they were deployed in phases rather than all at the same time.

The Secretary of Defence was also selective about the types of troops. Against the wishes of Franks and the other generals at the Pentagon, he was instrumental in holding up the deployment orders of about 36,000 troops in the Texas-based 1st Cavalry Division and the German-based 1st Armoured Division to ensure they missed the fighting. Such heavy units simply did not fit in with the new 21st-century warfare doctrine of agility and flexibility. Retired Vice-Admiral Arthur Cebrowski, a key adviser on the transformation project, neatly summed up the Rumsfeld vision of the first digital war: 'There's a substitution of information for mass.'

As war loomed closer, some well-sourced stories began to appear in the American media about space-age weapons that the Pentagon was planning to unleash on the hapless Iraqi forces. The most impressive among these was indeed the stuff of science fiction: a lightning surge of microwave power equivalent to the entire daily output of the Hoover Dam, which would fry enemy weapons and communications systems but leave the personnel operating them unharmed.

The off-the-record briefings from senior Pentagon brass left no doubt that the time had come to unveil in combat the so-called high-powered microwave weapon – or e-bomb. Every modern weapon system, air defence radar, command and control bunker and chemical weapons facility would be vulnerable, a declassified research paper by the former director of the e-bomb programme stated. 'In recent years, the modern battlefield has become a target-rich environment for high-power microwave weapons,' Colonel Eileen Walling wrote. 'Except for the standard rifle, knife, gun or grenade, virtually all military equipment contains some electronics.'

The US also wanted the world – and Saddam in particular – to know about its good old-fashioned brute force. In mid-March, as the military build-up in the Gulf reached its peak, the Pentagon released images of a test drop of its terrifying new 21,000 lb massive ordnance air blast bomb – Moab – the largest non-nuclear weapon in the world. The size of a large family saloon, the Moab was so big it had to be dropped out of a cargo plane by parachute. Its official military use: to penetrate deeply buried hardened bunkers and detonate with such a huge blast that any biochemical weapons agents would be vaporised instantly. Its unofficial use: to terrify Iraqi soldiers into believing they were going to be obliterated.

In the end, neither of these weapons was actually used. Their role was to enhance the propaganda element in the build-up to 'shock and awe': to persuade Saddam's forces to surrender before a shot had been fired. That may explain why the Pentagon let it be known that a Moab had been deployed as its forces were closing in on Saddam's home town of Tikrit. The expected resistance from the Republican Guard simply melted away.

When it came to the actual fighting, the backbone of the coalition military success was a technology developed after the last Gulf War, debuted in Kosovo and deployed properly for the first time in Afghanistan – the satellite-guided precision bomb. During Operation Desert Storm in 1991, only 10 per cent of the munitions dropped by allied aircraft were 'smart' weapons that could be steered to their target. These weapons relied on laser guidance, which, as allied commanders quickly discovered, could not operate in bad weather conditions because the lasers were unable to penetrate the cloud cover. They also struggled with battlefield smoke. So, despite the hyperbole of US and British commanders during their post-bombing raid briefings, many of these weapons missed their target and caused high civilian casualties.

The solution to this problem was a $20,000 add-on tail-kit that converted dumb bombs into precision weapons. Dubbed the JDAM – short for joint direct attack munition – the kit contained a navigation system and a tiny receiver that picked up signals from global position system (GPS) satellites. These signals guided the bomb to the co-ordinates programmed in before launch. Although the weapons did not have the pinpoint accuracy of the lasers – they were accurate to within a few feet rather than a few inches – the satellite signals were impervious to bad weather, smoke or sandstorms, allowing surgical bombing missions round the clock and in all weather conditions.

In Afghanistan, JDAMs accounted for 25 per cent of the 17,000 pieces of ordnance dropped. In Iraq, they were used in 80 per cent of bombing sorties, with US air force and navy aircraft dropping 5,000 – mainly 1,000 lb or 2,000 lb bombs – in the first 11 days of the conflict alone. The JDAM and Tomahawk cruise missiles had a crucial political role in persuading a sceptical Arab world and doubters back home that coalition forces were meeting their promise of surgical strikes against military and regime targets only. It became a daily ritual of the US Central Command briefing in Qatar for Brigadier General Vince Brooks, Deputy Director of Operations, to show reporters 'before' and 'after' photographs of precision bombing missions, showing single buildings being flattened while those to either side were untouched.

The Iraqis made a token attempt to defend themselves by using GPS jamming equipment to throw the bombs off course. But, according to US Central Command, the cheap Russian jamming gear proved ineffective, and coalition aircraft were able to locate and destroy at least six jamming vehicles. One was destroyed using a satellite-guided bomb, clearly unaffected by the jamming attempts.

The weapons are not foolproof, however. They have to rely on humans programming in the correct co-ordinates. It was a human getting the co-ordinates wrong that led to the bombing of the Chinese Embassy in Belgrade during the Kosovo war. This type of error may explain one or both of the missiles that hit two Baghdad markets, killing at least 66 civilians in the space of 2 days, although coalition commanders, backed by their political masters in Washington and London, maintained that it was just as likely that the carnage was caused by malfunctioning Iraqi missiles falling back to earth. As in the Afghanistan war, there were credible reports that US special forces, backed by extra-ordinary logistical and stealth-technology support, were oper-ating on the ground in Iraq to pinpoint targets for aerial attacks with smart weapons.

The use of sophisticated bombing technology was not confined to the Americans. The RAF went to war equipped with a series of new weapons systems in an attempt to recover its reputation after the embarrassment of its poor bombing performance in Kosovo, where poor weather led to 60% of bombs either missing their target or not being dropped because they could not be guided to their target.

This time round, British Tornado GR4s were dropping the new Enhanced Paveway bomb, introduced after Kosovo. Essentially, the weapon – which carries either a 1,000lb general purpose or a 2,000lb bunker-busting warhead – is a laser-guided precision bomb that has been turned into an all-weather munition with the addition of a satellite guidance kit. This meant RAF crews were able to continue flying precision bombing sorties unaffected by the sandstorms that raged across Iraq during the first week of the war, or the thick black smoke from burning oil trenches that shrouded Baghdad. At the height of the bombing, Tornado GR4 crews were flying 100 sorties a day using Enhanced Paveways to hit leadership targets, armoured positions and command and control sites in Baghdad, as well as attacking Iraqi tanks and artillery in the Faw peninsula in the south.

Meanwhile, RAF Harrier GR7s were, for the first time, firing Maverick anti-armour missiles to provide close air support to ground forces in the south and to destroy suspected Iraqi missile launchers as soon as they were spotted. The Maverick's introduction into RAF service was again a result of Kosovo, when the British found it extremely difficult to hit single targets, such as tanks or artillery, located close to buildings without risking high civilian casualties. The first British Maverick was fired on 21 March when a Harrier pilot destroyed a Scud missile-launcher which had been spotted 200 miles inside Iraq.

On that same night, the RAF scored its biggest PR success: the first combat use of its newest and most sophisticated weapon, the Storm Shadow air-launched cruise missile. Two Tornados launched the precision-guided, ground-hugging stealth weapons against sites in Baghdad as part of the massive 'shock and awe' bombing raid on the capital on the second evening of the war.

The moment was hugely symbolic. Storm Shadow – ironically, an Anglo-French project – had been due to enter service in late 2001, but was pushed back to late 2002, when it was delayed yet again. By the time the war started there were reports that it would be not be ready until October 2003, raising the prospect of yet another British defence white elephant. Instead, Geoff Hoon, the Defence Secretary, and Admiral Sir Michael Boyce, Chief of the Defence Staff, were able to trumpet this British success story to a sceptical public back home.

The PR potential of this opportunity could not have worked out better for the RAF had it been choreographed. The Tornados that launched the Storm Shadows came from 617 Squadron – better known as the Dambusters – and the mission coincided exactly with the 60th anniversary of the formation of the RAF's most famous bomber squadron. To underline the point, Wing Commander Dave Robertson, 617's commanding officer and the navigator of the lead Tornado on the sortie, told reporters at the Ali al-Salem airbase in northern Kuwait that he had dedicated the mission to the memory of the 53 members of the original crews who had died attacking the Eder and Mohne dams with bouncing bombs – another top-secret, hi-tech weapon – in May 1943.

At least 20 Storm Shadows, which cost about £750,000 each and which can be fired from up to 170 miles from their 'high-value, heavily defended' targets, were used during the campaign, and every one of them hit what they were meant to hit, according to the RAF. Major General Peter Wall, British Chief of Staff in the

Gulf, described the weapon as an 'outstanding success' that had been 'both extremely accurate and exceptionally potent'. The successful introduction of the Enhanced Paveway, the Maverick and the Storm Shadow gave the RAF a much-needed excuse to swagger after the ignominy of the Kosovo campaign. During a briefing in London, Air Chief Marshal Sir Peter Squire, Chief of the Air Staff, proudly announced: 'The combination of those three smart precision systems have given the Royal Air Force a step increase in our offensive capability and undoubtedly gives us a range of weapons which fully matches, frankly, the American range of smart munitions.'

The full impact of new technology on the war went much deeper than whizz-bang bullets and bombs. Away from the television-friendly action of precision strikes, Stealth bombers and gun camera footage, the Rumsfeld transformation doctrine required a more subtle but much more effective harnessing of America's cutting-edge technology that revolutionised the way its forces prosecuted the campaign. The aim was to follow another piece of Master Tzu's advice: 'Know the enemy and know yourself. In 100 battles you will never know peril.'

In military jargon, the approach was called network-centric warfare: the use of digital communications technology to provide each component of the military machine – command centres, special forces, surveillance planes, unmanned drones, strike aircraft or infantry units – with up-to-the-minute information on what is happening on the battlefield. This situation awareness gave the coalition forces the flexibility to respond swiftly and deal decisively with new developments, be it the sudden movement of Iraqi tanks out of Basra or the spotting of a ballistic missile launcher in the western desert.

The refusal of Turkey to allow US forces to invade northern Iraq from its territory meant that a key component of America's digital force was absent from the battlefield. The 4th Infantry – nicknamed the digital brigade – is the most technologically advanced ground force in the world. Its M1A2 Abrams tanks and Bradley fighting vehicles are equipped with a tactical internet system, known as FBCB2, that provides each vehicle commander with a scrolling map displaying up-to-the-second information on their location in relation to friendly units as well as the enemy.

While the 4th's multibillion-dollar armour was floating in containers in the Mediterranean waiting for a decision from Turkey, the technological campaign was well under way. During the last Gulf War, it could take anything up to 24 hours for data from military sensors – satellites and surveillance planes – to be downloaded and analysed and the target information sent to the shooters: strike aircraft, special forces or infantry. In practice, that often meant that the targets had long since moved on, especially the 'shoot-and-scoot' mobile missile launchers, which Saddam used to fire Scuds at Israel and other neighbouring countries. US aircraft failed to achieve a single confirmed kill on an Iraqi missile launcher in 1991.

This conflict was very different. Constantly patrolling the skies above Iraq were Joint Stars (joint surveillance target attack radar system) aircraft, converted Boeing 707s capable of locating targets on the ground, discerning whether they were wheeled or tracked, and tracking them when they moved. The co-ordinates of the target could be instantly sent down a datalink, via communications satellites, to the command centre and into the cockpit of the nearest shooter already in the air searching for targets of opportunity.

Special forces equipped with satellite communications and unmanned drones such as the Predator and Global Hawk were also constantly sending back information on Iraqi movements. As a result, the crucial sensor-to-shooter time was reduced from 24 hours in 1991 to a few minutes. 'Technology has made vast improvements to the way they generate bombing sorties,' said David Isenberg. 'Now they have the capability to reassign new targets after the plane is in the air, right down to the level of what munition should be used. That is a huge order of magnitude improvement in their flexibility.'

The most dramatic demonstration of this capability came on 7 April, when the US received intelligence that Saddam and his two sons had entered a restaurant in the upmarket Baghdad suburb of Mansour for a meeting with senior lieutenants. The intelligence was understood to have come from three sources: an Iraqi informer, a special forces soldier and a radio intercept.

It took about 30 minutes for the intelligence to be checked and the decision made to attack. A US B1B bomber, already in the air on its way to a scheduled series of air strikes, was fed the co-ordinates of the building and diverted to destroy it. Twelve minutes later, at around 3 p.m. Baghdad time, the crew released a package of four bunker-busting bombs, which replaced the restaurant and three neighbouring buildings with a 60 ft crater.

Ben Moores, European military analyst with the defence consultants Frost and Sullivan, said: 'We are living in the age of military revolution. Digitalisation is going to be as fundamental to the way wars are fought as the invention of the tank.' But that same incident provided a sobering illustration of an inherent danger: the lack of time to check that the information is correct. Saddam and his sons, according to British intelligence, had left the building minutes before the bombs struck. They survived, but 9 civilians did not.

While the US and British were keen to focus on precision smart weapons that helped reduce the risk to civilians, they were also using older, cruder and far more controversial weapons in Iraq. There was outrage when it emerged that the coalition had used cluster bombs against Iraqi forces around Baghdad and Basra, where the risk to civilians was highest. These weapons, though legal when used against military targets, have a high failure rate: anything between 2 and 20 per cent of the bomblets in current cluster munitions will not explode, leaving battlefields strewn with lethal ordnance. Yellow in colour and the size of soft-drink cans, they are attractive to children in particular.

Iraqis are painfully aware of the danger these bomblets pose long after a conflict has ended: and cluster munitions dropped during the first Gulf War are still killing civilians 12 years later. Last year alone, 2,400 bomblets were found. Some 1,600 Iraqi civilians have been killed and 2,500 injured since 1991. The

British military is so sensitive about these weapons that army headquarters in Kuwait immediately denied reports when they first appeared about their use in this campaign. The Ministry of Defence was later forced to retract that denial, admitting that RAF Harriers had dropped RBL755 cluster bombs on targets in southern Iraq. The weapons, which scatter 147 bomblets over a wide area, have an estimated 10 per cent failure rate. The MoD also said that British long-range howitzers had fired Israeli-manufactured L20 cluster shells at targets around Basra. The shells contain 49 bomblets and have a 5 per cent failure rate, although they are designed to self-destruct if they fail to detonate.

US B-52 bombers, meanwhile, were dropping new CBU-105 bombs – guided 500 kg cluster munitions – on Republican Guard tanks defending Baghdad, while American artillery units showered scores of cluster bomblets on Iraqi positions to the south of the capital, using the multi-launch rocket system. The US has faced fierce criticism over this weapon because the bomblets in the rockets do not have a self-destruct capability if they miss their target. Coalition commanders attempted to soothe the complaints by insisting that cluster munitions would not be used in areas near civilians. But the chief doctor at the general teaching hospital in Hilla, 60 miles south of Baghdad, said 33 civilians had been killed and 100 injured in a cluster bomb attack.

Humanitarian groups accused the coalition of breaking international law by persisting in the use of the weapons, and called for them to be banned. Richard Lloyd, director of Landmine Action, said: 'Dropping cluster bombs on Iraq contradicts any government claims to minimise civilian casualties. Cluster weapons are prone to missing their targets and killing civilians.' Unicef expressed concern that Iraqi children might mistake the bomblets for the identically coloured yellow food packets being handed out by US forces.

None of this cut any ice with Hoon, who enraged campaigners by suggesting on Radio 4's *Today* programme that the mothers of Iraqi children would one day thank Britain for the use of cluster munitions. He also told MPs that while there was a 'continuing problem' with the failure rate of the bomblets, their use was 'absolutely justified . . . because it is making the battlefield safer for our armed forces'.

Ministers also found themselves having to defend the use of another controversial piece of kit, depleted uranium shells and missiles. Adam Ingram, the Armed Forces Minister, revealed in a written parliamentary reply to the Labour MP Llewellyn Smith that British Challenger 2 tanks in southern Iraq had fired DU shells. 'The post-conflict administrators of Iraq will be responsible for monitoring DU levels in the environment and cordoning off and decontaminating sites of penetrator impacts,' Ingram wrote.

The war also demonstrated that, for all the zeal of the Pentagon hawks, overwhelming hi-tech firepower had its limitations. Five days into the war, US forces began engaging units of the Republican Guard's Medina Division dug in south of Baghdad and charged with defending the route north into the capital. Round-the-clock coalition air strikes targeted Iraqi air defence and command sites around the perimeter of the city, attempting to make the skies safe for attack helicopter missions to soften up the Republican Guard armour before the main ground assault.

Around midnight on Sunday 23 March, 32 AH64 Apache Longbows from the US Army's 11th Attack Helicopter Regiment launched an assault on the Medina Division's second armoured brigade. The Apache is vaunted as the most advanced attack helicopter in the world, capable of locating enemy positions, day or night, and launching its Hellfire missiles up to 8 km from the target. But the mission ended in humiliating failure when the helicopters ran into unexpectedly fierce fire from Iraqi fighters stationed on top of buildings and mostly equipped with nothing more than AK47 rifles and rocket-propelled grenades. The CNN journalist Karl Penhaul, who was embedded with the Apache regiment, said the attack left the Apache crews 'somewhat dazed, somewhat stunned'.

Of the 32 helicopters, his was the only one that made it through the battle unscathed. One was shot down, presenting a massive propaganda coup to the Iraqis, who paraded the captured pilots, Chief Warrant Officers David Williams and Ronald Young, on television. The US was forced to launch a precision missile to destroy the stricken machine before its weapons and other technology could be stripped by the Iraqis. The remainder were all riddled with bullet holes, sustaining up to 20 hits apiece, while one was so badly damaged it had to limp back to base in northern Kuwait on one engine. The incident reignited doubts about the Apaches' effectiveness. They are lightly armoured, they fly low and they fly slowly, making them extremely vulnerable to ground fire.

Such setbacks were not confined to the Apache crews. State-of-the-art command and communications technology helped the US 3rd Infantry, the main coalition advance force, to race north from Kuwait towards their ultimate objective, Baghdad, in just a few days. Some of the 3rd's Abrams tanks and Bradley fighting vehicles were linked to a sophisticated network, known as the tactical internet, which provided unit commanders with constantly updating maps showing real time information not only on their own position but also on those of their fellow units and the enemy. By removing the need for each vehicle to be in visual contact with the others, this allowed them to barrel across the desert with widely dispersed units – a massive improvement on the first Gulf War when allied armour had to move effectively in an unbroken line.

But the ability to move such a large force so rapidly over such a wide area created huge, apparently unforeseen, problems for coalition commanders. Supply lines, longer than in any previous war, were therefore more exposed to opportunistic attack from the flanks and rear by Iraqi forces employing guerrilla tactics. In these skirmishes, as with the Apaches, the coalition's technological advantage all but disappeared as lightly armed Iraqi irregulars mounted persistent sniping attacks before melting into the desert.

Regardless of such setbacks, there is little doubt that Rumsfeld and his allies believe his experiment was a huge success.

Defence contractors, such as Lockheed Martin and Northrup Grumman, are already jostling for position for the expected bonanza of hi-tech military contracts as the Pentagon 'analyses the lessons' of the Iraq campaign.

Dick Cheney, the US Vice-President, summed up the prevailing mood in Washington when he described the conflict as 'one of the most extraordinary military campaigns ever conducted'. In a speech to newspaper editors, he pointed out that it took half the number of ground troops and two-thirds the number of attack planes than in the first Gulf War to accomplish a much more difficult task in half the time. Even Sun Tzu would struggle to argue with statistics like that.

17 Dispatches

Am I to tell these things, or hold my tongue?

William Howard Russell,
Times correspondent during the Crimean War

At the moment when US forces swept into Baghdad and Iraqis began attacking the symbols of Saddam Hussein's rule, Syrian television interrupted its live coverage of the war to bring viewers a programme about Islamic art and architecture. The scenes in Iraq, apparently, were unsuitable for a state-run channel in an authoritarian Arab regime, so the war vanished from sight for five hours at its most crucial point.

In this campaign, like others before it, a media war was being fought alongside the military conflict. Whether it was in Al-Jazeera's pictures of US PoWs – retransmitted by CBS in America to a visibly stunned Donald Rumsfeld – or in the bombastic jingoism of the British tabloids, the truth was an early fatality. According to the western press, Saddam died on more than one occasion, Tariq Aziz defected, Umm Qasr fell and fell and fell again before it was actually taken, while Basra was said to be under British control when it patently was not.

On Arab screens, there was an image of a head of a child, aged about 12, split apart, reportedly in the US-led assault on Basra. Other scenes, too bloody for American and British audiences, came from northern Iraq, where US missiles targeted the Kurdish Islamist Ansar al-Islam organisation. On Arab televisions could be found a rallying call for suicide missions from Osama bin Laden. Arab satellite channels gave the impression that the Iraqi resistance had a chance of whipping the American forces, even when the war was in its final hours.

Probably the best story of the war emerged after the fighting stopped. It came from Abu Dhabi TV, a source of independent, uncontrolled news in the region. While everybody was wondering about Saddam's whereabouts, it ran footage of him in the Azimiyah district of north Baghdad, which the station said had been recorded on April 9, the day Baghdad fell with the toppling of Saddam's statue. The dictator rose from the sunroof of his limo to greet cheering Iraqis with his son Qusay at his side. There were images of a pot-bellied, olive-uniformed Saddam, along with a slurred, rambling call to arms. It was a great story. The subtext was that by evading a relentless manhunt and taunting his pursuers with occasional recorded musings, Saddam, like Osama bin Laden, has maintained a mythic status among Arab militants. Saddam would live on after his regime fell – an uncomfortable message to the coalition.

This was partly about different viewpoints, but it was also about ratings. In a global world, local sells. By western standards, at least, Al-Jazeera's coverage seemed unnecessarily intrusive as it lingered over the dead and maimed, whether Iraqi or American. What 250 million Arabs could digest would induce violent reactions in the West. If CNN brought you the first Gulf War, the Middle East's rolling news networks, Al-Jazeera and Abu Dhabi TV, brought you the second. These broadcasters and the increasingly muscular Arab press gave Saddam's regime a level of credence it perhaps did not deserve, but, most important, they allowed viewers to understand there were two sides in this war. Unlike in the first Gulf conflict, the huge scale of Iraqi military losses would not go unreported. This time there were pictures of missiles firing and guns blazing in emptied towns. There were shots of the dead and the dying. Truth may be the first casualty of war, but there is usually more than one version of the truth.

From live television pictures of battles to acres of newspaper coverage and internet headlines, this was to become the most scrutinised war in history. This was the ultimate in Reality TV. Viewers were able to watch bullets fly as reporters with hand-held cameras in the middle of the action beamed live shots to the world. Technology made this possible.

A journalist's kit has got smaller and lighter in the past few
years. Satellite phones fit in your pocket; digital cameras sit
comfortably around the neck. The videophone, with its jerky
images, can send pictures from the front line without a bulky
satellite dish seconds after events occur on the ground. But
what had not changed was the fog of war, which meant it was
hard to find out what was really happening. When the American
and British government and military were accused of obscuring
the truth, even lying, particularly in the difficult early phase of
the campaign, their guns were metaphorically trained on the
journalists. 'The UK media have lost the plot,' exploded Air
Marshal Brian Burridge, the Qatar-based commander of the
British forces. 'You stand for nothing, you support nothing, you
criticise, you drip. It's a spectator sport to criticise anybody or
anything, and what the media says fuels public expectation.'

Yet journalists still had to sieve fact from fiction, truth from
lies, propaganda from honest assertion. Reporters had to judge
how much to believe or disbelieve when fellow citizens were
risking their lives in combat. The death and pain were in our
name. Many of the weapons that caused the carnage in Iraq were
despatched from the Gloucestershire countryside. Journalists
could not reasonably turn their eyes away from the missiles
when they reached their hot and dusty destination six hours
later.

The sheer scale of the war-reporting effort distinguished it
from earlier conflicts. For the first time people had instant
access to round-the-clock reports from the military campaign,
mostly supplied by 700 correspondents 'embedded' with US
and British military units, who fed stories into a vast pool for all
media organisations to drink. An estimated 3,000 journalists
were dispatched to the region, the largest media war force ever
assembled, to talk for hour after hour on radio and television
even if they had little to say. Their problem was the volume of
'information', much of it conflicting, which made it difficult to
discern what was going on and impossible to fit dramatic snap-
shots into the big picture. The public had never received so

much detail – but was everybody well informed or simply baffled? 'Facts are very few and far between out here,' lamented Sky's Jeremy Thompson, in a classic understatement from the middle of the desert. 'It's a very confusing picture.'

Pictures of tanks rumbling along highways, explosions, tracer bullets, and breathless interviews at battle scenes, often conducted in the eerie green light of night cameras, dominated extended TV bulletins and rolling news channels. A senior Fleet Street editor was quoted as saying: 'These embedded pieces get to be like shots of vodka. Drink one and you think it's wonderful. Drink six and you get sick and woozy.'

The result was a series of gaffes, wrong stories and incorrect ticker-tape headlines running along the bottom of TV screens. Politicians blamed 'overenthusiastic reporters'; reporters said they had been fed the information by military and intelligence officials. Damage was done to all those involved. News media that had been led for months to expect the 'shock and awe' that failed to materialise should have been on their guard.

Early on in the blur of the fighting, confusion reigned. There were hyperbolic reports of two columns of tanks heading for coalition positions that were later denied. Admiral Sir Michael Boyce, Chief of the Defence Staff, announced that Umm Qasr had been 'overwhelmed', only for television screens a day later to be filled with a prolonged firefight between US marines and about 150 Iraqis. There were many excited reports of chemical weapon finds once the Iraqi army had been cleared from towns, none of which yielded anything more noxious than a pit in the stomach of the Pentagon.

Rixhard Gaisford, a GMTV correspondent embedded with the British, broke the news of the famous Basra uprising-that-never-was. He cited 'military intelligence' as his source – while Al-Jazeera's reporter in Basra, Mohammed al-Abdallah, rebutted the claim: 'The streets are very calm and there are no indications of violence or riots.'

GMTV was not the only news outlet dazed by the fighting. After the 'popular uprising' came the biggest tank battle involving British forces since the Second World War. A convoy of up to 120 Iraqi armoured vehicles was spotted breaking out of Basra in broad daylight on 26 March, heading south towards the British-held Faw Peninsula in what commanders described as an 'offensive posture'. TV news reports on that Thursday morning were filled with gripping accounts of clashes between British and Iraqi armour.

'British artillery and jets launched a fierce attack last night on a convoy of up to 120 Iraqi tanks and armoured personnel carriers seen pouring out of the city of Basra,' the *Guardian*'s front-page story said. The account was based on reports from correspondents with the British forces, who received details of the battle from commanders. Two days later the truth emerged at a military briefing. Rather than 120 Iraqi vehicles, 3 were involved, with blame conveniently pinned on an 'erroneous signal' from the coalition's electronic target indicators. It was, said US Brigadier General Vince Brooks, a 'classic example of the fog of war'.

The row over pictures of 5 US PoWs captured by the Iraqis underlined the global nature of television. They were carried by Al-Jazeera, and Downing Street and the White House said they contravened the Geneva Convention and 'requested' news organisations not to carry them. Governments argued it was Iraqi propaganda; most UK broadcasters replied that the public could distinguish between news and propaganda. British newspapers ignored No 10 and published the pictures. Sky News and BBC News 24 ran the footage. ITV used still pictures. US broadcasters were more circumspect, although CNN was to defy the Pentagon. The Pentagon said families of those captured should be informed first. A mother in the US, however, was to see the pictures on a Filipino subscription channel before receiving the knock on the door.

In the most media-addicted country in the world, America, the war brought out the best and worst of the media. While broadsheets produced reams of thoughtful, insightful coverage, television was disfigured by patriotism that shaded into press releases for the US army. It was perhaps a bonus that American TV stations removed their staff from Baghdad on safety grounds before the conflict began.

Some were braver than others. CBS, notably, played a tape showing American prisoners of war while Donald Rumsfeld, the US Secretary of Defence, was still in the studio. Interviewed later on CNN, Rumsfeld said: 'Television networks that carry such pictures are, I would say, doing something that's unfortunate.' During the Afghan war, some TV pundits had agonised about whether it constituted unacceptable bias to wear a Stars and Stripes pin in their lapel.

In the Iraq conflict, one television station appeared tather as cheerleader than impartial observer: Rupert Murdoch's Fox News was brash and crass to many Americans and certainly to anyone outside the country's 50 states. Its offering of American perspectives to an American audience often came over as simple-minded propaganda, replete with celebrity interviewers such as Oliver North.

Fox flew the flag constantly, literally and metaphorically, never hesitating to use words such as 'we' and 'ours' to indicate coalition forces. The team on its breakfast show, *Fox and Friends*, would criticise the journalists asking questions at the daily briefings in Qatar if they seemed unduly critical. 'Our show generally reflects the mood of America,' one of the *Fox and Friends* hosts, Steve Doocy, explained to the *Washington Post*. 'Right now, there is a wave of patriotism in the country. Our show is about patriotism.' After the Saddam statue was toppled in Baghdad, Fox anchor Neal Cavuto delivered a message to those 'who opposed the liberation of Iraq' and said: 'You were sickening then, you are sickening now.' Fox's audience almost trebled thanks to the war – putting it ahead of CNN and MSNBC. It is America's biggest news network.

The decision to take a huge number of journalists to the front line, embedding them with their units, was a big gamble for the two governments and the broadcasters and newspapers that accepted the invitations. William Howard Russell, grandfather

of war reporters, was embedded with the British army in the
Crimea 150 years ago when he asked his editor, John Delane:
'Am I to tell these things, or hold my tongue?'

Reporters, photographers and cameramen who ate, slept,
travelled and feared attack with the people they wrote or spoke
about were required to self-censor or allow an army officer to
put a red pencil through words. The distinction between warrior
and correspondent was an early victim of the system, first-person
plural emerging as the preposition of choice. Mark Franchetti of
the *Sunday Times* was with US marines when 'we invaders'
entered Iraq from Kuwait; Sarah Oliver in the *Mail on Sunday*
subsumed her gender as she opened her piece: 'We rode at
dawn, the men of the 1st Royal Irish . . .'

Chris Ayres, an embedded *Times* correspondent, admitted
the impossibility of remaining detached when he reported on
marines shooting Iraqis who failed to stop at a checkpoint. 'To
the marines – and to me – there was nothing gung-ho about it,'
he wrote. 'It was simply survival. Of course, I was hardly objective: as a journalist embedded with a front-line artillery unit,
my chances of avoiding death at the hands of a suicide bomber
were directly linked to the marines' ability to kill the enemy.'

Many dressed in the 'camouflage chic' of military fatigues,
particularly for pieces to camera, to underline their closeness
to the front line. At one point the MoD advised them to don
civilian clothing to demonstrate their non-combatant status in
the event of capture. Audrey Gillan, a *Guardian* correspondent
based with the Household Cavalry, found her dispatches being
delayed because they had to be read first by an officer who
hours earlier had been involved in the fighting. In a graphic
account of a 'friendly fire' incident in which an American A10
Thunderbolt aircraft machine-gunned a British soldier, she was
prevented from writing that troops had been told to light red
flares if taking fire from the coalition to prevent Iraqi forces
copying the defence.

Jamie Wilson, a *Guardian* journalist who listened in to the
operations room of HMS *Marlborough* as the codewords were

issued to fire the first salvos of the war, was allowed free run of the ship. Yet his mobile and satellite phones were removed, despite MoD promises that he would be allowed to use them. A minder listened in to calls back to London on the ship's secure telephone, and the commander insisted on reading everything Wilson wrote to check for 'factual errors' before it was sent to the newspaper.

The creation of 'embeds' did not prevent an estimated 2,000 freewheeling reporters, dubbed unilaterals, from giving independent accounts of what was going on in a conflict that claimed the lives of at least a dozen journalists. It was a bitter irony that for all the talk of chemical and biological attack, journalists died in accidents and in the line of friendly fire. ITV's veteran war reporter Terry Lloyd was the first to perish, thought killed by US marines who fired at his vehicle as he drove through southern Iraq without the 'protection' of coalition forces. Two of his colleagues, cameraman Fred Nerac and translator Hussein Osman, were posted as missing.

After Lloyd's death, General Franks was asked about the journalists who had been killed. He responded only that he did not know of any embedded journalists who had died. The message was chilling: embeds were part of the crew, unilateralists were at risk. An Al-Jazeera correspondent, Tareq Ayoub, was killed in a US airstrike on the organisation's office in Baghdad, despite the station supplying the site's exact co-ordinates after the channel's Kabul office had been destroyed by a cruise missile in 2001.

Friendly fire saw the Palestine Hotel attacked by US tanks. A single round killed cameramen Taras Protsyuk of Reuters and Jose Couso, who worked for the Spanish TV station Tele Five. Kamaran Mohammed, a translator with the BBC, died when the Americans bombed the Kurdish convoy in which he was travelling with John Simpson, the BBC World Affairs Editor. An Iranian cameraman, Kaveh Golestan, working for the BBC, died after stepping on a landmine.

War kills, and reporters were dying. The American journalist Michael Kelly, 46, editor-at-large of *Atlantic Monthly* magazine and a *Washington Post* columnist, died in a Humvee, Australian cameraman Paul Moran in an apparent car bombing. Julio Anguita Parrado, a reporter on Spain's *El Mundo*, and Christian Liebig were killed in an Iraqi rocket attack on a US forces operations centre south of Baghdad. The NBC TV correspondent David Bloom died of a blood clot while Gaby Rado, an ITV colleague of Terry Lloyd's, died in northern Iraq after falling from a hotel roof.

The US tank attack on the Palestine Hotel appeared to those inside as more than an accident. The American army captain who commanded the tank that fired the shell later told France's *Nouvel Observateur* that his men had seen sunlight reflected on binoculars on a balcony and believed an Iraqi soldier was directing incoming fire on the tanks. It was a bitter irony, noted the trade magazine *Press Gazette*, that

> in the first Gulf War, not one journalist was killed during the span of the fighting. Since then we might have thought we had learned more, not less, about the safety of journalists covering conflict. Certainly more money has been spent on training, greater awareness has been raised of the dangers, better equipment has been issued for those going out into the field to bring back the reality of war. Yet that ever-lengthening list of dead makes a mockery of all that . . . In looking for the truth, did we let them get too close?

The fatal attack on Al-Jazeera's Baghdad office fuelled fears that the US deliberately targeted the Qatari station because it refused to play by White House rules. Downing Street and the White House had questioned its independence, accusing it of being too close to the Iraqi regime, a charge that was undermined when it decided to pull staff out of Baghdad after a row with Saddam.

So did lightning strike twice – once in Kabul and now in Baghdad – or did Washington authorise action against a broadcaster that had been a constant thorn in its side? Iraqi TV and radio had been targeted earlier in the conflict, probably in breach of the Geneva Convention, which forbids military action against civilian targets, with commanders claiming it was a legitimate target because it was part of Saddam's communications network. The fact that Serbian TV had been blasted during the 1999 Kosovo war fuelled speculation that the second Al-Jazeera attack was no coincidence, but a deliberate attempt to silence a trenchant critic of Washington.

Media organisations were advised by the US authorities to leave the Iraqi capital before the invasion started, ostensibly on safety grounds. Also, the White House would have been aware of the potentially damaging impact of reports from Baghdad detailing the killing of civilians. A number of British newspapers, notably the pro-war *Times* and *Telegraph*, withdrew staff from the capital, but others, including the *Guardian*, *Independent* and *Mirror*, kept correspondents in the city to provide some of the most vivid accounts of the military onslaught, to the dismay of the coalition and, ultimately, Saddam's regime.

The public face of the media in Baghdad, and perhaps Iraq, was the BBC's Rageh Omaar. An Arabic speaker with six years of reporting, on and off, from Iraq had given him an insight into the regime. Yet some wondered if reporting restrictions imposed on journalists in Baghdad – government minders listened to reports with the threat of expulsion – could influence judgements. 'We also need to ask if some Baghdad reporters became seduced by the illusory rhetoric of the Iraqis. The BBC's Rageh Omaar, for example, seemed visibly startled at the final ease of the coalition invasion,' wrote Mark Lawson in the *Guardian*. 'As recently as the night before, he had been suggesting a fierce and confident regime. Did Iraqi media restrictions pollute the reporting?'

The heart of the military's media operation on the ground was a $1m press centre in Gen Franks's Central Command headquarters in Doha, Qatar. Inside a converted warehouse, Gen Franks or Brigadier General Vince Brooks or any of the other military figures dribbled out information in front of the world's cameras. If it looked like a Hollywood set, that was because it was. The backdrop was a $250,000 set built around tubular grey struts holding up five large plasma screens and created by George Allison, an art director who designed sets for Michael Douglas and George Bush. Above the podium was an eagle sitting on a Stars and Stripes shield with its wings outstretched to envelop a map of the Middle East and Arab world.

Announcements were timed to hit American breakfast TV programmes. Seats in the front row and questions were largely reserved for the US networks important to the White House. Robust questioning was treated with disdain; Franks preferred the milder style favoured by some US correspondents, including the poser, two days into the war, from a correspondent with the American network CBS: 'The campaign so far has gone with breathtaking speed. Has it surprised you, or is it going more or less as you expected?' Michael Wolff of *New York* magazine recalled how a *Newsweek* correspondent was denied the first name of one of the generals. 'The admonition is, "We don't discuss military operations," which obviously prompts the question, then why are we here?' wrote Wolff.

In Britain the political pressure on broadcasters, particularly the BBC, was more subtle than in previous wars, with Alastair Campbell, Tony Blair's spinner-in-chief, ringing editors in an attempt to influence coverage rather than writing threatening letters that might later be leaked. When tempers frayed, no punches were pulled. The Prime Minister's official spokesman branded a tabloid political correspondent 'morally repugnant' when he asked if Iraqi civilians killed by the coalition forces were counted as freed of Saddam.

John Reid, promoted during the war to Leader of the Commons, criticised the BBC's widely applauded coverage. David Blunkett, the Home Secretary, complained during a trip to the US that coalition troops were appearing as 'the villains', criticising what he termed the liberal and progressive media for its coverage. Jack Straw, the Foreign Secretary, wondered whether the Dunkirk evacuation could have been achieved in an age of 24-hour newsgathering. The MoD would undoubtedly have found it more difficult to portray Dunkirk, in which 68,000 Britons were killed or wounded over 9 days, as the great victory pulled from the jaws of defeat that it was presented as in an era before rolling news.

In the ratings war fought over Britain's airwaves, BBC and Sky were reckoned to have come out victors. 'Sky treated the war as drama and event, while the BBC consistently tried to reflect the controversial context of the conflict and the depth of opposition in Britain. The latter decision is perhaps journalistically more honourable, but Sky was better positioned to benefit when public opinion began to move in favour of the troops,' observed Mark Lawson.

Television eclipses almost any other medium in terms of its global reach. It may be this that pushed Blair and Bush to set up their own TV station after Baghdad's occupation, Towards Freedom TV, which opened with tapes of the two leaders separately seeking to assure the Iraqi people that troops had arrived as friends rather than foes. It was another shot fired in the battle for the most difficult terrain: people's hearts and their minds.

An undoubted media winner in Operation Iraqi Freedom was created by people's desire for instant and up-to-the-minute war news: the internet. Guardian Unlimited, for example, received more than 5 million page impressions on 20 March, the day the war began. Its traffic went up by 30 per cent. Other news websites, including the BBC, recorded big increases. War even outstripped sex as the web's most popular search term, according to internet service provider Freeserve. The web allowed people to satisfy their curiosity about non-western perspectives. Russia's intelligence reports could be found on www.aeronautics.ru – since GRU, the espionage arm of the Russian military, now publishes its analyses. It provided some of the most detailed reports of the fighting, though, unsurprisingly, it dried up once the Russians evacuated their embassy. Lycos reported that Al-Jazeera became one of the most searched-for names on the web.

Weblogs, created as diaries on the internet, also provided many with the authentic voice of battle. Of all the bloggers, an Iraqi known as Salam Pax (www.dear_raed.blogspot.com) became an international celebrity, if you can be so while remaining anonymous. Though it remains to be seen whether the 29-year-old is real or fictional, those who know Baghdad well say the day-to-day details contained in his online diary point to his existence. The blog of John Robb, a former US special forces officer (http://jrobb.userland.com/), was also considered essential surfing.

Despite the huge popularity of news websites, most war reports, particularly by embedded journalists, were filed to traditional news providers – meaning newspapers, television and news agencies such as Reuters or Associated Press. Although the second Gulf War took place in cyberspace, it seems the world will have to wait for another conflict for the first web-based war correspondent.

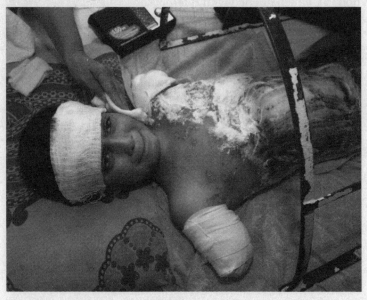

The Horror of War: Ali Ismail Abbas, 12, one of the conflict's enduring, terrifying images (Reuters/Faleh Kheiber)

If the blustering Iraqi Information Minister, Mohammed Saeed al-Sharaf, was the face of the Saddam regime until its fall, the picture of bewildered Ali Ismail Abbas was the symbol for many of the horror of war. His arms amputated, body seared by second- and third-degree burns, he was left an orphan by the US missile that killed his pregnant mother, father, brother and two sisters as they slept in a Baghdad suburb.

Two newspapers, the anti-war *Daily Mirror* and the pro-war London *Evening Standard*, launched financial appeals after readers moved by his plight sent cheques to help pay for treatment. The *Sun* set up a more general 'give a quid for an Iraqi kid' premium telephone line, considered in poor taste by many. The *Express*, possibly believing charity begins at home, founded a fund for the families of UK service personnel injured or killed.

The *Daily Telegraph* journalist David Blair wrote in mid-April how Ali Ismail Abbas had endured a succession of visitors from the international media and felt let down because numerous promises that he would be treated in the West had not been kept. 'You are coming to make fun of me because I have lost my arms?' he asked. 'Doctor, doctor, no more journalists please.'

18 The hot war

I learned the lesson of leadership from [Imam] Hussein, for he was wronged and hence loved.

Gandhi, Indian nationalist leader, 1869–1949

Political freedom arrived in Iraq as the presence of Saddam Hussein ebbed away. The Kurds in the north of the country were jubilant at the toppling of their most feared and hated foe. When General Jay Garner, the man America wants to rebuild Iraq, arrived at the picturesque lakeside retreat of Dukan he was greeted with cheers, hugs and a shower of flowers. This was liberation.

General Garner, whose official title is the Director of the Office for Reconstruction and Humanitarian Assistance, would have received a different message had he plunged into the Shia river of humanity that was meandering through the holy city of Kerbala. There, the sight of a million flagellating men and the sound of religious chants would have alarmed him. It certainly worried Saddam, who banned the rite and the march, which marks the most symbolic event in the Shia calendar – the death of Imam Hussein, the grandson of the Prophet Mohammed. On the outer wall of the Imam Hussein mosque in Kerbala, a poster from the Shia clerics says no one should organise marches or join a political party without their permission. Some pilgrims chanted anti-American slogans and a growing number of religious leaders were starting to make unnerving noises about the presence of US troops in Iraq. For them, this was occupation.

If that was a missive meant for George Bush, the President saw hope instead of fear. 'I love the stories about people saying "Isn't it wonderful to be able to express our religion, the Shia religion, on a pilgrimage this weekend" . . . It made my day to read that.' Others in Washington, perhaps with longer memories,

regarded the rise of the Shia as a sign of troubling times ahead.
America had been humiliated by a religious revolution in Iran,
the world's only Shia state. The most potent guerilla force in the
Middle East, Hizbullah, bombed the Americans and then Israel
out of Lebanon. Its shock troops come from Lebanon's Shia
south. Ominously, US officials were quoted as being taken by
surprise by the strength and organisation of the Shia groups
demanding an Islamic state. The *Washington Post* reported that
a Pentagon meeting had turned into a 'spontaneous teach-in'
on Iraq's Shias and how the US would try to contain fundamen-
talism in Iraq. One general concluded: 'This is a 25-year project.'

For others liberty would surely be followed by democracy, not
theocracy. Small political parties, once cowed by Saddam, were
bursting from the streets of Baghdad. 'We are back,' Faris Faris,
a member of the Central Committee of the Iraqi Communist
Party, told the *Guardian*'s Jonathan Steele as he watched comrades embracing each other on a Baghdad pavement beneath
red flags and a banner saying 'A free country for joyful people.'

The party took over an abandoned and looted building in a
city suburb formerly used by the Mukhabarat, Saddam Hussein's
security police, which had offices, safe houses and interroga-
tion centres all over the city. Old graffiti still cover the inner
walls. 'Always keep the enemy in your sights and don't let him
get behind you,' says one. 'We've not yet had time to paint it out,'
said a smiling Faris.

Other parties also set up shop in deserted premises of the old
regime. The Liberal Democratic Movement has taken over the
building formerly used by the Union of Iraqi Students. The
National Arab Democratic Movement is in a cultural centre.
Ahmad Chalabi, who heads the US-funded Iraqi National Congress, has set up in the Hunting Club, one of Baghdad's top
country clubs. The seeds of democracy were, undeniably, being
planted in Iraq.

America had chosen force to do so and bypassed the United
Nations. It created disorder in international relations and was
now trying to create order in the Middle East. But will America

hand over power to the Iraqi people, as President Bush has promised? Will he dare to? The West took hundreds of years to create what we understand as liberal democracy. The act of free elections, of the rule of law and of separating religion from the state, did not materialise in months but evolved over decades. How does a nation of 25 million – of whom 15 per cent are Kurds, 15 per cent Sunni Muslims and two-thirds Shia Arabs, while the rest are Turcomen, Assyrians, Christians and obscure religious sects such as the Yezidis – come together before it comes apart? What of Iraq's oil – which Dick Cheney says will be a 'significant advantage' in building democracy? Or of the plan to station thousands of American troops on Iraqi soil? All these questions are good ones, and only the future will provide answers.

For Tony Blair, the pain was worth the gain. His public position was that the war would take as long as it needed to. Privately, Whitehall expected Saddam to fall in around 14 days. In the end, it took just over a week longer. Although the quality of intelligence was improving as the conflict loomed, Saddam's thinking was still the subject of guesswork. As one senior Foreign Office official admitted: 'Our intelligence about his intentions was sketchy. You don't really know what is going on in his mind, you only get the odd still photograph. You cannot get spies in that close. You cannot get people who see him daily to work for another government.'

Blair did not expect the war to end in days, but did become worried that the troops were being bogged down. Every day he had one question for his intelligence people, until they got fed up with it: 'Tell me what the picture is. Is this Ceausescu in Romania or is this the Vietcong? In other words, is this a security apparatus that has a grip on a country that will fight to keep that grip, but actually has no popular support, in which case they will be removed; or is this a movement that actually does have some genuine popular support?' The intelligence officers replied every day that it was the former, not the latter.

Even among loyal ministers, there was a widespread sense that the government was heading into the unknown. 'Either

Tony knows something the rest of us don't know, or he's insane,' said one minister, just hours before the war started. The plan was for speed and flexibility. Geoff Hoon, the Defence Secretary, recalled that it was 'more like a decision tree in which you start at the top with lots of different options of how you get to the bottom of the tree – in this case Baghdad'.

But planning had been upset by the loss of a northern front because of opposition from the Turkish Parliament. Hoon was anxious about the change. 'The whole idea was to give Saddam a whole series of different challenges, not all of which he could handle simultaneously. The fear was that without the northern option, he would concentrate his forces south of Baghdad. With a sizeable contingent north, he would not have dared to do that.' Hoon argued strongly against a lengthy bombing campaign, and in favour of shifting the ground attack forward to the start of the campaign. 'We needed to secure the south quickly. It would have been catastrophic if Saddam had set alight the oilfields, or turned open the oil pumping stations and flooded the Gulf.'

Despite the element of surprise, the first few days were very tough. 'It was just losing so many people,' said Hoon. 'Due to the time difference I was being woken up in the middle of the night to be told of yet another disaster, a helicopter coming down, two helicopters crashing, a Patriot taking down a Tornado. It is hard enough to explain to families why people die in action, but in such cases there is an understanding of sorts. But when these accidents occur it seems so pointless.' When the British and Americans again met at Camp David, just five days into the war, there was intense discussion and a difficult mood between the two sides about friendly fire losses.

There was also, Hoon admitted, surprise at the level of resistance in the south. 'I guess we just had not used our imaginations to the extent we should have about the way the regime had a hold on the country. Naively we thought people would behave as they had in the uprising in 1991, but since then the regime had increased its control over the civilians and over the armed forces.'

The regime had embedded itself in the armed forces. There were examples of commanders around Basra giving up, but their forces continuing to fight, since they were taking orders from the regime and not the army. In the British military's eyes, it was the attack on Ba'ath Party headquarters and the apparent bombing of Chemical Ali that opened the door to Basra. In Hoon's judgement: 'We could have flattened the place, but had to be patient. The mood changed dramatically as soon as the city thought Chemical Ali had gone. The people were much more confident and willing to welcome troops in a way that they had not until then.'

The momentum of the American drive northwards won huge admiration inside the Ministry of Defence, even being described as 'a thing of beauty'. 'Rumsfeld constantly kept saying to the US military, "Keep going, keep up the momentum",' Hoon recalled.

British intelligence suggested that Saddam's plan was to let his army do what it could, but ultimately he wanted troops to fight street by street across Baghdad. This might have imposed a price on the democratic coalition that it could not afford to pay: the US and the UK could not sustain the possible number of losses involved, with all the international criticism of the number of civilians that might have been killed.

In the end, Saddam lost control. Hoon said: 'We had maps on the wall of these Iraqi divisions, including the Medina Division, but they were soon reduced into their component bits. The maps had no bearing on what was happening on the ground. The aerial bombing took a severe toll. Once Baghdad Airport fell that was a huge blow.'

Hoon, in an interview with the *Guardian* in late April 2003, said he did not know what happened to Saddam, whose fate was by then still undetermined. The British Defence Secretary was also baffled as to why Saddam never used chemical weapons.'He buried, and had hidden, all sorts of surprising military equipment, including quite sophisticated modern aeroplanes. We're not quite sure why he did it, but we think he thought he might have hidden material in the hope he was able to live to fight another day.'

Among the reasons for going to war, the most frequent justification was the threat of weapons of mass destruction. Tony Blair and George Bush sensed that unless the world was rid of such destructive devices, chaos would replace order. Yet, at the time of writing, none has been found in Iraq. There has been plenty of smoke, but no smoking gun. The war and its aftermath produced a dozen or so instances where coalition troops had uncovered hoards of suspicious powders and liquids. But none turned out be more dangerous than a toppled dictator. Perhaps Iraq simply has far fewer unconventional weapons than was suspected. But we were told that there were up to 500 tonnes of nerve and mustard agents, and 30,000 munitions capable of delivering them; that 25,000 litres of anthrax and 38,000 litres of botulinum toxin could be conjured up in an instant; that there were mobile or underground laboratories to make germ weapons. If so, why is it taking so long to find them? Another question left hanging.

What is left is an unintended, deserved vindication of the United Nations chief weapons inspector, Hans Blix. Rather than launch into a war, Blix wanted more time to complete his inspections. He was flatly denied this by, among others, Blair and Bush, who are now insisting, believe it or not, that more time is needed to find the lethal weapons. The failure so far to locate anything stronger than a cup of Arabic coffee does not mean none exist. But the longer this situation remains, the stronger the suspicion that, egged on by rabid right-wingers, the US and Britain greatly exaggerated the threat of weapons of mass destruction posed by Iraq. They were a convenient reason to bring down Saddam and, without them, there is still no answer as to why all those innocent Iraqi lives were extinguished to make the world a safer place.

This is the end of the beginning. The New American Century will ask much of the rest of the world. The fall of Saddam defines a new global era. As the world's hyperpower, America has chosen to eliminate rogue states that constitute no immediate threat – in contravention of the United Nations Charter. This is the hot war that replaces the cold one that ended more than a decade ago. If Iraq is any guide, Washington will pursue its aims regardless of the opinions of that country's neighbours, its own allies and the rest of the world's middling powers. Days after Baghdad fell, Michael Ledeen of the American Enterprise Institute, an out-rider for the American right, was advocating regime change in Syria and Iran: 'We cannot give them time to organise . . . attacks, while all the while developing the weapons we all properly dread.'

Whether America chooses to remake its enemies or simply destroy them will shape the course of world events for decades to come. In doing so, it may force the pace of European integration – to produce a post-national entity with enough clout to tackle the United States. It may also see nascent industrial powers covertly try to acquire the kinds of weapons that will deter acts of US aggression. About 15 countries, some as rich as Britain, others as poor as Pakistan, either have or are on the verge of obtaining weapons of mass destruction.

American actions may also breed hate and contempt for Pax Americana, for that is the epoch we are about to enter. Unless Washington succeeds in cleaning up the mess it makes, the American empire will be less about global fraternity and more about the projection of US power. We are present at the creation of a new world that nobody, least of all George Bush or Tony Blair, may want to live in.

The war in numbers

Casualties

2,320
Iraqi soldiers killed

9,000
prisoners of war

2,325*
maximum number of
Iraqi civilians killed

5,103
injured

128
US personnel killed

2
missing

554
injured

7
prisoners of war

30
British personnel killed

74
injured

700
journalists were
embedded with
coalition forces

13
killed in action

Research: Guardian research dept
Sources: Pentagon, Ministry of
Defence, Reuters, Standard chartered
bank, united nations
*Figures from iraqbodycount.net based
on independent sources

Military

300,000
coalition personnel are
in the region

45,000
from Britain

130,000
British and American
troops are in action

40,000
gallons of water were
consumed by coalition
forces each day

$6.77
the cost of each MRE
(meal ready to eat)

300,000
consumed daily

£45,000
cost of keeping British
soldier on operations for
a month

30,000
sorties flown by coalition
forces

$15,000
the maximum cost for
each bomber run

750
cruise missiles fired

$750m
the cost of missiles

Humanitarian crisis

$2.2bn
appealed for by the UN,
including $1.3bn for the
World Food
Programme

$55bn
the amount the US is
spending on fighting the
war

$275m
the amount the US
spent on aid to Iraq

$3bn
allocated by the
treasury to the UK's
military effort

£240m
allocated to the
numaniratian effort

$100bn
is the amount it will cost
to rebuild Iraq

6,000
tonnes of wheat flour
sent by World Food
Programme to northern
Iraq

420,000
people will be fed by
that

24m
people live in Iraq

Appendices

Timeline

Monday 17 March
- Search for a UN mandate for war ends in acrimony
- Bush to Saddam: quit Iraq or face war – an ultimatum opposed by Russia, France, Germany and the Vatican
- Robin Cook resigns from the cabinet

Tuesday 18 March
- Saddam rejects George Bush's 48-hour ultimatum to leave the country with his sons or face war
- US psychological warfare units bombard Iraqi troops with 1.4 million leaflets urging them to surrender
- All UN international staff quit Baghdad on grounds of safety
- Home Office Minister John Denham and Health Minister Lord Hunt resign
- UK parliament backs government's war plans after powerful speech by Tony Blair. A record number of Labour MPs rebel – 139

Wednesday 19 March
- Hans Blix delivers final inspection report to United Nations Security Council
- French, Russian and German foreign ministers issue fresh plea for restraint
- US and British forces move into demilitarised zone on Kuwaiti border
- Coalition aircraft drop 2 million leaflets on Iraq warning citizens they could become victims of Saddam's chemical weapons

Thursday 20 March
- US and UK forces move into southern Iraq and launch land, air and sea assaults

- US/UK forces attack the strategic Iraqi port of Umm Qasr
- Oil wells alight near Basra
- After attending EU summit in Brussels, Blair appeals to the nation in a TV broadcast to rally behind British forces

Friday 21 March
- Heavy fighting in south as British-led marines battle for Faw Peninsula and Umm Qasr. Basra becomes 'key aim'. US marine becomes first combat death
- Special forces fighting around northern oilfields. Thirty southern wells on fire
- Army units race towards Baghdad, halting at Nassiriya
- Iranian President says the war is 'satanic'. Archbishop Desmond Tutu says it is 'immoral'

Saturday 22 March
- Six British servicemen die when two Royal Navy Sea King helicopters collide over the northern Arabian Gulf
- Coalition forces advance deeper into Iraq, capturing some key oilfields and bridges, but face stiffening resistance
- Baghdad suffers fourth consecutive night of heavy air raids
- 200,000 march in London in biggest-ever wartime protest

Sunday 23 March
- US soldiers captured and shown on Al-Jazeera TV
- US and British forces held back in Umm Qasr by small Republican Guard force
- US forces halted at Nassiriya and Najaf, 200 miles and 100 miles from Baghdad. US marines seize Iraqi naval base at Zubayr
- US officials investigate claims that chemical weapons factory has been found near Najaf
- UK Tornado shot down by US Patriot missile battery
- 33 killed by stray US missile in northern Iraq
- Five journalists, including ITN's Terry Lloyd, reported dead or missing

Monday 24 March
- A British soldier is killed in action in Zubayr. Coalition forces try to locate two other British soldiers
- US forces bombard Iraqi positions around Baghdad and in northern Iraq
- Iraqi TV shows pictures of a downed Apache helicopter and video of two men it says are its crew
- Saddam Hussein speaks to the nation
- UN Secretary General Kofi Annan urges measures to supply Basra with water. EU officials say aid is starting to trickle into southern areas
- Five Syrians die in US missile strike near Iraqi border

Tuesday 25 March
- Reported uprising of civilians in Basra against Iraqi forces. British say Umm Qasr is 'safe and open'
- US warplanes bombard Republican Guard positions on approach to Baghdad and marines cross the Euphrates at Nassiriya
- Two British soldiers killed when their tank is fired on by another British tank
- US F-16 fires at Patriot missile battery in 'friendly fire' incident
- Fierce sandstorms hinder military operations
- Turkish Foreign Minister says Turkey looking to move up to 12 miles into northern Iraq to keep refugees out
- UN food agency makes the biggest single request for cash in its history – over $1 bn

Wednesday 26 March
- At least 14 killed in air strike on Baghdad market. Annan 'increasingly concerned' by growing civilian casualties
- US troops in big battle at Najaf, advance halted north of Nassiriya. US sends 30,000 reinforcements to Gulf
- Bodies of 2 British soldiers and 2 prisoners of war from Zubayr shown on TV

- Iraq will probably need the biggest humanitarian operation in history after the invasion, says the UN World Food Programme

Thursday 27 March
- 1,000 US paratroops secure northern airfields. US troops build up for battle at Kerbala
- British say they destroyed 14 Iraqi T-55 tanks and armoured vehicles in battle south of Basra – the biggest tank battle since Second World War
- Planes bomb Baghdad; aid agencies say security fears slow relief efforts as Basra residents flee fighting
- Tony Blair meets George Bush at Camp David

Friday 28 March
- British army reports 1,000 civilians attacked by Iraqi mortars as they try to leave Basra
- Market explosion leaves 52 dead as bombers and cruise missiles strike Baghdad in some of heaviest bombing of war. US drops two 4,500 lb 'bunker-buster' bombs on communications tower. Ba'ath Party office hit, 8 killed
- One British soldier killed and 2 seriously injured in 'friendly fire' incident

Saturday 29 March
- An Iraqi army officer kills 4 US soldiers in a suicide attack
- Al-Jazeera TV reports explosions around Mosul
- US orders pause in advance towards Baghdad because of supply shortages and Iraqi resistance
- Britain says Iraq's air defence commander has been sacked after Iraqi anti-aircraft missiles fall back into Baghdad

Sunday 30 March
- Former Foreign Secretary Robin Cook calls on Blair to bring Britain's troops home
- Truck ploughs into soldiers at US base in Kuwait, injuring 15

• Palestinian Islamic Jihad says it has suicide bombers in Baghdad after Iraq claims more than 4,000 Arabs are willing martyrs
• US helicopter crashes in southern Iraq, killing three soldiers

Monday 31 March
• Low-flying coalition aircraft bomb Baghdad and missiles hit the palace of Saddam's son Qusay
• US marines launch dawn raid on Shatra, targeting senior Iraqi officers including Ali Hassan al-Majid, the general known as Chemical Ali
• B-52 bombers attack Iraqi positions near Mosul and Kirkuk, northern Iraq, guided in by US-led forces
• Fighting raging near the site of ancient Babylon and other points along the Euphrates river. Advanced US units 50 miles from Baghdad

Tuesday 1 April
• US forces in clashes at Hilla and Hindiya as Republican Guard troops south of Baghdad are bombed
• US soldiers shoot and kill about 10 Iraqis at checkpoint. At least 11 civilians, mostly children, killed when US hits Hilla residential district
• 'Helmets off, berets on' order to British troops patrolling southern Iraq
• Iraqi forces launch a rocket attack on prisoner-of-war camp guarded by UK troops at Umm Qasr
• Desert Rats uncover arsenal of bullets, bombs and more than 1,500 mortars in primary school
• Vandals spray slogans at a British First World War military cemetery at Etaples in northern France. 'Dig up your rubbish, it is contaminating our soil,' says one

Wednesday 2 April
• Baghdad Republican Guard Division based around Kut 'destroyed'

- US forces advance from east and south. 3rd Infantry passes Kerbala, heads north
- US 101st Airborne troops attack militia in Najaf. Iraqi troops based in Tomb of Ali
- Baghdad under aerial attack. Red Crescent maternity hospital, the city's trade fair, and a presidential palace hit, killing several people, wounding at least 25
- Special forces rescue 19-year-old private, Jessica Lynch, held in Nassiriya for 10 days. They also remove 11 bodies, two of which are believed to be members of US forces
- The US authorises troops to detain civilians who 'interfere with mission accomplishment'

Thursday 3 April
- US within 6 miles of Baghdad, at main airport
- Republican Guard divisions head south and east to meet US forces
- More bombs dropped on Baghdad, power goes out in city centre
- Baghdad presidential palace raided by SAS
- US F-18 fighter downed, perhaps by friendly fire. Black Hawk helicopter lost
- In north, Kurds attack Iraqi front lines
- Turkish troops move to positions on Iraqi border

Friday 4 April
- US 3rd Infantry seizes Saddam International Airport, renames it Baghdad International
- 'Suspicious' chemical site discovered by troops
- 2,500 Republican Guards surrender near Kut
- Three US soldiers, a pregnant woman and an Iraqi man killed in car bomb at checkpoint
- Saddam Hussein live on Iraqi TV
- Bombardments of Iraqi positions in north and south of country

- Iraq says it will use 'martyrdom operations' against US forces
- In an open letter to be handed out by British troops, Blair pledges that post-war Iraq will be run by Iraqis

Saturday 5 April
- Coalition tanks enter Baghdad on what appears to be the first significant push inside the city boundaries, killing around 1,000 Iraqi defenders
- British troops find hundreds of human remains in a 'make-shift morgue' in southern Iraq

Sunday 6 April
- British troops move into central Basra
- US forces encircle Baghdad, raid city centre
- Kurdish fighters and US troops hit by friendly fire, killing 17, injuring 45 – including brother of the Kurdistan Democratic party leader
- US forces take Kerbala
- Russian Embassy convoy leaving Baghdad attacked
- US National Security Adviser Condoleezza Rice arrives in Moscow for talks

Monday 7 April
- US troops in tanks and armoured vehicles launch 'armoured raid' into centre of Baghdad
- British paratroops move into Basra to patrol old town. Presidential palace seized
- British say they have found the body of Chemical Ali
- 700 Iraqi opposition fighters, led by Ahmad Chalabi, arrive in Nassiriya

Tuesday 8 April
- Air attack on reported Saddam Hussein bunker
- US forces tighten grip on Baghdad, attacking targets in heart of city

• Two cameramen, from Reuters and Spain's Tele 5, killed after US tank fires on hotel housing foreign media; Al-Jazeera cameraman dies after US air raid
• Looting continues in British-controlled Basra
• The bodies of 11 British servicemen are flown back to RAF Brize Norton
• The WHO says it is concerned that Baghdad's hospitals are running out of supplies to treat casualties

Wednesday 9 April
• Jubilant scenes as US marines advance through east of Baghdad to banks of Tigris
• Iraqi crowd and marines demolish Saddam statue on live TV as crowds loot main government buildings
• Red Cross convoy trying to reach casualties comes under fire, killing a Canadian worker
• US warplanes attack Iraqi positions in Mosul, as Kurdish fighters and special forces seize targets nearby
• US-led forces 'actively engaging' Iraqi troops in Tikrit

Thursday 10 April
• Looting, civil disorder and fierce gun battles in Baghdad
• Kurdish fighters take northern oil city of Kirkuk. US reassures Turkey that American forces will be in control of the city and agrees to Ankara sending military observers
• Iraqi Shia leader Abdul Majid al-Khoei and aide murdered by mob in holy shrine at Najaf

Friday 11 April
• US and Kurdish forces take Mosul without a fight; mob goes on looting rampage and torches market
• Baghdad descends into anarchy; the Red Cross says the city's medical system has 'virtually collapsed'
• US says Iraqi leaders are trying to escape to other countries
• Bush says Syria must deny refuge to Saddam loyalists

Saturday 12 April
• Saddam's scientific adviser, General Amer Hammoudi al-Saadi, surrenders to US forces
• US troops tackle anarchy in Baghdad, Mosul, Kirkuk; plan night curfew in capital
• US forces seize one of last strongholds of Arab 'mujahideen' fighters in Baghdad after exchanging heavy fire
• Iraq's UN Ambassador, Mohammed Aldouri, arrives in Syria
• Jacques Chirac tells Tony Blair the UN should decide Iraq government

Sunday 13 April
• US troops fight remnants of Iraqi army in Tikrit
• Bush repeats charges that Syria may be harbouring Iraqi officials and chemical weapons
• Small arms fire erupts in Baghdad near Palestine Hotel
• Friction flares between Muslim Shia factions in Najaf
• Seven US prisoners found safe and well
• US officials say they have captured Saddam's half brother Watban Ibrahim Hasan al-Tikriti

Monday 14 April
• US marines and tanks seize Tikrit
• Donald Rumsfeld says Syria carried out chemical weapons tests in the past year and has let Iraqi forces enter its territory – both denied by Syria. Colin Powell says the US will examine other measures against Syria; the White House calls Syria 'a rogue nation'
• Tony Blair tells the UK Parliament: 'We are near the end of the conflict. But the challenge of the peace is now beginning'

The language of war

A thousand express trains rushing towards you
With no journalists embedded with the Republican Guards
outside Baghdad, the defence analyst Christopher Bellamy
gave a taste of what they would be experiencing when he
quoted a German veteran's description of Soviet artillery on the
eastern front in the second world war. It was like 'a thousand
express trains rushing towards you', Bellamy wrote, adding
that the US bombing was far harder and more accurate.

An ugly place
In descriptions of what it is like in Baghdad it seems to be
becoming de rigueur to describe life on the streets of the Iraqi
capital as 'ugly'. Major-General Vincent Renuart, director of
operations at US Central Command in Qatar, asserted:
'Baghdad is still an ugly place.' Similarly, when she was
questioned about the widespread looting in Baghdad, the
International Development Secretary, Clare Short, chipped
in with: 'Chaos feeds on itself and is a very ugly thing.'

Attrit
The military attrition of the English language continues apace.
Commanders in the field and armchair generals talked about
how British and US forces would 'attrit' the Iraqis. Unfortunately,
for the likes of General Wesley Clark, the former Nato supreme
commander, this word does not exist. Attrition is fine. But
attrit? That came from their imaginations.

Blue-collar warfare
After one US marine was killed and another injured in fighting
with Iraqi irregulars at a cement factory near Diwaniya, Lt Col
B.P. McCoy described the incident as 'blue-collar warfare'.
Blue-collar is taken from the world of industrial sociology to

denote skilled and semi-skilled workers, but to Lt Col McCoy it
was 'just the hard-grinding work of patrols'. The phrase might
reflect the bewilderment of US personnel coming to terms
with a war they had been led to believe would be easier. 'The
enemy we're fighting is different from the one we'd wargamed
against,' explained the senior US ground commander in Iraq,
Lt Gen William Wallace.

Blue on blue

The US has a stockpile of phrases to describe the all-too-
common tragedy of allied forces being killed by people on
their own side. Blue on blue, which made its debut after the
downing of an RAF Tornado by an American Patriot missile,
comes from wargaming exercises where the goodies are blue
and – in a hangover from Cold War days – the baddies are red.
Replaces the older term 'friendly fire' which, as Murphy's Laws
of Combat eloquently note, isn't.

Breaking the china

Facing starvation and the threat of disease, Basra's 2 million
residents were no doubt relieved to hear that Britain meant
them no harm. They may have been less happy to hear the
clinical language deployed by the British military to describe
their efforts to protect Basra's population. Air Marshal Brian
Burridge, the head of British forces, declared: 'When you go in
and sort out an urban area you are not out to break the china;
we want to win hearts and minds but we will have to use force.'

Cakewalk

It looks injudicious now, but this was used by Ken Adelman,
former assistant to the US Defence Secretary, Donald Rumsfeld.
'Demolishing Saddam Hussein's military power and liberating
Iraq would be a cakewalk,' Mr Adelman said in February. The
phrase, popular in Britain in both world wars, implies a very
easy task. It originated in a strutting dance popular in the
American south before the Civil War, when plantation owners
would have a contest for the slaves in which the prize was a cake.

Calibrate me, Dick

From Donald Rumsfeld – the man who brought you known unknowns and unknown unknowns – comes a phrase so disorienting in its weirdness that even seasoned Rumsfeldologists were taken aback by its increasingly frequent use at Pentagon briefings. Uttered one way, it sounds combative, like *Dirty Harry*; uttered another way, camp like *Austin Powers*. In fact, it appears to be just a hi-tech, precision-guided version of 'correct me if I'm wrong', the Dick in question being General Richard Myers, chairman of the Joint Chiefs of Staff. Worryingly, 'calibrate me' is also the name of a song by the scary indie rock group Atombombpocketknife. Could Rumsfeld be a fan? Typical usage: 'The Republican Guard has – calibrate me, Dick – they pulled south in the north and they went north in the southern portion of the country.'

Catastrophic success

Amid their excitement at taking on a depleted and demoralised Iraqi army, US commanders talked about sweeping triumphantly into Baghdad in a 'catastrophic success'. They were using a negative adjective – catastrophic – to emphasise the positive, in the way that anyone under 21 describes something that is 'cool' as 'wicked'.

Centre of gravity

'The Republican Guard is the real centre of gravity,' said one impressively erudite Pentagon official. 'If Saddam Hussein was popped today, they'd fight on.' Centre of gravity is an old concept in military terminology, coined by the 19th-century Prussian strategist Karl von Clausewitz (1780–1831), and which he called *Schwerpunkt*. It means the crucial point around which a battle or a campaign is decided. His book, *On War* (1832), is still viewed as one of the two great works on strategy in the western canon. The other is *The Peloponnesian War* by the Athenian writer Thucydides (400 BC).

Collateral damage
Labour's pugnacious John Reid early on announced the demise
of this chilling euphemism, which describes the deaths of
innocent people in conflict. 'I do not like this terrible military
phrase, collateral damage,' he said. No longer would military
spokesmen be able to stand on a podium, far from a war zone,
and dismiss innocent deaths in abstract terms, as they did in
1999 when US warplanes fired on a convoy of ethnic Albanians,
believing they were Serb forces. The change of language did
not, however, herald a change in military tactics, according to
Reid, who said the world should prepare for 'unavoidable
civilian deaths'. While his new phrase is more honest, some
may wonder whether it says much for Anglo-American 'smart'
bombs, which are meant to hit solely military targets.

Culminating point
In military terminology, attackers reach their 'culminating
point' when their supplies and energy are depleted to the
point when they can no longer overcome enemy resistance.
'There are some tough days ahead,' predicted one senior US
general. 'I think this whole thing is at the culminating point.'

Deconflicting the airspace
Baghdad was not the only victim of allied bombing. The
English language took a fair pounding when commanders
announced that they were 'deconflicting the airspace' over
southern Iraq. Lt Gen David McKiernan, the land war
commander, unveiled this phrase to describe the complex
process of ensuring that the vast array of weaponry fired into
southern Iraq did not collide. 'I want to make sure that the fires
are fully co-ordinated and deconflicted,' he said.

Embedding
Charmingly horticultural metaphor for the US military's
approach to handling journalists in the war with Iraq. Since
Vietnam, when the government blamed reporters for fuelling

anti-war protests, access to front lines has been severely
restricted. Gulf War correspondents in 1991 mostly followed
the action via flipcharts and videos in briefing rooms. Not this
time: at least 700 reporters, American and non-American, were
'embedded' inside US troop units, eating and sleeping among
soldiers. Commanders hoped the 'embeds' would correct Iraqi
media deceptions and show US forces were abiding by the
laws of war. Debate is raging among US journalists, though,
over whether the embedded media just end up taking root,
losing their objectivity.

Evil ones

Saddam Hussein threw George Bush's favourite insult back at
him. In a television address, he branded Bush and Tony Blair
the 'evil ones' who were no better than 'lowlifes and enemies
of humanity'. Such language must have been familiar to Bush,
who condemned Osama bin Laden as the 'evil one' after the
11 September attacks.

Exporting the risk

Used by US troops in Iraq in relation to procedures at checkpoints for handling civilians suspected of being irregular
forces such as Saddam's Fedayeen, Ba'ath Party 'enforcers' or
suicide bombers. Reflected American nervousness about the
unexpected character of the war and difficulty of winning Iraqi
hearts and minds. 'Exporting the risk' seems to mean shooting
whoever is approaching and asking questions afterwards –
probably the mind-set that led to the death of about 10 people
at a checkpoint on Route 9 near Najaf, the worst single case of
civilian deaths admitted in the war.

Eye-raq

In a troubling development for those already concerned about
US domination of the coalition attempting to topple Saddam
Hussein, British officers appeared to adopt the American
pronunciation of the country they were invading. Captain
Al Lockwood, one of the spokesmen for British forces in the

Gulf, gave the new spoken form its first outing on BBC Radio 4's *Broadcasting House* programme.

Fixing

The US and British forces surrounding the southern towns of Nassiriya and Basra were, the military said, fixing them. This did not mean they were already engaged in repairing buildings damaged in battle. Rather, they sealed off the perimeters to neutralise any Iraqi troops still inside the towns without having to risk engaging them in potentially costly street fighting, so that the main advance could continue north towards Baghdad.

Foxhole

US and British forces probably never believed they would have to resort to sleeping in foxholes, a term coined by American troops in the First World War. Wary of sleeping in tents, which could reveal their position, troops took to digging shallow trenches or pits in the sand that give them some cover from enemy fire. Reinforced with sandbags, foxholes can be deeply uncomfortable, particularly when there is heavy rain.

Geographic piece

Victory is all about winning over people not places, went the cry in Washington. At one point, military planners said they could declare victory even if they had not captured every 'geographic piece' of Iraq, as long as they had secured key territory and wiped out most Iraqi resistance.

Golden bridge

British forces, who eschewed American slash-and-burn tactics, tempted Iraqi forces out of Basra by making them an offer they could not refuse: stay in the city and be shot, or cross the 'golden bridge' out of Basra which will ensure your survival.

Granularity

In the fog of war everyone looked for detailed accounts of the battles on the ground in Iraq. The granularity of this war was not the sand that covers most of the country, but these details

that proved so elusive. Both the military and the press were
obsessed with the search for granularity. But practical problems
with communications from soldiers in the field to their
commanders and restrictions from London and Washington
on the flow of information meant it was an endless search.

Holocaust

Naji Sabr, Saddam Hussein's Foreign Minister, warned
reporters in Baghdad that foreign Arab volunteers and Iraqi
forces would lay the groundwork for a 'holocaust' for US and
British soldiers. 'Every day that passes the United States and
Britain are sinking deeper in the mud of defeat,' he said.
Holocaust, from a Greek word meaning 'burnt whole', means
destruction or slaughter on a mass scale, such as a nuclear
holocaust. Normally used with the definite article to refer to
the extermination of 6 million Jews by the Nazis during the
Second World War.

Hot contact point

How do you describe the uncomfortable business of casualties
in a low-key way? 'A hot contact point is where our soldiers are
getting shot at,' said a British sergeant, manning a checkpoint.

Jewel in the crown

English romantics who long for a return to the days of empire
will be heartened by the reappearance of this phrase which
once described Britain's greatest imperial possession: India.
Rather than describing a glittering land, this now refers to the
less glamorous surroundings of Baghdad Airport. 'It is a jewel
in the crown to the coalition,' Group Captain Al Lockwood said
of the airport, where the burnt-out shells of Iraqi aircraft could
be seen.

John Major good

Civilians in Iraq learned a few choice phrases with which to
greet the coalition troops. A favourite of some of the Marsh
Arabs who live off the Baghdad to Basra highway upon meeting
British soldiers was: 'Bush good, Blair good, John Major good.'

In Baghdad one US serviceman, Jerry Duval, from Cyclone Company of the 4th Battalion, 64th Armour Regiment, was delighted when a child welcomed him with: 'I love America, Bruce Springsteen, *Born in the USA.*'

Killboxes
Some might regard this term as a refreshingly honest departure by the military, which has a habit of cloaking its work in abstract language. To others, it will be seen as disturbingly bloodthirsty. Killboxes are grid squares, measuring 35 square miles, into which RAF Tornados fire their Paveway laser-guided bombs. A 'hot' killbox contains a specific target posing a direct threat to troops. This is a far cry from the 1991 Gulf War, when US commanders laughed as they replayed cockpit video clips of pilots dropping their bombs.

Kinetic targeting
Current preferred euphemism for dropping bombs. When aircraft drop leaflets on Iraq asking the military to surrender and radio stations broadcast anti-Saddam rhetoric, the generals describe it as soft targeting. When fighter jets and cruise missiles destroy targets on the ground, the military calls it 'kinetic targeting'. For the military, it is an unusually simple and vigorous description of the destruction they are about to deliver. It also spawned a spin-off early in the war: the tens of thousands of US and British troops poised to attack Iraq were simply waiting for permission to 'go kinetic'.

Les belligérents
Massively adopted by the French media as shorthand to describe the armed forces, and by extension the governments, of the United States and Great Britain. A poll in *Le Monde* said a third of the French disapproved of what les belligérents were up to and only a slender majority (53 per cent) hoped they would win.

Liberation bounce
Not a patriotically named 20s-style dance-floor move popular among Washington's more swingin' neo-conservatives.

Instead, this was the phrase some used to describe what war planners hoped would be a sudden surge of welcome by ordinary Iraqis towards US and UK forces once the population realised there was no chance of Saddam regaining his grip on power. As Joseph Wilson, the former acting US ambassador to Iraq, put it: 'One of the things that we do want, it seems to me, is . . . a positive liberation bounce out of this as we settle into the hard task of restoring democracy or representative government to this country.'

Live from Baghdad

Regulation phrase of the day for TV and radio anchors the world over, this one should be treated with caution – particularly in Swaziland. Questions were asked in Parliament after state radio's alleged war correspondent in the Iraqi capital, Phesheya Dube, was spotted strolling round his home town at the weekend, and scandalised MPs realised his breathless 'live reports' were in fact being broadcast from what one parliamentarian described as 'a broom closet' at home in Mbabane. The programme's host, Moses Matsebula, had none the less frequently expressed concerns on air about his courageous correspondent's safety and well-being, at one stage advising him to 'find a cave somewhere to be safe from missiles'.

Manoeuvrist approach

Commanders adopted one of the oldest military terms to describe the battle unfolding in Iraq. A manoeuvrist approach, they said, described the flexible tactics that allowed commanders in the field and at the main headquarters in Qatar to adapt their plans in response to events on the ground.

Mercenaries

A gratifyingly colourful foray into the grey world of military jargon by the Iraqi Information Minister, Mohammed Saeed al-Sahaf. Contrasting the hordes of American and British troops attacking Umm Qasr and Nassiriya with the Iraqi 'heroes' defending the towns, he told reporters: 'Those mercenaries and hired guns are seeing death in front of them . . . We have drawn them into a quagmire and they will never get out of it.'

Methodical slugfest

Armchair generals occasionally abandon their caution and come up with lively terms, even if they stretch the English language to breaking point. Gen Wesley Clark warned that US forces would face a 'methodical slugfest' in the battle for Baghdad if warplanes did not destroy the Republican Guard. A slugfest covered 'combat at close quarters [with] significant risk', he wrote.

Mirror-imaging

This comes from the world of policy analysis and intelligence assessment. 'Many people in the administration had a very strong political agenda, which was inspired by the Iraqi opposition, and by western mirror-imaging, assuming they want what we want,' said Anthony Cordesman of the Centre for Strategic and International Studies in Washington. Nicolo Machiavelli warned against assuming that your adversary would never do something you would never do. It could be dangerous if applied, say, to Iraqi readiness to use chemical weapons. 'Mirror-imaging – projecting your thought process or value system on to someone else – is one of the greatest threats to objective intelligence analysis,' a senior CIA officer, Frank Watanabe, wrote in 1998. Failure to avoid it led the US to believe that Japan would not attack Pearl Harbor.

Mouseholing

This apparently innocuous term has sinister connotations. It describes one of the most horrific elements of urban warfare in which troops do not enter houses from the front door, for fear of triggering trip wires. Instead they blow holes in side walls, invariably causing numerous civilian casualties. Mouseholing was last seen in the Israeli assault on Jenin, where tens of Palestinian residents were killed.

Nahnoo hoonaa limoo saa edu tek

Is this a language invented by British squaddies to hide their
inner thoughts? Sadly, the explanation is more prosaic. This
was the sound made by British troops on the outskirts of Basra
as they attempted to pronounce the Arabic for 'We are here to
help you.' The attempt by squaddies to ingratiate themselves
with the residents of Iraq's second city, by painstakingly reading
from a special card, left locals mystified. 'What is he saying?
Is it English?' one driver asked a Reuters correspondent.

On to Richmond

Vietnam was not the only painful chapter in US history to be
recalled as America came to terms with the horrors of another
war. One armchair general went back 100 years before Vietnam
to draw parallels between today's Iraqi campaign and the
American Civil War of the 1860s. The unnamed general told the
Washington Post that he saw a parallel between America's
difficulties in taking Baghdad and the initial 'on to Richmond'
strategy of Union forces in their attempts to take the Confederacy
capital. This descended into a strategy of 'Kill the enemy army
first', the general said. 'The civil war lasted four years,' the *Post*
helpfully reminded its readers.

Open sources

Amid the fog, or sandstorm, of war the military often do not
have a clue what is going on. This is the term used by military
spokesmen when they have to rely on reports by journalists to
tell them what is happening.

Pac-Man

Republican Guards dug in around Baghdad were little more than
dots on a computer game in the minds of US commanders. Describing the tactics of US forces massed outside the Iraqi capital,
one retired general recalled the 1980s arcade game Pac-Man,
in which a big hungry dot races around a maze gobbling up
smaller dots. 'I think you should Pac-Man the ring around
Baghdad,' General Barry McCaffrey told the *Washington Post*.

Poke in the eye

The initial lightning thrust through Baghdad by US tanks was
replayed under camouflage of several euphemisms. Officers
at US Central Command relished it as a 'poke in the eye' for
the Iraqi regime, implying a deliberate insult to Saddam. This
amounted to an advance on the cautious process of . . .

Poking a toe

Wary of storming Basra, British forces initially adopted a softly-
softly approach as they tried to take control of Iraq's second
city. Poking a toe described this process, which contrasted with
the less subtle tactics of US forces.

Rapid dominance

This, according to the Pentagon's current philosophy, is what
follows from a successful 'shock and awe' offensive designed to
terrify the enemy into submission. Both terms were coined by
the military strategist Harlan Ullman in a 1996 National Defence
University book. 'The idea is to hit the Iraqi military and political
structure at all the critical nodes and links with unbelievable
intensity and unbelievable force and simultaneity,' he explained.
'That induces paralysis, desperation and a sense of extreme
vulnerability. In essence you change their will and they
surrender.'

Real-time television connections

Had the military dreamed up a grand phrase to describe those
'embedded' television reporters providing live pictures to
24-hour rolling news channels? Not quite. This described the
unmanned aerial vehicles flying over Iraq that beamed live
pictures back to base, known as 'real-time television
connectivity'.

Regime target

Even with harrowing pictures of young victims of allied
bombing in Basra, Britain and the US insisted that they were
only striking Saddam Hussein and the infrastructure that
supported his regime. These were, in the military parlance,

regime targets, which included presidential palaces, the army, security service and intelligence headquarters.

Sensitive site exploitation
General Tommy Franks, the overall commander of coalition forces, coined one of the more memorable military terms of the campaign. Troops would be performing what he called SSEs – sensitive site exploitation. This described the delicate process of examining suspected plants containing weapons of mass destruction. No doubt such a technical term would come in handy if the allies failed to detect any weapons of mass destruction, whose alleged presence in Iraq provided the pretext for war.

Shoot and scoot
What do you do when the world's largest military power marches into your backyard? Take potshots and scarper as quickly as possible is what the Iraqis did, in a tactic known as 'shoot and scoot'. The term first came into use during the first Gulf War to describe how Iraqis would fire mobile Scud missiles in the western desert then drive off before the US could respond. British and US forces also used 'shoot and scoot'. In the battle for Baghdad they fired Paladin howitzers from launchers which could be moved quickly to avoid detection.

Situational awareness
Air Marshal Brian Burridge achieved a first when he admitted that the military had a habit of using jargon. Troops, he declared, would have to be aware of their surroundings when they attempted to take Baghdad. 'It is a question of developing absolute situational awareness, as we say in the jargon, so that we know what is going on.'

Snake in the desert
Many of Iraqi Information Minister Mohammed Saeed al-Sahaf's verbal assaults on the invaders contained references to serpents. 'They [US forces] are a snake moving in the desert,'

he told a press conference. The day before he told his audience: 'We're waging a war of attrition against this snake, and we will be victorious.' The metaphor appears to be a favourite. One soldier found a Ba'ath Party pamphlet by Saddam Hussein – *Principles, a Way to Life, and its Crown* – in a building. It included the admonition: 'Don't provoke a snake before you have the intention of cutting its neck.'

Stay behinds

Iraqi forces that lay in wait for US convoys travelling the lengthy supply lines from the south up to the outskirts of Baghdad were called 'stay behinds'. This did not denote any cowardice on the Iraqis' part, but rather a grudging US respect for troops who fight on alone to try to attack and disrupt the supply lines.

Strike package

Before anyone gets too excited, this is strictly a military term to describe the vast array of hardware and technology supporting the bombing raids. When people watched vast B-52 bombers taking off from Britain, or their vapour trails high over Iraq, they were only seeing part of the bombing campaign. The 'strike package' includes fighters, reconnaissance and early warning radar aircraft, and air-to-air refuellers, an RAF speciality.

Supply nodes

This term describes the latest rage in the Pentagon. As troops surged through Iraq towards Baghdad they established small battlefield depots, known as supply nodes, to provide supplies for their forces. These were abandoned when troops moved on.

Swamps

Mohammed Saeed al-Sahaf showed that he too had been leafing through the Bush dictionary of insults. Iraq, he declared, had lured British and American troops into 'swamps' from which they would never return. This had shades of President Bush's pledge, after the 11 September attacks, to 'drain the swamp of terrorism'.

Thunder run

As a demonstration of death-or-glory bravado, the initial
incursion by Abrams tanks into Baghdad was saluted by
those who recognised that it could have ended in disaster.
One American newspaper reported that soldiers in the tanks
called their mission Operation Thunder Run. A thunder run is
a term in white-water rafting for shooting the most treacherous
rapids. The term also crops up as a monumental, final bar
crawl before leaving a posting, said to originate in the Korean
War.

Thwack

Officers in the RAF, the most junior of the three armed services,
sometimes become a little over-excited. One officer could
barely control himself when he described how RAF Harriers
opened fire on an armoured Iraqi convoy leaving Basra.
'The army and air force had a thwack at them and they didn't
get anywhere, let's put it like that,' a senior RAF source said.
'I think they got thwacked.' Naval and cavalry officers would
regard such language as vulgar.

Tip-fiddle

From the acronym TPFDL, which stands for time-phased
forces deployment list, which in turn means the detailed
blueprint of a US military campaign. The tip-fiddle stipulates
who is to go where, and when they are to get there. The tip-
fiddle for the current Iraq campaign was, apparently, Number
1003 and angry military top brass in Washington accused
Donald Rumsfeld of having fiddled with it.

Traction

New favourite word of Sir Jeremy Greenstock, Britain's UN
Ambassador, who used it before the conflict had started in
the battle to get a second UN resolution, to describe Security
Council members' responses to the six 'benchmarks' proposed
by London in what diplomats helpfully called a 'non-paper'.
'If this gains traction . . . then the co-sponsors would be prepared

to drop' any mention of an ultimatum in the resolution, Greenstock said. Diplo-speak, meaning either that the proposal might be 'pulled along' or – a more vivid alternative dictionary definition – that it would gain 'adhesive friction', like a good set of tyres on a steep road. Sample sentence: 'If the benchmarks in this non-paper gain traction we could have it in blue by the weekend.'

Training wheels
Paul Wolfowitz, the US Deputy Defence Secretary, compared the running of Iraq to a child learning how to ride a bicycle. It is important, he said, that a civilian administration is set up as quickly as possible before the country becomes too reliant on the coalition. 'It's like the problem if you leave the training wheels on a bicycle too long, the kid never learns to ride.'

Unintended consequences
Searching for ever more abstract terms to cover the brutal business of killing civilians, the US deployed this phrase. Insisting that coalition forces were unlikely to have been responsible for a missile attack on a Baghdad market, General Vince Brooks, the Deputy Director of Operations, warned that sometimes civilian deaths were the 'unintended consequences' of an attack.

Uprise
Gen Wesley Clark maintained the military tradition of mangling the English language. 'They didn't uprise,' he complained to CNN about the failure of the people of Basra immediately to fulfil the coalition's expectations of an uprising against Saddam Hussein. 'The simple fact is that the liberation didn't quite occur.' His remarks came amid a war of words among America's armchair generals over the relatively light numbers of troops sent to Iraq.

Vertical envelopment
The Pentagon's term for the preferred method of outflanking
Iraqi forces by flying troops over them and then attacking from
the rear or the sides.

Vietnam Redux
As one of America's grandest columnists, R. W. 'Johnny' Apple
could be relied on to coin a suitably historic phrase to describe
Saddam Hussein's tactics. 'Mr Hussein seems to have decided
that he can turn this war into Vietnam Redux,' Apple wrote in
the *New York Times*, of the Iraqi guerrilla raids against British
and American forces. He argued that Saddam, like the Vietcong,
was willing to suffer heavy casualties and to give away territory
to gain time. To cap that, he was doing his best to isolate the
US on the world stage.

Yapping like a rabbit
Gore Vidal, the grand old man of the American literary left,
coined one of the more eloquent, though cutting, phrases of
the war. 'How embarrassing for Blair, Prime Minister of that
once great country, to be yapping like a rabbit in support of
our war,' Vidal said to cheering supporters at a rally in Santa
Monica. As a man of letters, Vidal is unlikely to have been
inspired by the Chas and Dave song, 'Rabbit Rabbit Yap Yap,
Rabbit Rabbit.' Perhaps he was thinking of the noises male
rabbits make after mating.